The NightWatchman

Lorna Couillard

WORKBOOK PRESS LLC
187 E Warm Springs Rd,
Suite B285 Las Vegas NV 89119 USA

Website: https://workbookpress.com/
Hotline: 1-888-818-4856
Email: admin@workbookpress.com

Ordering Information:
Quantity sales. Special discounts are available on quantity purchases by corporations, associations, and others. For details, contact the publisher at the address above.

ISBN-13: 978-1-963718-16-4 Paperback Version
          978-1-963718-17-1 Digital Version

REV. DATE: 06/13/2024

The NightWatchman

By Lorna Couillard

Dedication Page

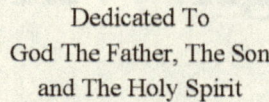

Dedicated To
God The Father, The Son
and The Holy Spirit

Preface

What is the purpose and focus of this book, and most important thing to be conveyed throughout? I'll begin by making clear what it is not. It's not an attempt to create a legacy, to form or uphold a reputation of any fashion. It's a narration, some of it in journal form, of a journey of an obscure, ordinary person, whom God has, for His own purposes, made Himself known to; and His consistent hand of guidance, discipline, and work of His calling on my life.

Does God take notice of ordinary, obscure people? Does He call them, and use them for very specific purposes? I can say with assurance yes, He does.

It's the account of Jesus' power to forgive, and set a sinner free. To bring deliverance from alcoholism and occult activity that held me bound from a young girl, to the age of twenty five, and his working to bring me into freedom, and of use for His service.

This is a compilation of events, dreams, visions and manifestations throughout my life that have come true, and answers to specific prayer/fasting and intercession. The calling that was placed on my life from birth, that evidenced itself as years unfolded, of an intercessor and watchman for specific things God revealed to me over the years, that were His intentions and desires for ministries, individuals, and nations. In each of these events, God has used them as teachings, to help me to understand His Person, His mind, and His heart in a greater depth. This is an ongoing calling, that changes and deepens with each year.

It is a testimony of God's hand on one person, who has desired to follow Him, no matter where He leads. To surrender my desires, my will, and my life; as His servant. In these pages there are accounts of victories shared, and failures, and the depth of spiritual warfare in standing in faith for some of the things God placed before me, and to believe Him for. Many times God's people do not see victory in their intercession because they stop, and give up before God is able to move the circumstances and people to see the answers come. I've prayed/fasted and believed God sometimes for years, before the answer became reality. Each time, it was another learning experience. The serious intercessor and watchman will find this a pattern of their life. All the great intercessors of the Bible found this to be true; Abraham, Moses, Daniel, Jeremiah, as examples.

It's my hope, and prayer that the Holy Spirit will use it, and whoever reads this will find within it something of use in their walk with the Lord, and their prayer life. That the presence of God will witness to the reader.

And, that they will find that God is keenly aware, interested, and has a unique plan for every individual he's created. We are fearfully and wonderfully made. In His eyes, there is no respecter of persons. God is more than able to make Himself known to anyone, who will seek Him with all their heart. If they do, they will find Him, and this will be fuel to their spirits, to seek Him even more. I've not come to the end of my hunger for Him. The more I know Him, the more the fire of desire burns in this heart.

The greatest desire for this book is to bring glory to only Jesus Christ. To make known His ability to change any life, and make it useful for His service.

-Lorna Couillard-

Introduction

In 2002 an event took place that was a significant move of God in my life, and I still have the notes in my journal describing what happened. I'll share the majority of the actual event, and then explain its meaning in regards to this book now.

"On a Monday in the early part of the month of April, 2002, I finished a riding lesson with one of my young students, and got in the car to keep a meeting that was set up by my pastor's at the church I was attending. I didn't bother to change, just kept on my work clothes and boots. I looked like just another working farmer.

The weekend before, I had attended a small Christian gathering in Hardwick Vt., at an evening service, and listened to a man with a prophetic and teaching ministry. The next day, Sunday my pastor spoke to me and asked if I would be willing to meet this man in a private meeting during a week day. I wasn't given any details, and I wondered what he could possibly want with me, but I nodded and agreed to meet with him, and the date was set for Monday later in the morning.

I found the residence given to me in Morrisville Vt., parked in the front and went to the door. I was directed to the back of the residence and asked to follow the paved walkway. I followed it around to what appeared to be a small garden area. The walkway led up to a doorway; as I was instructed, I just walked in to what appeared to be a small meeting room. A chair was at my left, and at the other end of the room two people were already seated waiting for me. A woman sat at my left, with a door behind her that led further into the building. At my right, also at the other end of the room sat Mr. Davis, the man who had asked for this meeting. I never met him before, only having heard him speak at the Saturday night meeting, and what my pastors had shared with me about him. The heavy presence of the Holy Spirit was among us; I silently asked Him to guide me in this situation.

Then Mr. Davis spoke: "Thank you for accepting my request, please have a seat."

I sat at the chair to my left, and continued to wait on Mr. Davis to continue.

"I know you are wondering what the purpose is for this meeting. I'll try to be to the point, and brief. The Lord has laid you on my heart for some time, and has a few things He'd like me to share with you, if you don't mind."

I gazed steadily at him, and said, "Yes, I'm willing to listen."

He began "I asked the Holy Spirit to confirm to me what he's given me. When you walked in, you were holding a Bible, and a large journal under your arm, that's one confirmation which I'll explain later. First, I'd like to relay something I believe God has shown me about you, and when I've finished, please feel free to tell my I'm crazy, or I've heard from the Lord".

I said nothing, but nodded to continue.

"You've had a very difficult life, Satan has tried to kill you many times. From a baby, you've had dreams and visions that have come true and do to this day. You are a seer, and prophetic, but keep it mostly to yourself because of unbelief and misunderstanding with people. You write them down in your journals, when they come to pass. Some of them are far in the future, but you will see them. You've gained a level of authority in prayer and spiritual warfare because of your obedience when your husband divorced you shortly after you were saved. You continued to pray for him and believe for your marriage to be restored, which it was. But, even in this, you have been met with many adversities, and battles. Your husband almost died from a heart attack, your fasting and prayer kept him alive, and still going today. You're still believing for his salvation. Satan hates you for this. You've had much jealousy, and contention with people, because you won't compromise the word of God, but you're standing on it has given you a place of authority that most never understand." He stopped and looked in my eyes for my response.

"Yes, you've been shown the truth. Now, what's the real purpose for this meeting?"

He looked down at a piece of paper in front of him, and continued. "First, the Holy Spirit has asked me to tell you, He'd like you to write a book. I don't know about what, but he's asked me to share this with you. It may confirm to you what He's already been speaking to you."

"Yes, but I've been putting it off. My feeling is-does this world really need another book?"

Dave Davis looked at me; "If God wants you to do it, there has to be a good reason. Ask the Lord to help you get it done."

I remained silent, and waited for him to continue.

He went on, "The Lord wants you to do spiritual warfare against the spirit of Jezebel over New England. He has told me to pray with you for it to be done, and how to go about it. If you agree to do it, it will open the heavens for a greater harvest of souls into the Kingdom, before the Lord returns."

He had no way of knowing that in 1988, I had traveled with my younger sister to the Hegewisch Baptist church outside of Chicago, and during the three days there, they had teaching every day on the Jezebel spirit by Win Worley, and that God had spoken to me to make this a special matter of prayer over my area when I got home. He was confirming again, what I had been told many years earlier.

After a year of fasting and prayer, and seeking God for how he wanted this intercession to be done. It was accomplished during a 3 day stay at an Inn in N.H., in June 2003, between the nineteenth through the twenty-first. I still have the journal notes of that intercession, and the Lords direction in it.

He continued on; "Because these are the end days, you will see an acceleration of trouble, and misunderstanding. The years you've learned to stand on God's word, and stand-alone if you must, will be a matter of course in your life. Few will be willing to hear or heed the scriptures, and you will continue to be labeled too dogmatic, and legalistic. We will add this to the time of prayer, for needed strength to see you through. As Jesus said, some of your enemies will be those in your own household. Satan will be relentless in using people to falsely accuse you."

It would take too long to go into great detail on this, but what he spoke has come to pass completely.

"Lastly-you will be a powerful witness against the Masons, Jehovah Witness, Buddhism, and Mormons in New England. Do not be discouraged at not seeing outward results, it is the obedience of boldly proclaiming the truth of what scripture teaches, and exposing these false religions and cults for what they are that the Lord is concerned about. On the day of Judgment with the truth you proclaim-anyone who has seen it and read it, will have no excuse."

Sidenote: In the two websites I created and maintain, http:// twosparrowsministry.org/ and https://www.thenightwatchman. org/ , there are multitudes of sound biblical teachings by reputable Bible teachers, and videos that boldly proclaim the error of these false religions, and cults, and I know many people have read and listened to them. This has been fulfilled in the past seven years.

He stopped, and questioned with his eyes, whether I agreed with his statements. I answered simply "Much of what you've spoken has already been confirmed by events you had no way of knowing about. I have no doubt the Lord is speaking through you. However,

I don't feel adequate for the job."

Dave Davis smiled slowly, "None of us are, but when we pray together I'll ask the Father to equip you with all you need to accomplish these things, and for angels to assist you. With God, nothing is impossible".

We stood and gathered together in the center of the room, and held hands. The presence of God intensified. He began to pray:

"Father in heaven, all you've shared with me concerning Lorna, she witnesses to in her heart, but is feeling the pressure of our weakness, we are only humans. Lord, I ask for you to fill her to overflowing with your Holy Spirit and the boldness to proclaim the things you've commissioned her to do. I ask you to send the angel Gabriel and Michael to assist her in the intercession against the spirit of Jezebel over New England. Help her to accomplish this, that Satan would not succeed in hindering it to be done. Give her the needed wisdom and discernment to accomplish this task, for the souls of many who will be set free, saved and brought into your Kingdom. In Jesus name, amen."

We hugged, spoke a few moments, and I turned to leave. His last words to me were "Remember, in eternity, it will all be worth it."

I looked at him, and his wife, nodded, then opened the door and left. The gravity of this meeting and its purpose has been part of my life ever since.

After eighteen years, since this meeting, the book still hasn't been written, until now. There's been much wrestling in the Spirit and prayer over this. I've got material everywhere, in journals, on my computer, and in private letters. What God would want shared, will not be easy to decide-there's been a lifetime of answered prayer, and experiences that God has used to teach me His ways-which I'm still learning every day.

But, how far God had to go to reach me, and the life of sin he saved me from, will also be told. Not to dwell on it, but to show the extent God will go to rescue somebody, and what He can do with anybody who will turn and surrender their life to Him. As this story is told, looking back to the past before my salvation will be like telling of a dead person, because that person is dead now, and has been for a long time. Much of the section before my salvation will be written as an observer, an outsider. Simply relaying what happened. When one becomes born again, and walking in the salvation and freedom that Jesus provides, our past is dead to us, only to be used as reference, and the lessons learned during that time of darkness.

When we are saved, God has cast our sins in the depths of the sea, never to be remembered again. Unlike people, God forgives, and forgets our sins. He never brings them up to us in condemnation again. His word gives us the promises of His love, mercy, and restoration to our lives. From the point of our salvation, if we hear any condemnation coming at us, we can be assured Satan is using that person to heap guilt on us, and bring destruction to our souls if he can. We are to reject it, and refuse to receive it, at all costs. Whom the Son sets free, is free indeed. His word gives us full authority to stand against all condemnation of our past, and reject it-no matter who it is that's trying to heap it onto us again; including pastors or leaders of a church. It takes discernment, prayer, and going to the word of God to see if someone is giving godly counsel, or condemnation. There are times when it's necessary to shut the door to people who attempt to undermine us, in order to walk in freedom with the Lord, and fulfill His will in our lives. The devil will use anyone he can, to pull you back into the world. In the power of the Spirit, we are to resist it, no matter who it may be.

The experiences are in the book are true, but the names of some people may not be shared, out of consideration to them. When sharing specific dreams, visions, answers to intercessions, care will be taken to provide dates, and details to validate the truth regarding them.

Over the years He's shown me His word is true. He's a God who does not lie. He means what He says in His word, and He can be counted on. He is a God of infinite mercy, and love. But, He is holy. When we understand that He is a holy God, we begin to grow in understanding His heart and His Person. I've been given glimpses, and will share some of what I've come to understand, to this point. But, the mystery of His Being will never be fully known here. Only when we reach the other shore, and see Him, face to face, will we behold Him, in all His glory.

~Lorna Couillard~

ONE

TURBULENT BEGINNING

On January 20, 1953, Dwight D. Eisenhower was sworn into office as the thirty-fourth president of the United States; it was also the same day I came into the world. I was born in a hospital in Schenectady New York, the fourth child of seven.

My parents were both hard working people, with only an eighth grade education, my Father worked as a laborer in carpentry or in warehouses. His last employment before his retirement was as a boiler operator in a bottling plant, that made soda's. Mother worked part-time cleaning houses in some of the richer housing developments to help make ends meet. Both of them came from poor families in the Adirondacks. Dad had twelve other sisters and brothers, and Mother was the fifth of six kids in her family. Their lives were very difficult growing up during the Great Depression. It caused much of the drinking problems in my Father, as well as the arguments and conflicts between them. All they ever knew was hard times, and making choices made many times ruled by emotions, which is almost never a good idea. Many times it caused a lot of regrets.

This is why there were many contradictions and paradoxes that went on throughout the years. Mom and Dad loved each other but little money, hard times, and seven kids to raise in this environment caused discouragement, resentment, and a lot of conflict. My Father drank just about every weekend, sometimes more. This caused arguments that escalated and would sometimes go on until morning. Each of us kids learned to do what we had to survive in this environment. We each found an outlet and a way to cope.

Each of us had a very distinct personality with different interests, and we didn't always agree with one another. We learned to deal with the differences between us by getting occupied with the things we enjoyed and were drawn to. We found peace between us this way, most of the time.

Unfortunately, some of the activities we got involved in caused a lot of heartache, and trouble for us as the years went by.
We did not go to church, Father denied any faith in God. Mother did know the Lord, but did not go to church because of trouble caused by gossip, which she didn't want any part of. Dad was also relentless in making her life miserable if she did. She brought the Lord into her life, and ours by putting gospel hymns and music on the record player and singing along with them, sometimes for hours. She often said it helped keep her sanity and give her peace. She also talked to us kids about the Lord often, telling us short stories from the Bible and telling us we needed to let Jesus in our hearts. Her simple faith in God was a solid stability we learned to lean on during the times Dad would be on a drinking binge, or when they'd have another long argument; with the long resentments and silences that often followed.

My earliest memories are from age three. I began to be aware of my surroundings, and developed significant desires that molded the pattern and journey of my life.

On my third birthday, Mother gave me a doll. I opened the box, moved the tissue away, looked down at the dead eyes of the doll looking back at me, left it in the box, and shut it again.

"What's the matter, don't you like the doll?" Mother asked.

"No, its eyes are dead."

My parents looked at each other then back at me.

Dad said, "This girl knows what she likes, and what she doesn't, might as well listen to her."

Mother picked up the box and took it back. I don't know what she did with the doll. But I was never given another one.

Not long afterward, Dad came home from work with two new books under his arm. After supper that night, he picked me up, sat me on his lap and opened the book in front of me. It was full of beautiful colored pictures of ocean life of all kinds. Fishes, whales, star fish; many, many kinds of creatures. He read to me out of the book what each one was, as he pointed them out to me. I was fascinated and loved every minute of it. In the midst of this, Mother came and stood behind us in silence.

My Father turned and looked up to her and said "I believe we've found something Lorna likes better than dolls."

Mom smiled with a twinkle in her eye. From then on, I looked forward to books at birthdays and Christmas.

During those growing up years, before the age of twelve, I spent many winter nights either in my parents room on their bed, or my own room, when I finally got one, reading. I loved it. I was able to be transported to far- away places, and read exciting accounts of people's lives, especially in history books of the Revolutionary war period, the Civil War, and the expansion of the West, which I've been drawn to all my life. Between this and a love for exploring the forests around our house in summers; I was never bored. My parents often had to go hunting for me. They learned to expect this from me. When I'd be gone till way past dark, they'd send one of my younger brother's to find me.

Another significant event in my third year was a trip to a farm Dad took me to, that began a life-long desire and love of horses. As he drove to this farm, he told me we would see horses and he'd let me pet one. I had only seen horses in books. I was so excited, my heart was racing. He parked the car, put me in his arms, and we went to the barn. A man greeted Dad and they talked and visited My eyes went to the horses in the fields on both sides of their corrals. They were quiet, and so beautiful.

The man then looked at me and said, "Would you like to ride one?"

"Oh, Yes!"

Dad chuckled and waited with me still in his arms, as the man went back into the barn. In a few minutes he came out with the most beautiful palomino horse. Golden with a pure white mane and tail. He told my Father he was a stallion but very mild and tame, and if he'd hold me while I was on him, he would lead the horse for me.

My Father placed me on his back and told me to hold on to the mane as I rode; his hands holding me firmly around my waist, and I held on. I was full of total joy. The owner led me the entire length of the driveway, stopped and let me enjoy petting the great muscled neck, and talking to the stallion. Then he led me back to the barn. That day was the beginning of a life-long love of horses, and a desire to one day own and train one as a companion. There were times in my life that I thought this would only be a dream, never to be realized.

Whenever they could manage it, my parents would take us camping in the Adirondacks, where they both grew up as kids. There are many memories of wonderful family times, fishing, swimming, telling stories after eating around the campfire, and nighttime escapades that brought laughter. At the end of all this, we'd sing along with those who played guitars and fiddles. Through all the difficult times, and the hardships they endured, my parents did all they could to bring joy, fun, activities and love into our lives. We learned to come to understand why at times Dad or Mom would be so discouraged, and depressed, or make wrong decisions. We learned to try to put ourselves in their place, and not hold their weaknesses and faults against them. Because, when we saw how much they sacrificed and went out of their way to bring us so much joy, we knew they loved us. We knew we were wanted, and we came to see through their eyes.

It's with sadness that I look back on those years. I understand how much our lives could have been different if we'd allowed the Lord to be the center of our lives, and followed His ways. How much grief, suffering, and loss we would have avoided. Decisions that would have been made differently, if we applied wisdom; doing things God's way, instead of letting emotions, sin, and selfishness rule us. But, that's what happens when people live in blindness and darkness, which we walked in.

When I began school, events took place right from the start, that would make lasting impressions on me, both good and bad.

Already at five I spent a lot of time reading books, loving all kinds of subjects, I wanted to learn. Being with the other kids was good, but I didn't have any desire to stay with groups. At break time, I'd go to the swings, or talk with the other girls, but when I saw them teasing other girls or making fun of people, I didn't want anything to do with that. I'd walk away and go back to the swings, or go back to the school, and read.

But, as time went on and I went into first and second grade I began to pay attention to the cruelty the kids treated some of the other's with. The boy's especially. Some would go in gangs, and pick on the smaller, more timid ones. They'd surround a kid, and hold him by force while the other's would kick, and beat, him and I watched as they sometimes would beat the kid until he almost passed out. This went on in the school yard just about every day. As I grew and became more aware of my surroundings, and what these kids were doing, I realized I did not like this one bit. I went to the adults a couple of times and pointed out what these bullies were doing, being cruel to the littler kids, but quickly found these adults didn't seem to care, and soon found myself labeled a "troublemaker" for saying anything about it. I learned that the bullies usually win out, unless you became one of them, or found other avenues to escape.

One day, I again saw girls taunting another smaller timid girl, who didn't know how to stand up for herself. I asked myself "Why am I here? I hate this cruelty, and what these kids are doing, and I don't know why I am here." I went home that day, and found my Mother in the kitchen. She was cooking. I sat at the table watching her. She turned to me with a question in her eyes. I looked at her and asked "Mom, why am I here?"

"Why are you asking that?"
I told her what I had seen at school, and that it happened all the time. I said I didn't fit in. I couldn't stand the cruelty.
Mother's gaze saddened. "I'm sorry you have to go through that. But first you must learn not to be like them. What they are doing is wrong, and the adults are wrong for allowing it. Do what you can to get away from those kind of kids, and find other things to do. Learn to not be like them. Don't let them ruin you. I'm doing all I can to teach you to respect and treat people right. You do belong. I and your Father love you. Remember that."

Throughout my school years, I had to remind myself of this, many times. But, the conduct and behavior I witnessed during those years, has left lasting impressions on me to this day. I saw the reality of what sin does to people, how it destroys lives. It almost destroyed mine. It has shown me how Satan uses many schemes and manipulations aimed at the very young, to begin his destruction in their lives. Many times, the parents are not aware of the level of demonic activity children are attacked with. But society eventually reveals the results in ruined marriages, divorce, physical violence, drug and alcohol abuse, and destroyed lives.

Society also does all it can to hide, and excuse the cruelty, brutality, and underhanded tactics of kids and adults alike. Children learn very quick to be like the grownups that influence them. The bullies in the school yard become the adult bullies out in the world. Many become the corrupt leaders, and use the same tactics of control, cruelty and intimidation to get their way; all the way to the top of the ladder, and don't care who is destroyed in their path.

Many marriages are destroyed for the same reason. The school yard bullies grow up to be the wife beaters and child abusers. But as a small kid, finding myself in this situation, it caused me to seriously wonder what I was created for, because I knew I didn't want to be like what I was finding myself in the middle of every day. I came to dread school, but kept it to myself. The question I asked My Mother however, stayed with me. Very soon an event would take place that would put me right in this same cycle of destruction. Satan never plays fair, and never gives warning, when he makes plans for our ruin. He hits us where we least expect it, and by people we may trust and look up to. This was to be the case for me in a few years.

In the middle of my seventh year, early one summer morning, I laid in my bed asleep and had a dream. I still remember it to this day, as if it had happened yesterday. Years later, I would come to know it was from God, and see the fulfillment of it. But for most of my early life, it simply remained stamped in my mind, as if it had been branded into me. It had been; it was the call of God on my life. This is how it went:

The dream was in vivid color. I was moving forward in the air across a land beneath me that was lush and green, with mountains, lakes, rivers, and pastures. Cattle and horses were in the fields. The sky was clear blue.

As I continued to move across the land, looking down, I became aware that someone was behind me, traveling with me. I could feel

His presence as he began to talk to me. His voice was very deep, with kindness, but also authority. He told me one day I would live here in this land below, and would do service for Him there. He said He'd be with me and would show me what He wanted me to do. I listened, still looking at the beautiful land below me as we moved over it together. I asked him "where is this?" "This is Vermont". Then, as we moved across the land, his voice became indistinguishable, I no longer understood what he was saying, it trailed off. I awoke and found myself back in my bed looking at the ceiling.

I don't know how long I laid there remembering the dream. After a while I heard our rooster crowing in the back yard, and smelled bacon coming from the kitchen. Mother was making breakfast. I jumped out of bed, and went down stairs to the kitchen. Dad sat at the table with his first cup of coffee, Mother was at the stove. I blinked at them, Dad smiled and asked if I was hungry.

I didn't answer, but asked "Can you tell me where Vermont is?" I thought Vermont was another country.

Dad looked at me with a smile in his eyes, looked at Mother, then back at me "Vermont is the next state over from us. We're not very far away."

Mother looked at me and asked "Why are you asking?"

"Because I dreamed about it, and don't know where it is".

They looked at each other again, with questions in their eyes, but said nothing. A couple of days went by, and Dad came home with a map of Vermont. It had another map on the back of the entire country, and Dad showed where New York and Vermont were; up in the far right of the country. He pointed out the border between us. I registered all of this in my mind, but never spoke of it again to them.

Many years later, this dream was fulfilled. After many heartaches, trials, and wrong decisions, much that I had brought onto myself. Through all of it, God used it to move me into His will, and teach me many valuable lessons, that have molded me to this point.

At age ten, I began to spend a lot of time reading about and drawing horses. In my heart I wanted one very badly, but knew we didn't have the money for one so I didn't ask. I didn't want to make things hard on my parents. But I couldn't think of much else, but horses. My parents decided to do something for me that is forever etched in my heart.

Late one summer afternoon, my Father came home from work, found Mother and said "It's a nice afternoon, let's go for a ride." They told me they needed me to go also. I was not going to refuse, and got quickly in the back of Dads Chevy. He drove along a country road till he reached a large horse farm. He pulled in the driveway, and stopped in front of the barn. He spoke to an older man who led us to a stall toward the back. He opened the stall door, and a large solid black mare stood quietly, munching on hay. The man asked Dad if he wanted to ride her home. Dad said yes. The man took the mare, saddled her, and gave Dad riding instructions.

I was so young, it didn't dawn on me what was happening until I saw my Father get on the horse, and begin to ride her in the small corral attached to the barn. Dad got off, and the two men finished making the sale transaction. Then, saying thanks and a brief farewell to the man who sold her to him, Dad got back on the mare, and told my Mother to follow along beside him, as he rode her home. I sat in silent amazement, and joy. Mother got in the driver seat, started the car, and drove ever so slowly, as Dad rode the mare down the road, five miles home. It took what seemed a very long time. It was almost dark when we finally got to our driveway.

The courage and extent my Father and Mother went to give me my heart's desire never left me. They both made these kinds of sacrifices for each of us as we were growing up. It caused us to love them and respect them, in spite of the times when drinking, fighting, and turmoil took place. We learned to weather the bad times with the good, and stick together. That's what families do.

At twelve, my life revolved around doing what was necessary at school to get by. At home, life revolved around being outdoors from dawn till dark. There was always something to do. I rode my horse during the summer months and into the fall, until the snow stopped me. But this summer, something happened that proved to be a very subtle, direct attack of Satan on my life, that was meant to destroy me, and it almost worked. He doesn't care who he uses. Many times it can be in our own families.

My Mother had an older brother who was respected, because of his military history. He had fought in WWII both in Germany and Africa. He also sang, and played several instruments, leading his own country and western band. He lived in the Adirondacks, and many people went to hear him play for many years. But he was also a mason, and a Rosicrucian; both satanic cults. He was deeply involved in both of them, and tried to influence members of my family a lot. Mother was easily influenced by him, and though she said she believed in Jesus, his influence worked to damage her faith a great deal. Her love for him as her brother, and his strong personality worked to damage many of us, along with me, for a long time.

As I write this, I have a younger brother who is deeply involved in the freemasons. I've tried to talk to him several times, to no avail. The last conversation we had on the phone several years ago, he stopped me, and hung up. We've not talked since. I've had to pray for him and put him in God's hands. This uncles evil influence in our lives is, I know, what did this to him. I can only pray that God will in some way get through to him, and open his eyes to their deceptive, lying practices, and turns away from them, and truly gets saved. In the meantime I grieve for him, and all others who get trapped in these evil secret societies. Jesus is all truth, there is no lie in his mouth, He can be trusted.

One day, riding back to the house, I saw my uncle was in the yard. He had come to visit Mother. As I rode up the drive to the house, he stopped in front of me, wanting to talk.

I smiled at him, and greeted him.

Looking up at me he said "You know, there's many things you could be doing, besides riding horses. You are old enough now, that you ought to be thinking about things other young women are doing."

"And what would that be?" I asked.

"Don't you have any desire to go out with a boy?"

"I haven't really thought about it."

"Well, that's what I mean, you're at an age now, that it's time to think about becoming a grown woman."

I looked at him, but said nothing. My stomach was in knots, but not knowing why.

He turned to go in the house, "I'll talk to your Mother, and see if we can help you get started in finding someone to meet."

How I wish I had turned away from him that day, and rode away instead of stopping to listen to him. How I wish I'd never allowed my Mother to make the decisions for my life, that would start me on a road to destruction. But a twelve year old girl doesn't have the discernment to know what the adults around them may be scheming for them. In a short time, I learned to be much more aware of people's conversation, and the layered intent behind it.

This began a turn in my life I've regretted to this day. Within a few weeks, one Saturday afternoon, my Mother came to me and started talking about how much fun it would be for me to start to learn to socialize with others, and go to parties once in a while. I listened, not really sharing her point of view on it, but at twelve, my mind couldn't clearly comprehend what she was telling me.

Then she began to reveal the agenda she planned for me. "I've set out a pretty dress for you, it's new, you'll love it. Go in and take a bath, change into the new dress. I'll fix your hair, and you can put on some of my perfume. Your uncle is going to come and pick you up, and take you with him to the place he's playing tonight. You'll be able to sit right next to him at his table with all the others who play with him, and there's a young man he'd like you to meet."

This was the beginning of a very long downward road that led me into deep sin, sexual abuse, alcoholism, and almost total destruction.

He arrived, and I went to his car with him. Mother came out and watched as I got in, then turned and went back to the house. I rode with him in silence, feeling very insecure, and somehow lonely. When we arrived we went to the front table where his band was. I sat listening to a maze of noises in a darkly lit room full of tobacco smoke, loud country music, people laughing, drinking, cussing, flirting with each other, and belching. I was miserable.

The young man I was introduced to was eleven years older than I. He had been in the military, and acted more as an older brother, than someone who'd desire company with someone like me, a kid. Satan loves it, when the innocence of a child, blinds them to the evil intended for them.

He was very quiet, gentle, and kind. He bought me a drink, just a coke this first time. After talking for a while longer, he took me to the floor, and taught me to dance. He held me close, but careful not to use any force. He asked more questions, and seemed genuinely interested in what I had to say. Of course, this registered to me that I was important to him. It fed my foolish young heart with the delusions that only childish innocence can create. My uncle kept careful watch from the platform where he played with the band, but didn't interfere. When the evening was over, the young man said he had enjoyed my company and would like to see me again, if I was interested. I said yes, and went home with my uncle.

Within a few months, he was coming to my house and picking me up and taking me to the places my uncle played, but we didn't always stay there. By now, I was drinking wine, and mixed drinks, and each night sexual foreplay was getting deeper and soon the foreplay was molestation. By the time I reached thirteen, my virginity was lost. Now the relationship revolved around sex, drinking, and partying. He had bought a small piece of property in the Adirondacks close to where my uncle lived, and said he wanted to marry me after I graduated from school. I knew this was not going to be for at least five years. I asked him if he would wait that long for me, "Oh yes, of course". I felt a heaviness in my heart, but didn't want to allow myself to pay attention to the warnings going off inside me. I kept it to myself. It was just as well. It didn't take long before the truth revealed itself.

After a two year stretch of partying, along with working on the house he was building, and other projects he was involved in; we both learned how different we were in personality and desires. I had given up my horse, and regretted it. My school work suffered because of the turmoil of the relationship. I was deep in sin with layers of manipulations, schemes and corruption in my daily life. Now I was drinking every day, to get through the day at school. Many at school took drugs; my choice was drinking. My attitude was, whatever works for you.

During all of this, I spent a lot of time with a girlfriend, who lived nearby. Her Mother was divorced, and delved in sorcery, the occult, tarot cards, Ouija boards, seances, tea leaves, and many other demonic activities. She was very interested in supernatural powers, no matter where they came from. As an ignorant pagan, I had an interest also, and started getting involved in doing some of the things they were into, to see what it was really all about. This took me into an even deeper level of evil, and Satan used it greatly to almost destroy me. But even in this, God used it to be a source of learning later, in order to be of service to Him.

My boyfriend started becoming sullen, and the meetings with him became tense. I could feel a distance between us, and knew something or "someone" had caused this distinct change. Sex wasn't fulfilling him now, and I knew it. I was just fifteen but now knew the feeling of being the used woman. I knew it was only a matter of time, and he would be gone. I was right. Shortly after he left for good, he married another woman, and they moved into the house we had worked on together.

I became more involved with my girlfriend and her Mother, and their occult activities. I was drawn into it to the point that we were seeing and experiencing manifestations of demons. This supernatural activity drew us deeper into the evil aspects of spells, incantations, curses and controlling people through sorcery. By doing this, we opened ourselves up to being demonically attacked, and put ourselves in bondage to Satan.

I will tell anyone who reads this now; what you are doing with occult practices, Ouija boards, and all manner of divination is going to destroy you. You are putting yourself in bondage, this is Satan's goal. Jesus Christ came to set us free from all of this. Repent, ask Jesus to forgive you, and ask Him to wash you from your sins. He can and will. But, we must turn from these evil practices and reject all forms of occult activity. God's word is clear on this:

Deu 18:10 There shall not be found

among you any one that maketh his son or his daughter to pass through the fire, or that useth divination, or an observer of times, or an enchanter, or a witch,

Deu 18:11 Or a charmer, or a consulter with familiar spirits, or a wizard, or a necromancer.

Deu 18:12 For all that do these things are an abomination unto the LORD: and because of these abominations the LORD thy God doth drive them out from before thee.

Deu 18:13 Thou shalt be perfect with the LORD thy God.

The more we read, and practiced these demonic activities the more manifestations we experienced. Lights flickering on and off, noises and voices from what we learned were demons, we learned to send curses and hexes on people and more. But, in our darkness, we failed to understand the cruelty of what we were doing when it affected other's lives. Involvement in these things causes our hearts and souls to become cold, callous, and destructive, because that's exactly what Satan's nature is, totally evil. Jesus describes him well:

Joh 10:10 The thief cometh not, but for to steal, and to kill, and to destroy: I am come that they might have life, and that they might have it more abundantly.

One Saturday night, after we had been out dancing, drinking and partying we went back to my girlfriends house. Her Mother was also with us. She had met a black man who said he was a witch doctor from Haiti. He said he knew how to put people in trances, and send spirits into them and give them greater power in the supernatural. She brought him back to her house that night. I was there, and he said he wanted to do a spell on me, to give me greater power. I said ok. He had a candle put in the center of the table, and lit it, then he started chanting and told me to look him in the eyes while he put me into a trance, to put the spell on me. I sat looking at him, watching him over the light of the candle while he chanted. This went on for several hours. I became irritated, and said "I don't think you can do anything".

He became very angry, hissed at me and said "What power is it that you have? I've never had trouble like this before".

"I don't have any idea what you're talking about, I don't have any power I know of, I'm just tired of this, and see you really can't do anything."

He glared at me again, with total disgust "I don't know what power it is you have, but wherever it comes from, it's greater than any spirit I can call up."

Years later, after I was saved, delivered and baptized in the Holy Spirit, the Lord showed me that on that night, He had sent an angel to stand against the evil spirits that black man was trying to call up. That God himself was protecting me, and covering me with a shield against the spells. It's just one of many reasons I totally trust God today, and praise His Name forever. He is worthy of all praise.

Along with these demonic involvements, my own family also became involved in these occult practices in my parents' house. We fooled around with Ouija, tarot cards, and seances. We opened the door to Satan and invited him in to our homes, our lives, and put ourselves in bondage. This caused every one of us many sorrows that could have been avoided if we had turned to God, applied the word of God to our lives, and turned away from those evil practices.

My older sister one day came to our house, and told us of a mirror that her Mother in law gave her, and that she was uneasy about. She said it made shivers go up her spine, she thought it was hexed. I went to her house and looked at it, and said, "I'll take it home and use it in my bedroom, I'm not afraid of it."

It was absolutely the wrong thing to do. That same night, I awoke and saw a glow coming from within the mirror. My hair prickled, I laid there feeling fear rising in me, not knowing what to do. I finally fell asleep, and had a dream, I should say a nightmare. I saw a bald headed man in the mirror rotating around, until his face came to the front, it was a hideous, grayish white. He looked as if he had died and come back to life. Then I was at the bottom of what looked like a swimming pool, and looking up, I saw a young woman floating face down, her eyes open in death. In horror, I realized the woman looked just like my younger sister. In the future I would realize the significance of this, but for now it just made my blood run cold. God never let me forget it, and for good reason, which will be explained further on.

I woke up in a cold sweat. By this time, it was morning. I got up, took the mirror off the wall and went downstairs. I told my parents what had happened. My Father took it with him and said he would destroy it. We never saw it again, but the damage was already done.

The mirror was indeed hexed. They call these Scrying mirrors. Witches and Satanists use them. My sister's mother in law told her it had been used in casting spells by a man in New York City. She had given it to my sister knowing this. She wanted to cause her trouble for my sister. I, in my arrogance and ignorance had taken it to my house, and caused more demonic bondage in my own life, and my families; along with everything else we were already doing to ourselves. I was in for many years of grief, turmoil, and suffering in my life because of involvement with these evil practices. A door for even more demonic oppression in my parents' house had been opened, and everyone in that house suffered because of it, in many ways.

We were blind, living in rebellion, ignorant, and foolish. Satan laughs at people like this, hoping to keep us bound until we die, and land in hell. How I praise the Lord, for His goodness, mercy, and ability to open our eyes to the truth, if we will allow Him to, and be set free from all of it.

Needless to say, this life of demonic influence, my promiscuity, and lack of moral direction sent me into a spiral of depression and wrong choices. In my heart, I felt I had already gone too far, had lost too much, and would never gain any sense of integrity or purpose again.

Several times in high school, opportunities came my way that I allowed to slip through my fingers. I had talent in drawing and painting, my art teacher at school sent some of my work to Norman Rockwell, and he sent one of his personal agents to my house to talk to me, and my parents. He said they wanted to help me go through Mr. Rockwell's school for illustration. My Father took out a loan and helped me get started into it. But the mixture of being involved with the wrong people, my own lack of self-worth, the influence of the demonic activity I was involved in, all played a part in my not applying myself. I never finished the courses.

The high school librarian knew I had talent in drawing, and gave me special attention and opportunity to create window displays monthly on special subjects, and those with historical significance. I ruined that because I wouldn't apply myself, and allowed other kids to influence me to not be serious about it. There are times when opportunities come our way only once, and if we don't take advantage of those special open doors, we lose them. But, I've also learned that God is a restorer of broken dreams and broken lives, as I'll share as this story goes along.

In the meantime, my life was going to spiral down even further into a pit of chaos, turmoil, and sin. My choices and those who influenced my life, were going lead me into despair, hopelessness, and one failure after another. This is exactly what allowing sin to rule you does.

But, as the reader goes on, focus on how far down Jesus will go, to reach somebody bound by sin. It is truly mind boggling. After all these years, I still wonder at His mercy, love, and power to forgive any sin. All we need to do, is call out to Him, He's only a prayer away.

TWO
WRONG CHOICES

Sixteen, the age when many girls live in the fast lane. The center of attention evolves around school events, boys and weekend parties with girlfriends, the prom, and petting their egos. On the hunt for the best perfumes, makeup, the latest styles, what's in fashion. By this age, they have honed their skills in manipulating their parents to get what they want; regardless whether they could afford it or not. No one really takes each other seriously. After all, what's a little fib to make the story a little more interesting. Lies weren't really lies, just little exaggerations. By the time many of these girls become adults the pattern of this kind of living is set in them, and no one thinks anything of it. This is womanhood and what is expected in society. I quickly learned to never believe any of them, and made it a point to avoid lasting relationships. I'd watched the tactics of these girls as they would feign friendship with a girl in public for a short time, then tear her to pieces when she was out of sight.

My Mother often said to me, we are fortunate if we have a handful of real, true, friendships in a lifetime. This was one thing my Mother said, I know is true.

I hated this aspect of being a young girl, and did not share the dreams or goals most girls my age strove for. But, I wasn't any better. I had developed a cynical, angry trait in my character, that I still have to pray about often; and ask the Lord for balance in my life. By this time, I'd lost all innocence, felt I had gone too far, and ruined any chance of ever having any lasting happiness. I drank almost every day, especially weekends. During our parties, and going to the bars, we'd hook up with other's like ourselves. Like spirits attract like spirits and congregate together, either for good, or evil. At this time of my life, it was perpetually evil.

I was still going to my girlfriends house often. We'd spend weekends using the tarot cards, Ouija board, and whatever else we felt led to do; along with the usual drinking, rock music, and getting together with boys. Her Mother was out dancing at these times and getting drunk also. Several times she became pregnant. There were a couple of quiet adoptions that took place, which was not talked about. Life would go on afterward as if it never happened.

Several times my girlfriend would talk about two brother's she had, that I'd never met. One was older than her by a couple of years. She spoke of how he had been on his own for a while, traveling in the south, and had come back to New York. One of the weekends we were together she asked me if I'd be interested in meeting him. I'd been alone for almost a year by this time, but inside I felt reluctant to get involved with anyone who may have serious intentions. I said no at first and hoping she would forget about it. But a couple of weeks later, she asked me again. I finally agreed.

She set the meeting up for me to come to her house on a Saturday afternoon during midsummer break. When I arrived he met me outside. We walked for a while and he told me some things about himself, the places he'd been, and his goals at that time. I listened, not really wanting to share much about myself. At the end of the meeting, we parted, not making any commitments between each other, which was fine with me.

Soon however, he called me at home one evening after school. He asked a lot of questions, and seemed genuinely interested in what I had to say, and shared some things with me that gave some inclination we had some things in common. A relationship began to form, and the calls continued to come every few days. After about a month of this, he asked if I'd be interested in going out, just for dinner and a ride in the country. I thought about it for a few moments, then agreed. That meeting began a lasting bond, and we got together as often as we both could. But, with no moral compass, or upbringing, and still living in sin; I allowed sex to be a part of our relationship. By this time, knowing most of the kids in school were doing the same thing, it seemed that nothing was wrong with it. This is what living in sin, and darkness does. It blinds us to the truth of the consequences of our actions. I learned the hard way, there are many consequences that sometimes affect the rest of our lives, even after we are saved.

He came to me one day, and asked if I'd marry him. My girl friend tried to talk me out of it. She said she knew him better than I did, and felt I would be making a mistake. I considered what she said, and found it odd that her Mother, who knew her son better than any of us, said nothing, and gave no advice. After a short time of mulling it over in my heart, I told my girlfriend I decided to marry him. She didn't agree with me but said nothing more.

In mid-July 1970 at age seventeen, we married in a small Methodist church near my parents' home, and the reception was held in their house right after the service. My new husband had been working on a dairy farm in northwest North Carolina. He had come to New York with friends he knew, who drove up for the wedding. Within an hour of the reception, I had to change out of my gown, which was left with my Mother, into regular clothes, for a long trip by car with him and his friends, back to North Carolina.

I embraced my parents. Mother was crying in silence, Dad was somber but said nothing. My other sisters and brothers embraced us. There were smiles, but serious eyes. The younger ones were mostly silent, not knowing what to say or do. I hugged them knowing it may be a very long time before I saw them again, or ever. The significance of this moment was beginning to reach my heart. My life was going to change forever. Looking again at my parents, I realized, they *did* know all this, and were trying to look happy, for me.

I had packed a small suitcase to take with me. I took it and got in the back seat of the car; for a seventeen hour journey back to North Carolina. I looked in the rear view mirror, and saw Dad holding Mother around the waist. They waved as we began driving away. My heart was torn and wrenched with many feelings. But there was no turning back now, the journey had begun.

Tired from the long trip through the night, we arrived at the mobile home of the people we were with. They took us to the dairy farm my husband worked at. It was very old, the boards were without insulation of any kind, many of the cracks in the walls were wide enough to see to the outside. The first night there, I slept very little, listening to strange noises from animals in the forests surrounding the house. The next day was spent cleaning until my hands bled. But, as an excited new bride, I didn't care about the cracks in the walls.

Within a couple of weeks my husband began talking about his boss, the man who owned the farm. He said the man wasn't happy with his work, and he needed to improve, or he wouldn't keep him on. I said nothing, waiting to see what happened. In less than two months, he was fired. We spent the night we were evicted sleeping on the ground behind a high school building. We were fortunate it was just the beginning of September, and still warm at night in the south.

We had very little money, and owned an old car that used a lot of oil. We made it to a town that had many furniture mills. We went to several real estate agencies who listed places for rent, and found a basement apartment that we could afford, and moved in. John was able to walk to many of the furniture mills, and found work in one of them on the third shift. We settled in, and I began again to clean up the "new" place, and make it a home.

Within a few weeks I began to feel nausea's. It continued to worsen, with vomiting, no appetite, and not able to hold anything down.

We went to a local hospital. A doctor examined me and took several tests. In a short time he came back, telling us I was pregnant. I was stunned. Before we were married, I had gone to a doctor in New York and had an IUD inserted to prevent getting pregnant. When I told the doctor this he shrugged and mumbled about them not staying in place at times. My husband's countenance changed, and became very dark. He said nothing until we got back to the apartment.

When we arrived back home, then he lit into me "How did you let this happen! I told you I'm not ready to have kids, we can hardly take care of ourselves! How could you be so stupid?"

Suddenly, I felt his hands on my shoulders, pushing me down and into the chair behind me with violent force.

The realization came, "This man does not really love me, and now I'm alone in this mess." I didn't move, just waited to see what he was going to do next, and forming a plan if the violence got worse.

He bent over slightly, glared into my eyes, and said, "This is your problem, not mine." He turned, slammed the door and left.

It was mid-afternoon. I sat there for a while, still sick to my stomach, but not wanting to sit there any longer staring at the walls alone. I put on my jacket, put my wallet in my pocket, and started walking to the middle of town. It soon became evening, the sun was going down. In this town, gangs of mostly black people usually roamed the streets, and the news on TV always issued warnings to not be out alone after dark. I kept on walking, I didn't care. I saw several of these gangs in the distance, but none of them came near me that night. I know now, God was walking with me, but I didn't know it then.

Late into the night, on a dark street, standing between the glow of city lamps, I looked up, and for the first time prayed to God. "I'm not afraid, but I don't know what to do. If you're there, would you please show me the right thing to do in this." That was all. I turned and walked back to the apartment. Reaching for the door knob, I knew what to do. From then on, I started planning and saved all I could of my tiny allotment for groceries, for a bassinet.

We were only in that apartment two more months when my husband decided it was time to move again. This time to a farm about 25 miles away to a house owned by another farmer. He kept the same job at the furniture mill in town, and rode to work with other guys who worked in the same place. I was beginning to show in pregnancy, and Thanksgiving was soon coming. I hoped there would be no more moves until the baby was born, but this was not to be.

Through that fall, and early into the spring, I enjoyed the beauty of the country around the house we lived in. There was no extra money, but I had found a very pretty pond behind our house. A dirt road went down to it, and I used it often for the exercise, sometimes taking a fishing pole and bringing back dinner.

But my husband was restless again, and talking about wanting to move and get another job somewhere else. My heart sank. I had no choice in the matter. He was just informing me what was going to happen, not asking what I thought of his intentions. We had no phone, there was no way to call any of my family for counsel, or help of any kind. I braced myself for what may happen.

One morning in early March, I looked out the dining room window and saw several vehicles coming up the driveway. Looking closer, it was my family! My parents, older sister, two brother in laws, and my eldest brother in three vehicles. One was a truck big enough to haul our belongings. I was big with child, but ran to the door, and out into the driveway. They all got out, talking and laughing at the same time. My Father and Mother embraced me, and told me they decided to take me back home with them; so I could have the baby in safety. They said they couldn't stop thinking about me being here all by myself, and had to do something. God's goodness working in those we love, we often don't recognize. My husband wasn't given any choice in the matter. The men didn't ask him if he liked the decision. He simply was told I was coming home with them, and he could too if he wished. He made no dispute, and started helping pack the truck with our belongings.

We moved in with my parents in their upstairs rooms. The stress of moving so many times during the pregnancy brought on a lot of anxiety, causing me to go several weeks beyond the due date. Finally the doctor said he would have to induce labor, and make sure the baby delivered safely. On May 8, 1971 at around 7:00 p.m., Carrie was born, slightly blue, but perfectly healthy. I awoke to see her crying loudly on my chest. The nurses took her, bathed and placed her in a tiny pink bunting, and put her in my arms again. Pure joy in those precious moments.

In a few months, my husband began talking about moving back to the Carolina's again. My parents were not happy about it at all, nor was I.

But, with a six month old baby girl in my arms, we packed the car we owned with what would fit, and made the journey back to North Carolina. We only stayed there a very short time. Again leaving, this time for Mrytle Beach South Carolina. There he found an apartment about five miles from the beaches, and found work.

During this time my eyes were opened to more of the real personality and character of this man, and it changed my own character. I became determined, calculating, driven, and focused on one thing; raising my daughter, and some way, somehow, getting out of this hopeless existence.

One afternoon, he came home earlier than usual. I could tell he'd been drinking. Carrie was 15 months old, just starting to learn to walk. I was folding clothes, coaxing her to hold onto the furniture, and take a step. He sat down, looked briefly at her, then said to me,

"When you're done with that, let's get cozy".

I knew what that meant, and didn't reply. I wasn't really interested. He saw this, and spoke up again.
"We had a pretty good porn party at work today, and the boss let us off early so we could enjoy the rest of the day free."

I turned and looked at him, "What?"

He repeated the statement.

"What goes on at these "porn parties"?"

He smiled, "We get pizza's, sandwiches, snacks, and booze, and the boss puts a video on of some hot pornography, then we have a ball".

"How long has this been going on?"

"Guys just about all over down here in the south do this, it's everyday stuff."

My stomach churned into knots. I was getting sick, he may as well have told me he was committing adultery, because that's what it was; and he'd been doing it from the first year we were married.

"Have you been with any other women?"

He looked down at his feet, no answer. I didn't need to see anymore, I knew. I went back to folding the clothes and talking to Carrie. This was the beginning of the end of the marriage.

Several months later, again, he let me know it was time to move on.

Each time it was either the job, or the people causing the decision to move on "the job has no future", "it doesn't pay enough", "the boss is an idiot and doesn't know what he's doing". I had learned the pattern well. The Bible describes the kind of person I was married to, which defined him to me years later as I looked back on these dark days of turmoil and insecurity.

**Jas 1:8 A double minded man is unstable
in all his ways.**

Shortly before he left to find another place to live, he brought home a man about the same age as my husband, and introduced him to me. He shared some of his life, or what he *said* was his life. Most people in general at this time gave vague, general information about themselves, and you learned not to probe very far. You never really knew if you were being told the truth, and learned not to pursue it. Just live and let live. So I listened, and he became a frequent guest. The two of them would go off together sometimes for the entire day, leaving me and Carrie alone. Once I got in our car and followed them, far enough behind so they didn't notice me. They went to one of the beaches, and were playing, laughing and socializing with other's they seemed to know. I had Carrie in my arms and walked up behind my husband. The guy he was with spoke to him that I was there.

He turned around and when he saw me, he flew into a rage, telling me I had no right to follow him, to get out, and go back home. The people he was with just stood watching, saying nothing. I left, and indeed learned to never do that again.

Not long after, they both left together, telling me they'd be back to get me, when they found jobs and a place to live. They were headed for Columbia South Carolina. He told me he'd call me when they found a place, and let me know when to start packing to move. The day after they left, the power company turned off my lights. It was mid-day when they did this. I was 19, with a broken down car that ran, but needed oil put in it every 50 miles. Carrie was now 19 months old. I got out some candles, expecting to have to find a way to live without power until he called and came to get us. That same evening, just before sundown, there was a knock on the door. I opened it to see my parents standing there. My mouth dropped in amazement. I motioned for them to come in, and told them what had happened.

Mother's response was simple, but so true.

"We just knew something was wrong, and had to come. It must have been the Lord speaking to us."

Dad was furious, "I want you to pack your stuff and come back to New York with us. You can't raise a baby like this."

I knew how he felt but wasn't sure what to do yet. He helped me pack our belongings and leave it there for either my husband or someone else to take care of it. The next several days, we spent going to the beaches, and enjoying time together. Then my husband called to say he was ready to come for us. Dad got on the phone and told him he wanted to drive me and Carrie to where he was, and asked him the directions. When he got off the phone, he turned and looked at me and said, "Before I take you there, are you sure this is what you want to do? I think you should still come back home with us, and leave him to do whatever he wants." My Mother looked at me. I saw she agreed with him.

My heart was torn. I agreed with my Father's point, but the natural desire for stability, and a father for Carrie won out.

"No, take me to him, and I'll decide what to do when I see what the situation is."

Dad drove the 120 miles to the city. It was late afternoon when we finally found the street and house number with the directions given to him. I stayed in the car. Dad went in first, to find out if my husband was really there. He didn't come out to greet us, we went in ourselves. The majority of our belongings were still in Myrtle Beach. Dad told him this, and also told him he was leaving me there against his better judgment. My husband never looked him in the eyes, but nodded that he knew what was meant.

As my father pulled out into the street, I stood holding Carrie in my arms, waving my parents goodbye. Again with no clear direction of our future. All I knew, was to try to meet each day, and get through it.

It was in Columbia I started drinking again. When I found I was pregnant with Carrie, I had stopped. I wanted to be a good Mother, and go back to school, be a nurse or learn some other skill, and better myself, for her. But now, looking around at the environment facing me, knowing he was hooked on pornography, and having sex with not only other women, but also this "friend" who now was a part of our life, whether I liked it or not. I gave up inside, and started drinking to get to that numb place again and kill the pain. The worst was yet to come.

I found a job at a seven eleven job, as a night manager, 3:00 to midnight shift. I only needed to pay a babysitter a couple of hours, until my husband picked up Carrie and took her home for the night. Our lives were pretty much separate now, and he did what he wanted. It wasn't uncommon for my husband to leave on a Friday, and not come home till Monday, never explaining where he went, or with who. I didn't ask.

One night at work at almost midnight, closing time; two tall black men wearing stocking masks came up around me from behind, grabbed my ponytail and dragged me to the front behind the desk. One of them pointed a gun at my forehead, pressed it into my skull, and demanded I open the safe and hand over all the money in it. I did, as they cursed me and telling me how lucky I was that they didn't blow my head off. I was not afraid, and spoke back,

"If you do, you'll not get away with it."

I handed the zippered cash bag over to them, knowing that earlier, as I usually did, I had actually stashed the most of the money in the trash can in a paper bag. Only at the very end of the shift I added it to what was in the floor safe. They grabbed it, running for the door, and cursed me one more time as they disappeared into the night. This was one of several times in my life the devil has almost killed me. I knew it must have been God who saved me, but I was still in too much darkness, to give him the thanks he deserved.

Finally the day came, that I knew would. Once again my husband had been gone for over 3 days, with no word of where he was, or with whom. I sat looking at the walls of the apartment and Carrie sitting alone on the floor, playing quietly with a toy she especially liked.

"I can't live like this anymore." I thought, I knew I had to make a change for my daughters sake, this was no life for a little girl. I decided to call my parents and make arrangements to go back to New York, and make a life for us there.

Dad said to expect a check within a day from Wells Fargo. He'd paid for a greyhound bus ticket home to Albany, and would be waiting to pick us up when we arrived. I packed what I could fit into a large green trunk, and one suitcase that was allowed on the bus with small toys, clothes, and food for us both on the trip.

When we arrived at the station there was Dad, hands behind his back, quietly waiting for us. There is no greater sense of security, than when you know your loved, and cared for by family. I've known that love, and cherish it tremendously. I look forward to that great reunion, on the other shore in heaven when I meet those loved ones again.
I was back again in my old room, with a small bed next to mine for Carrie. I found work as a cashier in a local grocery store and worked all the hours I could, saving money for whatever opportunities

I may encounter and improve our life. I wanted to forget my husband, erase the past completely and start new, and that was the focus of my time and energy now.

In a couple of months the phone rang. Mother answered it, it was my husband again. My Mother looked at me with the phone still in her hand.

"You don't have to talk to him, I'll tell him you're not here."

I almost said yes, but reached out and took the phone, and gave a cold greeting. He began asking for forgiveness, and "could we try again" was again his approach. This time I flatly refused, and told him I had no more interest in going on with the relationship. It was dead to me now and he should find a lawyer to finalize a divorce. I hung up before he had a chance to dispute anything.

But as I knew would happen, he continued to call. Weeks of this went on, listening to him tell me in convincing terms that he wanted us back, he would settle down, there would be no more moving. He'd find a home for us, and we'd repair the love he had damaged. I caved in and told him to come up if he really meant it. Within a few days, he was at my parents door again. My parents had nothing to say. They were not happy about it, but just accepted it. I didn't blame them.

We spent time talking and settling disputes between us. I made it clear I wasn't interested in moving south again, and he knew I meant it. My oldest brother, a very caring man, came to us one night, and told us he wanted to try to help us get a home, and stability for Carrie. He took us to a mobile home sales park. We looked at several small mobile homes that would make a good starting home for us, and we chose one. My brother gave us the down payment, and helped us get it set up in a nice park in a rural area, with a large back yard. It looked like our lives were going to start to improve, and we'd have a solid future as a family. It was not to last.

After the life of turmoil we had been through together, I wasn't interested in getting chummy with neighbors. I had to work, and found a night job as a waitress at a local diner. My family helped take care of Carrie on the nights I worked. On the few days I had off I just wanted to be home with my daughter, and have some peace. My husband was never content with this. Our personalities were very opposite. He always wanted to get involved with weekend parties and in other people's personal lives. I knew this kind of thing almost always ended in eventual strife, misunderstandings, and trouble. I didn't want it. This caused arguments again and I could see increasing distance from him, and signs of the same patterns emerging from him from the past. He started being gone Friday nights, that increased to the entire weekends. I wasn't told where or who he was with, I didn't bother to ask. I kept working long hours, and staying home. I was drinking heavily now, just to exist and get through life.

My Father had gone through lung cancer surgery, and long sessions of treatments and partial recovery. They weren't able to get all the cancer; he died five years after losing his lung. But we were fortunate to have been able to spend those last years with him. Both my parents were going through great turmoil, I could not put any more burden on them. I didn't talk to either of them about what my husband was doing again. But something in deep inside told me, this was the last time.

One summer night he came home with a couple I'd never met before. He said they wanted me to go with them to the movies at a local drive-in close by. I got in the passenger seat in the front, the couple were in the back, my husband did the driving. Shortly after the first movie began, I realized what we were watching was a triple XXX rated pornographic movie, and there were three of them to sit through. I couldn't believe what was happening to me. I sat in silence, not knowing what to do. The scenes before me were so filthy, so hideous, I began to cry.

John looked at me laughing. "Hey, this is to get you softened up. Let's trade partners. Try it, you don't know what you're missing."

I looked at him "You have become nothing but an animal. I want to go home."

"What's the matter, why does it bother you?" He laughed again.

I got out of the car and started walking home. The drive-in was five miles away from my house. I didn't care, I'd walk all night if I had to. But soon he pulled up beside me, stopped, and told me to get in; he'd take me home. I got back in, and sat in silence until we pulled into our driveway. I got out and told him not to come back, I was finished. He laughed again, "You've said that before".

"This is the last time I'll say it, don't come back."

It was the end, I wanted it to be.

Ironically the day after he left, my lights were turned off again, just as they had been in Myrtle Beach, South Carolina. This time it took several months of working overtime and saving to pay it off, and get the lights back on. He had taken out a loan for a motorcycle about a year before he left. A man from the bank came to the door one day telling me I had to pay his overdo motorcycle payments. My answer to him was "You're not getting any blood out of this rock." He knew I meant it and left. I never saw him again. From that time on it was a matter of closing all the doors to the past life with him, and never look back.

Writing this after so many years is not pleasant but necessary; because it's all part of the plan of God to rescue me and my daughter. God may use it, to rescue you.

THREE
HITTING BOTTOM

S ignificant events began to take place that would change the course of my life forever. God placed people in my path, and moved in my circumstances in profound ways, to use every means he could to bring to me out of darkness. To cause me to begin to open my eyes and see the path of destruction I was on, and make changes in my decisions that would open the door for God to get through the unbelief, cynicism, and rebellion that had blocked Him from being able to reach me up to this point.

Each day now revolved around working at night, coming home, drinking to unwind, and try to go to bed and get some sleep. Carrie was now three, and would spend the nights I worked at my parents' house, a short walk down the road from me. They were always there and willing to help, even in the midst of their own problems, dealing with Dad's health problems with lung cancer.

There had been numerous times in my life I now know God had used other's to be a witness to me. But during my teen years, and then married to a man with no stability, moving pillar to post; I'd become very harsh, and brushed them off with a cold rebuke. I've prayed and asked the Lord to forgive me for those times. One day I'll have the opportunity to thank them for having the courage to say anything to me, and for their prayers. They were not in vain.

During one shift at work, a tall dark haired man got out of his truck, and headed for the door to come in. I glanced his way, but was busy with a diner full of hungry drivers, all wanting service. I'd not seen this man before, he was quiet, and had a demeanor about him of inner strength. He sat at the counter and asked for a cup of coffee and a sandwich. I tended to him and went on working.

When he got up to leave he left a tip, but then looked up into my eyes, and very directly said,

"You seem very sad, I can understand why, glancing quickly to the full, noisy room. But there' someone who cares very much for you, who can give you the love and purpose you need to get through, and give you hope. But most important, eternal life."

He handed me a small piece of paper that looked like a check. It said "To Whosoever will COME" at the bottom at the signature line it said "The Lord Jesus Christ".

His eyes were full of love and strength at the same time. He never flinched when he spoke to me, as soon as I took it and read it, he turned and went out the door. I never forgot his courage and conviction. God used it for years to speak to my heart, in my darkest of days. I watched him walk back to his truck. I was angry with him, and almost threw the tract in the trash, but something stopped me, I couldn't do it. I kept that tract in my wallet for many years after I was saved, and prayed for that man every time my eyes glanced at it. None of us will ever know in this life, until we are in heaven, what one simple act of obedience can do to make a change in someone's life.

About the same time, one Saturday afternoon a school bus came down through our lane. It was the Sunday school bus driver from the local Baptist church that picked up kids and took them to church on Sunday's. I wondered why it was here on a Saturday. As it went down the road, I noticed it stopped at several other mobile homes along the way. The man got out to talk to some people who were in their yards outside. I went back inside, deciding to get some things done on my day off. About an hour later I hear a knock on my door. It was the Sunday school driver. With a smile on his face, he asked if I had a few minutes to talk. I had no desire to talk to him, and quickly thought of something to make an excuse to shut the door. He sensed my reluctance.

"Would you rather come out in the yard, and just talk for a few minutes?"

"Ok".
I stepped out, shutting the door behind me, leaving Carrie in her room playing.

"I see you have a young daughter, and she doesn't go to school yet, I don't believe. I'm wondering if you'd be willing to let her come with us to the church on Sundays and join the kids in Sunday school class. It would give you a break and I'm sure she would enjoy the fun with the other's. You are very welcome to come also, we'd love to have you."

As he talked I considered what he was saying. Carrie was an only child, only three and it would be an outlet for her to join with other's and bring some joy into her life. I knew he was right.

"Alright, but will adults be there to watch over her during the time she's there? I need to know she will be safe at all times."

"Oh yes, there will never be a time when she would be out of sight of someone responsible. We make very sure of that."

I could see his sincerity, so I agreed to allow her to be picked up the following Sunday. It was to be a small part of her life that brought enjoyment, a time of innocent fun, but most of all, learning about the love of Jesus, and bringing the light of His life into her little soul. I wasn't willing to go, I was still drinking, working many hours, and didn't feel people would accept me in this state. I didn't have the desire to go through the possible rejection.

God was doing all He could to bring light into our lives, a step at a time. The years of turmoil, sin, and the consequences of it, had finally brought me to a place of being willing to listen, and open the door of my heart; at least a crack.

It had been about eight weeks now since my husband had left, and I began to feel the familiar signs of being with child. Inside I hoped it wasn't so. I waited, hoping the nausea would go away. It didn't, and certain foods became inedible to me again. I knew I had to find out for sure and deal with the truth, if I was pregnant. I made an appointment, and went in within a few days. Yes, I was pregnant. I went home, sat down, and started drinking until late into the night.

One of the sad realities of my childhood was watching the way the women in my family dealt with hard times in their lives; I allowed it to mold me into the same patterns of letting my emotions rule me. My Mother and two older sisters both had ongoing troubled relationships with their husbands and relatives. I watched this over the years, and it affected me, and not for the good. They each had the tendency to use moodiness, revenge, long silences and manipulation to send their messages, or retaliate and use as weapons against their husbands and boyfriends. They all went through breakups, long silences, divorces, then they'd get back together, and try to
patch up the relationship again. I learned to be the same way. After I was saved, God dealt with me a great deal over this, and disciplined me consistently about it.

I didn't go to anyone in my family to talk about this, they were all in situations just as bad as mine. I was alone and had to make my own decisions in this problem.

I knew I wasn't making enough money to keep the mobile home, my daughter, and have another child.

Satan never fights fair. He is a dirty fighter, and will hit you the hardest, when you're at your weakest. Jesus says it well when he tells us Satan comes to kill, steal, and destroy. As believer's the battles we wage here aren't against flesh and blood. It's against the principalities and powers of darkness, who are relentless in their attempt to destroy people; created in the image of God, and made for his glory and purpose.

I do not care what society thinks of what I've just said. I'll admonish the reader to open their eyes, and be willing to see this world as God sees it. And as far as society goes, millions of Harry Potter books fly off the shelves and kids around the world are delving into the supernatural in every aspect. Satan has been very successful in gaining possession of kids, and many parents have not only allowed it, but encouraged it.

I did not know any of this yet., I was alone, discouraged, depressed, and still allowing sin to run my life. I sat there that night and evaluated my situation. I decided the most important thing was to not lose the daughter I had, and doing what I'd have to do, so that didn't happen. Getting up and turning off the light on the way to bed, I planned to call the doctor, and make another appointment to see about an abortion. It seemed to be the only answer.

At this point I'm going to interject something that the world is very good at covering up. I don't excuse the women who intentionally get pregnant to stay on welfare, and have one child after another, to stay on it and not work. But neither should the man get off free as a bird. Many women who have abortions are pushed into it by the man involved, and threatened if they won't go through with it. Most men don't care and make it clear they don't. Some men force the women they've gotten pregnant to have an abortion, and threaten them with violence, if they refuse. Some women have lost their lives for not being willing to have one.

After I was saved the Lord showed me his heart about this. He holds the man just as responsible for the abortion as the woman. On Judgment day if he hasn't repented of his part of it, God will judge him on it. It was just as much his baby, as the woman's.

The ungodly who have multiple abortions are heaping much judgment on themselves. I find it very disturbing listening to some women who've admitted having three, four, sometimes even more abortions, and say it never bother's them. It is chilling to listen to women like this.

When I walked into the waiting room it was only a short time before I was taken to the office. The nurse asked me if I was still living alone, and a few questions about my family and their situation. She asked if I was still working, and if I needed any financial assistance. I said no, because at that time, if single women received assistance from the government there was a real possibility of social services taking the children and I knew this. I wasn't willing to let them have that option. Then she started explaining the process of having an abortion, and if I was sure this was the route I wanted to take. My heart was very heavy but I said yes. She began relaying the form that needed to be filled out, and the appointment set up with Planned Parenthood not far away from where I lived. The appointment was set up, and I went home. I was torn inside.

The day it was to be done I walked into the waiting room. I was surprised to see a large number of women there. It saddens me even now, many years later. I now realize the significance of what I was seeing. So many women, both married and unmarried, choosing to end the life of their child for many different reasons. I hold no condemnation toward them, only sadness and grief.

When I was called the atmosphere was very business-like. People were polite, but there was no smiling interaction, just focusing on getting the procedure done.

It was painful, and in time to come, I would realize how much it would cost me. I lost three other babies, never being able to carry one to birth the rest of my life. Years later, a doctor found damage was done from the abortion, and questioned if the damage was caused intentionally.

I drove myself home alone. I had taken off several days, knowing I'd need to recover. Then the daily routine resumed, between work, caring for my daughter, and trying to keep a roof over our heads.

My Father was in and out of the hospital at this time, going through procedures dealing with lung cancer. My Mother was under tremendous stress, still having two teenage sons at home. My younger brother was giving her a lot of trouble she couldn't cope with. He was gone most of the time and getting into trouble. One day he told them he had made arrangements to go to Texas and stay with relatives there. My parents gave him their permission. It seemed like the best option to take. Otherwise he was going to get into trouble anyway. He did get into many mishaps there also. But he's still in Dallas, married and rooted to the area.

Because of this situation with my parents, I decided to not tell them about the abortion. I couldn't put any more burden on my Mother, it would have been too much for her.

I'm going to take some time here to minister to women, in hopes God will use it to help someone who may find themselves in a similar situation as I was. To give you some encouragement, hope, and persuade you to not do what I did.

First, if you are pregnant, single, or married but the man is gone, there is someone who cares about you and your situation. God cares.

No matter how desperate your condition may be, if you will look up, and simply ask the Lord for His help to have the baby and make the right decisions, he will make a way for you. Don't listen to the voices in your mind telling you ending this pregnancy is the only answer. They aren't coming from the Lord, but the enemy, and your own discouraged soul. You're battling hopelessness. If you open your heart and talk to God and ask Him to help you, He will guide you. He'll help you find a way to keep the baby, or put it up for adoption. Killing the baby is not the answer.

Let my wrong decision be an example to help you make the *right* decision. In years to come, you'll know the value of it. And, you'll never go through the heartache of living with the regret of knowing you've destroyed a life.

To any who may read this and feel I did this because of not liking children, not wanting another child, of just wanting to live a party life, you couldn't be more wrong. But there are no words that would make any difference. God knows what my situation was, and what was in my heart. He's made this clear to me, and affirmed His forgiveness to me many times. Only other women who've made the same mistake, and now realize the wrong of what they did, can understand what I'm saying.

When I was first saved, the Lord guided me to passages of scripture and used it to heal my spirit. I still go to it and remind myself of what the Holy Spirit taught me, and ministered to me with it. I'll share it here and pray the Lord uses it to bring the same healing and mercy to you.

In the gospel's, we are told of Jesus appearing after he was risen, to Mary Magdalene. There's two accounts, in John and Mark:

> But Mary stood without at the sepulchre
> weeping: and as she wept, she stooped
> down, and looked into the sepulchre, And
> seeth two angels in white sitting, the one
> at the head, and the other at the feet,
> where the body of Jesus had lain. And

they say unto her, Woman, why weepest thou? She saith unto them, Because they have taken away my Lord, and I know not where they have laid him. And when she had thus said, she turned herself back, and saw Jesus standing, and knew not that it was Jesus. Jesus saith unto her, Woman, why weepest thou? whom seekest thou? She, supposing him to be the gardener, saith unto him, Sir, if thou have borne him hence, tell me where thou hast laid him, and I will take him away. Jesus saith unto her, Mary. She turned herself, and saith unto him, Rabboni; which is to say, Master. Jesus saith unto her, Touch me not; for I am not yet ascended to my Father: but go to my brethren, and say unto them, I ascend unto my Father, and your Father; and to my God, and your God. Mary Magdalene came and told the disciples that she had seen the Lord, and that he had spoken these things unto her. John 20:11-18

I never cease to marvel at the tenderness, and love which the Lord speaks to her. But even greater how the Lord uses this to remind me that the same tenderness and mercy is extended to me, and to anyone else who will simply receive it. He brings me back to these passages again and again to pour into my heart it's truth, there is now no condemnation to those who are in Christ Jesus.

In this account we are shown by example; they who are forgiven much, love much. This woman knew she was a sinner. She made no attempt to excuse or deny her sins. She loved and adored the One who had the ability to set her free from her sin and restore her. Even death could not keep her away. She would do what she could to honor the body of the One she adored, no matter the cost.

Those with the calloused heart of the pharisee will never understand this kind of love. They reveal their true spirit by the cold, calculating gazes, and
standing afar off, so as to not be contaminated by such a sinner.

Now, the account in Mark:

> Now when Jesus was risen early the first day of the week, he appeared first to Mary Magdalene, out of whom he had cast seven devils. And she went and told them that had been with him, as they mourned and wept. And they, when they had heard that he was alive, and had been seen of her, believed not. Mark 16:9-11

Think of it, this woman had been possessed of seven devils. The first thing she does after this meeting was go and try to tell the other disciples, she preached. They, because of the hardness of their hearts, didn't believe her. But the greatest emphasis the Lord brought home to me was, this woman was the first person he appeared to, and spoke with, not the disciples, not even Peter.

As a new believer and just recently forgiven of so much, there were many times waves of guilt and shame from my past would almost overwhelm me. Every time, the Lord would direct me to these passages and those of the Apostle Paul, and how before his conversion, he had persecuted and imprisoned many Christians, and caused many of them to be killed. The Holy Spirit repeatedly brought me back to these passages and prompted me to do study them. He would stamp the truth in my mind; what he did for them, he has done for me.

These verses have truths in them that could take weeks to teach. I've only touched the surface of what could be shared. But, let it be a start, to

give you a glimpse of the heart of Jesus, how every individual is valuable to him, no one is more important to him than another. When we come to him for salvation, we are all equal in his sight. As the scripture makes so clear to us, let it sink into our hearts:

> 2Co 5:17 Therefore if any man be in Christ, he is a new creature: old things are passed away; behold, all things are become new.

Indeed, what does this verse truly convey to us, what does it proclaim for us? The miracle of a renewed spirit. Let's break it down.

If any man be in Christ, he is a new creature. Because, crucified with Christ, buried into his death, we have died with Christ, and risen to walk in a new life. The old life ended when we died and were buried. Born anew, we are new creatures who must live a new life. See Rom 6:6, 6:4, 2Co 5:14 Once we've placed our life and trust in Jesus Christ, what does scripture teach us concerning our position? Paul shows us our standing is with Christ, seated in

heavenly places:

> Eph 2:1 And you hath he quickened, who were dead in trespasses and sins;
>
> Eph 2:2 Wherein in time past ye walked according to the course of this world, according to the prince of the power of the air, the spirit that now worketh in the children of disobedience:
>
> Eph 2:3 Among whom also we all had our conversation in times past in the lusts of our flesh, fulfilling the desires of the

flesh and of the mind; and were by nature the children of wrath, even as others.

Eph 2:4 But God, who is rich in mercy, for his great love wherewith he loved us,

Eph 2:5 Even when we were dead in sins, hath quickened us together with Christ, (by grace ye are saved;)

Eph 2:6 And hath raised us up together, and made us sit together in heavenly places in Christ Jesus:

Together with Christ — The Head being seated at God's right hand, the body also sits there with Him. We are already seated there IN Him ("in Christ Jesus," Eph 2:6), and hereafter shall be seated *by* Him; IN Him already as in our Head, which is the ground of our hope; *by* Him hereafter, as by the conferring cause, when hope shall be swallowed up in fruition. What God wrought in Christ, He wrought (by the very fact) in all united to Christ, and one with Him.

Eph 2:7 That in the ages to come he might shew the exceeding riches of his grace in his kindness toward us through Christ Jesus.

Eph 2:8 For by grace are ye saved through faith; and that not of yourselves: it is the gift of God:

Eph 2:9 Not of works, lest any man should boast.

> **Eph 2:10 For we are his workman-ship, created in Christ Jesus unto good works, which God hath before ordained that we should walk in them.**

Now as new creatures in Christ Jesus, we've placed our lives in His. He now owns us. We are servants, not to sin any longer, but to serve the Lord, in righteousness, and holiness.

As he quickened Christ and raised him, so when we were dead in sins he gave us spiritual life by the gospel and lifted us to a new life. "We were planted in the likeness of his death and resurrection.

In Eph. 2:10, we're told we his workmanship, created for good works, not evil words, and we should walk in, hold a pattern of good works in our life.

Once we were servants of Satan when we walked in darkness. But now we walk in the light of Jesus Christ, and in the freedom He brings.

This brings clearer explanation to what Mary Magdalene's and our position is now, once we are set free by the Lord. Now we are co heirs, and Citizens of heaven.

As I took these verses and allowed the Holy Spirit to teach me, cleanse me, and renew my mind, my spirit responded with joy.

If you've lived deep in sin, and now as the prodigal son Jesus spoke of, want to come home, He's waiting with open arms.

Corrie ten Boom made a statement that's very true; "There's no pit so deep, that God's love is not deeper still."

It doesn't matter what you may have done. Jesus loves you as much as he does Mary Magdalene, Paul the persecutor of Christians, Matthew the tax collector, or Moses the murderer. If you will receive it, there's forgiveness and mercy for you, and room for you, at the foot of the cross.

"There is no pit so deep, that God's love is not deeper still."

Corrie ten Boom

FOUR
A FORK IN THE ROAD

Life settled into a routine of working, household chores, caring for my daughter and trying to give her some sense of stability. We walked to my parents' house just about every day, to see how Dad was doing and if there was anything I could do to help. It also gave Carrie time with her grandparents. I had every other weekend off and if I could afford it, would try to take her to a nearby river that had picnic areas. We could spend the day outdoors together, fishing and having a lunch. She loved those times, and would watch the wildlife, and run and play. My family also came often, and we'd plan a barbecue and roast marshmallows over the campfire. With little money, we learned to do things together and make our own fun.

Mother had a beautiful voice, and at times she would get out her guitar and we'd sing together favorite hymns, and country songs at the kitchen table, and make a special meal and dessert. I have special memories of doing the same things in my childhood, and wanted Carrie to have these times to help her get through this difficult part of our lives.

Between these events and her time at Sunday school, she seemed to be mostly unaware of the turmoil of a divorce, and a mother who had to be gone at work. I intentionally chose working nights throughout the years, in order to allow her to be with family I could trust. A few times I tried babysitters but this did not work. I found many of the women I worked with chose this shift for the same reason. We agreed it was worth losing the evenings home, for the peace of mind knowing our kids were with people we trusted.

One Saturday afternoon on one of my days off, I sat on the front steps watching Carrie play with her cat and some toys in the yard. I looked up to see the church school bus coming our way. I surmised he was seeing if he could get more kids to join the Sunday school class and pick them up. Sure enough, he slowly made his way down through, stopping and knocking on doors, and speaking to other's out in their yards. When he reached the end of our lane he turned around and came back up through on my side. When he reached my front yard, he stopped the bus, got out and walked up, stopped and smiled.

"Nice day to be out, enjoying the sun."

"Yes, I wanted to give Carrie a chance to get some fresh air before going in to make dinner."

"I understand."

He paused watching her for a moment, then began again.

"I know you haven't felt you could come to the services up to now, but I thought I'd invite you again. You might find the people are very understanding. I know your daughter would love it if you were with her."

I could see this was taking a lot of courage on his part to do this.

Quietly I answered. "Thank you, I can see your point, but I just don't feel I can do it right now."

"Ok, in a while, I'll ask again. But if you don't mind I'll ask you another question; have you thought of asking God for help? He cares very much for you, and if you'd talk to him about your problems, I know he'd listen, and believe you'd find things would start to change."

"I've heard this from others but I'm going to be blunt with you. If God really exists, why does He allow so much evil and suffering to go on? No one has been able to answer that for me in a way that makes sense. I have to be honest; I don't believe God cares, and I know people don't. You don't know what I face every day. If you saw the work conditions I face every night I work you'd know what I mean. I walk on concrete floors all night, listen to the dirty jokes, take the insults, and come home exhausted; to face my issues here alone. Then get up, and face another day just like it. If I told you what my life has been like up to now, you probably wouldn't believe it, and I wouldn't blame you if you didn't want to hear it."

The smile was gone from his face, but he looked steady into mine.

"No, I don't understand, but I do believe God does. Where do you work?"

I told him the name of the diner, he knew immediately where it was.

"I'll stop in sometime, and have a cup of coffee with you. But in the meantime, I hope you'll think about what I said. The Lord does care, very much, and I'm praying one day you will realize it."

"I'll consider what you've said, but right now, I'll still say no about services."

He nodded and went back to his bus, and drove slowly out of the park. I sat watching Carrie still playing on the grass, feeling unsettled but not knowing why.

The sun was setting. "Come on Carrie, let's pick up your toys, and bring in the cat, it's time for dinner".

She tried picking up the cat, who weighed almost as much as she did. We both laughed together. I took the cat and she gathered her toys. As the man had just tried to give me some sense of God's love when he spoke to me, watching my daughter as she went up the stairs before me, gave me a glimmer of what he meant. A great wave of love for her swept over me. Surely, God had shown me great love, in this bundle of joy.

Shortly after this, on a Saturday I had to work, another significant event took place, which began a complete change in the direction of my life.

The evening was getting noisy and busy, there was no time to pay much attention to any one person, everyone wanted service "right now".

As I weaved in and out of the tables, I glanced up to see a man come in I'd never seen before in the diner. His countenance was rugged, but there was a kindness about him, also determination and strength. I saw he sat at my side of the diner. When I had the minute to do it, I went to take his order. I gave him a menu and said I'd be back shortly.

When I came back he ordered. I sent it in and went back to my other customers. I noticed him looking at me a couple of times, but thought nothing of it. When his meal was ready I brought it to him and asked if he needed anything else.

"If I do, I'll let you know."

I nodded and went on with my work. The room began to empty out, the rush was about over. In between these waves of crowds I'd do cleanup jobs. I glanced at this man to see if he was getting ready to leave, but he seemed to be in no hurry. I went to him and asked if there was anything else he needed.

"No, but the reason I'm waiting around is my truck is broke down out in your yard, and I'm waiting for a guy I called from the pay phone outside. He's coming to work on it, and hopefully get it started."

"I see, do you live nearby?"

"I live in Vermont, just getting back from a beef run from out west".

"Well, I hope things go well for you. Let me know if there's anything I can do to help".

"Thanks, I appreciate it".

I went about my business, and he saw the man he was waiting for out the window and left. I thought of the hardship he was dealing with, and hoped he'd be able to get home soon.

About an hour later, he came back in and took a seat at a booth, glancing my way as he walked by.

Something about this seemed very strange to me, and became somewhat suspicious. Walking over to him I asked if he lost something or needed something more to eat to take with him.

"No, the guy I called is working on the part now that needs to be fixed. I'll be honest, I'd like to sit and talk to you when you have the time, or when your shift is up. I don't mind waiting."

I looked at him for a moment, I didn't know what to say. This man was a complete stranger, but I saw something in this man that made me trust him, at least enough to talk.

"I've got a couple of hours to go, you don't want to wait that long I'm sure."

"It depends on how long it takes the man to fix the engine and get it going for me. But I'd still like to talk to you if you're willing."

There were people needing to be served, and others wanting to be checked out, so I quickly nodded a yes to him, and went back to work. He went out again, tending to the repair man working on his truck. When my shift was done we sat in a booth with a cup of coffee; he started first.

"My name is Lyndon Couillard but everybody calls me Lynn. I live in the eastern side of Vermont near the New Hampshire border. My parents grew up there, and raised us kids in Bradford Vermont, where I live now. I graduated in 1968 from the Bradford Academy. Then went into the Air Force. They sent me to Vietnam then Alaska. I just bought a piece of land north of Bradford, back in the woods. I don't know if you'd be interested in living that kind of a life, but this tells you what kind of guy I am."

I sat and listened to this stranger tell me in very open, honest terms; his background, and goals.

"You seem to know what you want in life".

"Going overseas helped me get this way. When I left, I wasn't sure what I wanted to do with my life. But seeing the things I saw over there and experienced, brought me full circle. I want a home back in the country, where I can raise animals, beef, have my own place, and peace."

"Those are great goals. You'll make someone a good husband, if you decide to marry".

"Haven't got to that point yet, and I want to be sure of who I choose".

"I don't blame you, it's too important a step".

Then he looked at me and asked "Are you married?"

"Not anymore, I'm divorced." I made up my mind while listening to him that everything about me would be put out in front, and there would be no lying. I knew now he was fishing to see what kind of person I was, and I didn't want to give him a wrong impression, that I was some special woman. I briefly told him I had a small daughter, was living alone nearby close to my parents, and wasn't involved with anyone. I let him know I probably wasn't the kind of woman he was looking for. I got up and let him know I needed to get home to my daughter.

"I understand, thanks for talking to me."

I said goodnight and left. He went to his truck, which was now fixed and running. He got in and pulled out of the yard, giving a short honk from his horn as he drove out onto the road. As I drove home I thought, whoever that man married, she would be a very fortunate woman.

A couple of nights later I was working a Wednesday evening shift, it was about sundown. The diner was quiet with only a few customers toward the back booths eating dinner. At the counter I looked up to see the Sunday school bus driver walk in, take a stool and ask for a cup of coffee. I poured one for him, and placed the cream and sugar in front of him if he wanted it.

He smiled, took a sip from his cup, and asked if I had a minute to talk.

"Yes, it's quiet, I've got a few minutes."

"As I look around and see the environment, I can understand now what you were telling me when we talked in your yard. I can see why you'd find it hard to believe God cares. But though your situation is hard, and what you go through every day is more than I admit I could do; you may be failing to understand that it's not

God's fault you're in this place. He gives us free will, and we make choices. I know it's hard to hear this, but you can see it's the truth, if you're willing to admit it to yourself."

I didn't want to hear what he was saying, but nodded in agreement. I felt anger rising in me, because I didn't like hearing it; but I let him go on. He could see my reaction, and spoke kindly, but firmly.

"You're not to blame for all the circumstances you're in now, but you don't have to stay in them either. You can decide to make changes, set goals, and start working toward those goals. Change doesn't come overnight, and anything good usually comes by hard work. You walk these concrete floors and are doing what you can now, but you can begin to make decisions to get out of this situation. It doesn't have to be your life forever. You're depressed and discouraged, but with God's help things could change. But you need to take the first step, and open the door of your heart, and let Him in. If you do, you'll find your circumstances can change, for the better. God is for us, but he never forces himself on us. He waits for us to open our hearts, and ask Him for help in our lives".

As he talked many emotions went through me. His words rang true, I knew he was telling the truth. It sent a glimmer of hope into my heart. At the same time anger continued to build. There was a war going on inside me, a spiritual battle that I now know was an all-out duel between the demonic holds in my soul, and the Holy Spirit using this man to get through the layers of hardness, sin, and discouragement. I could clearly see the love and sincere concern in his eyes as he spoke to me. These many years later, my heart still prays for him. He may be in heaven now, and one day I intend to find him and thank him for his steadfast witness to me.

He stood up, paid for his coffee, and again asked if I'd consider joining Carrie and come to services on Sunday. Again I said no, but my heart was heavy. My mind and soul was in turmoil, and he could see it.

"I may not understand fully what you're dealing with, but God does. I'll be praying for you. I hope one day you'll let Him help you, and allow him in your life. I'll pray for that day to come for you."

We never spoke again. But it's a memory I keep, and will never forget. God answered his prayers, fully.

Shortly after this, on another Saturday I worked, late in the evening the door opened, and Lynn walked in. I was at the cash register. He looked at me as he walked by, heading to a booth toward the front. He smiled, and I sensed an air of determination about him. He held some magazines under his arm, and set them on the table in front of him as he sat down. I went over and asked what he'd like to eat. He ordered and I told him it would be a while because we were busy that night.

He grinned and said "That's fine, just give me something to drink."

I managed to get his meal to him, but then it took quite a while till I could take a break. Finally a lull came. I ordered a small meal, and took it with me to sit with him. He didn't waste any time, he opened one of the magazines, and started right off. "Since we talked last, I've been going over a lot of floor plans for the house I'm going to build on the property I just got. It's not going to be easy, because it's going to go over the top of an old foundation that I'm repairing. I'll have to make some adjustments on the measurements, but I've found several in here that could work, and wanted to show them to you, and see what you think".

I sat watching him, listening to him go on with such excitement and happiness. It boggled my mind. "What? I thought, Why is he telling me all this? Why does he want me to see what he's planning to do? The implications of what he was really doing, I couldn't allow myself to even consider.

I looked at him and said "Have you shared your ideas with someone whom you're interested in?"

He looked directly into my eyes "I'd like to show you these because I'm letting you know, I'd like you to share it with me."

"You don't know me, nothing about me really. How can you say you'd like me to share a life with you"?

"I've seen other women, and watched you enough right here, to give me a good idea what kind of woman you are. I know we need to spend time together and talk, and learn more about each other. But in my heart, I see in you what I've wanted in a wife".

My head and heart was spinning. I couldn't believe what I was hearing.

This dark haired rugged man, who I knew was hardworking and very intelligent, was giving me a very clear, direct proposal before we had even had our first date. I couldn't help but smile at him, he didn't seem to care that he was doing things out of sync.

"Wait a minute, wouldn't you want to spend at least one night out talking and getting to know each other a little better?"

"Oh sure, I know that's important, but hey, we both really know each other already, don't we."

I shook my head, still smiling "Yes, but don't ask me how I know you, but we do connect, don't we."

"We sure do, and my thought is, why waste a lot of time, when we both now we are meant for each other."

So, before we had our first date we sat in a booth at the diner looking over building plans for a house he was just starting to work on. He showed me several and asked what I thought of them. We talked about our likes and the things we didn't like. We discovered we both were into a country look with lots of wood and beams on the inside. We ended up going outside and talking, standing next to my car for a long time. Finally I said I had to get home to Carrie. This made me realize a question I knew I had to ask.

"You know I have a small daughter. Do you really want to get involved with a woman who already has a child?"

"I love kids. I'm looking forward to meeting her when you're ready".

I got in my car and watched him as he waved and went to his truck. We parted, going separate directions home. My heart was racing, my stomach churning. I had never felt like this in my life. For the first time I realized I was truly in love, real love from the heart.

The next time he came, after work we went someplace else, and sat alone for a very long time, talking about many things. He spoke of his time in Vietnam, and some of his experiences there. Then when he served in Alaska. He talked about his parents. I could tell he loved them and respected them. This meant a lot to me, it showed me the goodness of his character. He talked about his interests; hunting, fishing, raising animals and a wide range of other interests that were the same as mine. He asked questions, and really listened. He was interested in my family. I briefly told him of my Father, and his battle with cancer. Also Mother and the hardships she was going through, and my sisters and brothers. He said he'd like to meet them, when I felt it was the right time. I said I'd talk to them and let him know.

There was an easiness, and peace between us. Our souls began to merge, we knew our desires and interests were very much the same. We were at home with each other. The things we shared at this time melded us together forever. A sound love grew, and a companionship that sealed our spirits and we became one, before we were married.

As misunderstandings and people came into our lives who brought division that almost destroyed us, the bond of love couldn't be broken. It endured.

In heaven, I'm looking forward to sitting down and talking with him as long as we need to, to go over the times when we were in the worst battles of our lives together. We will know then the mistakes we made, and things we should have done differently, and people we should not have allowed to influence us.

The next time he came, we made plans for him to come to my house and begin to meet my family. We set a time on a Saturday that I didn't have to work. He said he'd do the shopping on the way, and pick up some nice steaks and we could have them for dinner at my place, if I didn't mind him cooking. I was surprised to hear him say he liked to cook, and did often. So that's what we did, and after the meal we went to my parents. My Father liked him right off, Mother did also. They talked and got to know each other. Before we knew it, it was late. Carrie needed to get to bed.

She had taken to Lynn immediately, and jumped into his open arms. After she was tucked into bed, we went to the living room to talk. After a long visit, and setting up the next time to meet he went out to his truck, and headed back to Vermont.

Several meetings took place after this with my family. My oldest brother Allen, my older sisters and their husbands, and my younger brothers and sister. He quickly was considered part of the family. They loved him. They said it felt like he'd always been a part of us.

One day Lynn looked at me and said "I'd like you to come to Vermont, and meet my family. I'll give you the directions, and make sure they're clear enough so hopefully you can find us."

Yes, I knew it needed to be done. I agreed. He drew the directions on a map, and the routes and intersections for me. I had a twinge of uncertainty, but made up my mind I was going to do this even if I got lost. I told myself to consider it an adventure. It proved to be one.

On a Saturday in early November of 1975 I left Carrie with my parents, and told them I'd be back before Monday. Early that morning I started out, excited as a school girl, but also full of questions that I knew would only be answered when I met his parents and sisters. He had let me know he had two, he was the only son.

Several times along the way I made a wrong turn, but backtracked and found the correct route again, and continued on. Finally I arrived at what Lynn showed on the map was Lebanon New Hampshire. Once I arrived there, it was due north on the interstate. I got on and kept going, arriving in Bradford, and continued following the directions till I found their house, just about a mile from the exit.

He met me with a smile in his parents yard, then took me in through the kitchen door. His parents greeted me, directing me to their living room, and we sat and talked for a short while. They were polite but quiet. They asked questions which I answered simply and directly. His Mother said they wanted me to stay for dinner. I said that sounded fine. His oldest sister came at this time and greeted me, asking more questions. I could see and sense quite a bit of probing. I expected it. I just answered their questions honestly, and let them make their own assessments. However, this meeting didn't have the same atmosphere of acceptance, or at-home feeling. I decided to be quiet and not offer a lot of chatter. It needed to be up to them to either accept me, or not. I wasn't going to push myself onto them. Over time, they came to understand this about me.

After dinner the conversations once again continued back in the living room. They talked about their early years, the first homes they built, the hard times they went through, how Lynn's Father established a motel in town, and ran it for quite a few years, then sold it and made other investments. His sister talked of her job as a nurse. She seemed very proud of her work, and her husband's work as an electrician. As I continued to listen I got the sense of how important money, and prestige was to them. Positions in the community, and the influence money brings was how they gauged a person's worth, and their position in society. I knew it would be best to listen more, and say less. I needed time to find out how to relate to them, and not put myself in a position I'd regret. I had learned the value of letting others talk.

The next morning it was cloudy and calm, and a light snow was falling. After breakfast with his parents he said he wanted to take me to the land he had purchased. I was looking forward to it but tried to hide my excitement. I didn't want to give away these feelings going on in me, that I didn't even understand myself. I didn't want to get my hopes up to only have them be crushed. I was going to be very cautious and quiet. But it wasn't easy.

We got in his truck, and he drove slowly up a two lane quiet highway headed north to the small village of East Corinth. At the end of the street, a right hand turn went onto a dirt road and an uphill grade. We drove along the three miles to the intersection known as Cheney Four Corners, in the township of Newbury. It was a one lane dirt road that had once been a carriage road that connected onto other routes over the mountains. It was very rugged, bumpy, and hadn't been kept up. His land was the last property, we were at a dead end of the road. Later, I would learn the road continued past us, veering in several directions, and a small cemetery was just beyond us, on the same side of the road. Through the years, we cared for it, planted trees there, and I used the trails many times walking, riding, and enjoying the peace of the forests.

We made it to the end of the driveway of his land and got out. It was still snowing, no wind, so still, and quiet. He looked at me, took my hand and we walked up the trail to where the foundation was. I could see the work he had already started, and the land around it was being bulldozed and graded to make a lawn.

When we got to the foundation he turned and asked "Well, you can see how far this is from any real town, do you think you could live like this, and be happy?"

I knew from his eyes, he was going to take the answer I gave right then. I looked around at the forests, and the work that would need to be done. To work on this, and at the same time continue to work on developing our relationship as we went, was going to be a mountainous challenge. But my heart was already bursting with joy. The decision for me, was simple.

"If we are together, that is what will make me happy. We will make this a home, and give it all we have. It will be beautiful".

We embraced as the snow covered us. For several moments we stood in the silence holding each other, not saying anything. Nothing needed to be said. Our hearts were doing the talking, and the land we stood on, was bonded between us.

The next year would be one of tremendous effort, fun, long hours of hard work, planning, arguing about what would go where, then laughing it off and taking a break.
Every weekend we'd meet at the property, and sleep on the ground. I cooked meals over an open fire, unless we decided to go for dinner somewhere. But most of the time we didn't want to go anywhere. We wanted to spend our energy getting work done on the house, not wasting time traveling back and forth needlessly. Monday mornings we went back to our jobs, till the next weekend. We worked around the clock many days, and only took real time off, when our weary bodies told us we had to.

As we moved along with the house, we also planned our wedding, and decided to have it in the house. We didn't care if it wasn't completely finished. We felt we could get the basic structure up, and have it livable by late fall, so planned on a November wedding.

On November 27, 1976, we were married by one of his family members who was a minister. We cleaned the house, cooked for our own reception, which was held in our unfinished kitchen, and the ceremony was in the living room. The house was full of people. It may have been the most informal wedding in a long time in the area, but we didn't care.

For us it was a celebration of our lives, and our future in the house we built with our own hands. We continued to work on it for several years. For five years Lynn brought home rocks of different sizes and shapes to add to the fireplace he was making by hand. It was nine feet long, and went to the ceiling, fourteen feet high. It was beautiful when he finished it. He was proud of it, and had a right to be. The mantle piece was a huge log from a tree Lynn cut off the property. He took off the bark, sanded it, and sealed it with a clear preservative. It gave the fireplace a bold, rugged beauty.

The first winter Lynn still drove tractor trailer over the road, mostly out west hauling beef, and frozen meats back to Vermont, but also other products as well. I spent that first winter keeping warm with a wood stove. Lynn would cut enough for the week before he'd leave me. He was usually gone a week, sometimes more, if he had deliveries from several mid-west destinations. So I was alone a lot. But there was so much to do I didn't spend any time feeling sorry for myself. I had a home, I could work as much as I wished and could explore my surroundings with Carrie, walking the trails in the woods and sleigh riding on the hill in back of our house. There was no time for boredom.

As we interacted with people he knew, and they'd come for dinner, visit, or help us on projects, several times they and people in our family said of us; "You are like two cyclones that have merged together". Yes, we loved each other, but we both also had very strong personalities. When we didn't agree it was like two storms colliding. In the next several years, this would be the case, and bring a lot of heartache and trouble to us both, and take us through divorce, and back.

God used my Father's last year of life in 1977, to begin to deal with both of us on many levels. Dad suffered a great deal that last year, and it forced us to face watching someone go through the valley of the shadow of death, and watch what it did to him physically. We watched his body deteriorate, become weak and lose the strength to do what people take for granted when they are healthy. We couldn't ignore or look away when we went to visit and saw what he had to deal with every day.

I was working that year at a veneer mill. When Fridays came, after my shift, I'd drive to New York just about every weekend, and see what I could do to help Mother, and see Dad. I knew it would be the last year, and decided to be with him as much as I could. I saw how it affected Lynn. He had a very hard time and felt very awkward the times we visited Dad in the hospital. I could see he didn't know how to act, or what to say.

From the Lords point of view, every soul must come to the realization that they are going to die. No one wants to talk about it, and everyone does all they can to avoid it. People will change the subject, laugh it off, whatever they have to do, to not look at it. But it doesn't change the fact, we are all going to die. Sadly, the vast majority reach their day of death, totally unprepared, which Satan strives for. It's his goal for us to find ourselves in hell.

In the months to come, God would use Dads suffering and death to force us to look at disease, suffering, and consider our own death; to wake us up, and force us to think about the fact, that one day our time to die would come. We were about to go through the school of life, death, and fixing our eyes on eternity, and that we must face it ourselves one day.

**Heb 9:27 And as it is appointed unto men
once to die, but after this the judgment.**

FIVE
THE VALLEY OF DEATH

In the early spring of 1977 my Mother called one day, and said Dad's doctor had let him know his cancer had come back, was found in his lymph nodes, and he was terminal. They said they didn't know how long he had to live, but estimated less than a year. I asked her if she felt up to having him come to our house for a visit one last time. She said yes and that the doctor had advised him to do as much as he felt he could for as long as possible. She said she'd talk to the rest of the family and let me know when they could come.

A couple of weeks later she called back and asked if coming the next weekend would be ok. I said sure. She let me know one of my oldest sisters and her husband were coming also in their own car, to help along the way, and be a part of the visit. Lynn and I were happy to hear it. We told them to be prepared for a good time and some good food.

When they arrived we had to walk out to the main road, about a quarter of a mile from the house. It was officially mud season and our one lane road wasn't maintained by the town yet. We had to park our vehicles off the side of the road and walk to the house. They arrived on a Friday night and we were waiting for them in our truck when they came. As we walked to the house we could see the difficulty Dad was having. He had to stop a couple of times to rest and get his breath. We told him we were in no hurry, it was a nice night for a walk.

We sat around the supper table that night, talking about the doctor's diagnosis, and the expectations in the coming months. We were all open, realistic people, and talked about serious issues in just that manner. We made no attempts to cover up the situation, or try to ignore it in a childish manner. Dad wanted to be able to talk and say what was on his mind, and we wanted him to. It was important to settle everything he could while he had the ability to do it.

I could see he was weary from the trip, Mother was too. We let them know they could have Carrie's room for the night. They went upstairs early, letting us know they'd look forward to the morning coffee. We had made a comfortable bed for my sister and brother in law in the living room, then sat and visited for a while before going to bed. We shared our feelings and planned ways we could help Mother during this hard time. We knew the coming months would be more difficult as days went by. We admitted we didn't really know the best ways to help, but would deal with things as they came up. We all knew we were going to be facing something none of us had any experience with; death.

We had a great time throughout the weekend. I cooked meals I knew my parents liked. Home-made pies I knew Dad liked; apple was his favorite, and Lynn's, so they were ready with their plates when it was cut.

Dad and Bob spent time with Lynn, and he took them to town on business and his regular errands. They came back laughing and it was apparent they enjoyed each other's company. Bob and Lynn had developed a bond like brother's and had taken an approach together of being a source of strength and fun for Dad, as grown sons.

Mother and I and my sister did the house chores; cleaned up the kitchen, and planned the dinner for later, along with a lot of visiting. I asked Mom how she felt, and what we could do to help her during the coming months. She was as uncertain as we were about how to be prepared. I could see the sadness that the last 4 years of suffering had brought to her. She had been with

Dad through the lung cancer surgery, and the months of recovery afterwards. It had taken a toll on her in many ways. Weariness was etched in her face.

I let her talk and share her thoughts, glancing out the window noticing it was now a sunny warm morning. As we finished our talk I made a suggestion. "Let's take advantage of the warm sun, and take a walk down past the cemetery."

They knew where this was. Both spoke at once "Sure, that sounds great."

When we made our way back to our driveway, the men had returned. The joking, good humor, and friendship between them was like glue to the family structure. The rest of the weekend went fast. Before we knew it, Monday morning had arrived.

Though Dad had enjoyed the time with us, he was tired and out of breath. I could see the evidence of what the cancer was doing to him. We didn't dwell on it. We just faced it and dealt with it. As he sat at the kitchen table getting ready to walk back to the vehicles, he looked at us and said what we had known, but kept to ourselves up to this point.

"This will be my last time here. I've enjoyed it and was glad I came, but I know I won't be able to make it again."

Sadness permeated the room, we just nodded. We all knew he was marking time and saying what needed to be said.

As we walked slowly back to the vehicles, again he had to stop several times.

"Just a year ago, this would have been no problem for me. This tells me what I'm going to be dealing with soon. I worry about your Mother."

I looked in his eyes "All of us will be here for her. We'll do what we can to help, but none of us really know what we'll face, until we are there."

"That gives me some peace of mind, it's not going to be easy for any of you. But just know, I love you all."

Each of us looked at each other and him, and said almost as one, "We love you too, don't worry."

We hugged and planned a time when Lynn and I could come to New York and visit; then stood watching as they drove slowly away. Lynn took my hand, Carrie walked close beside us, in silence. The inner strength of this man brought the stability I needed and depended on during this time.

The next several months I made the trip to New York mostly every other weekend, and stayed until Sunday, driving back home late in the afternoons. I was still working a full time job at a veneer mill in Bradford, and would leave from there Friday evenings and make it to Mother's house about sundown. We'd visit for a while before going to bed, planning for the next day. Sometimes Dad would be in the hospital getting treatments, but when he was home we didn't plan any activities that meant traveling. He was getting weaker by the day. We made adjustments according to what he could deal with, and felt well enough to do. As time went on even enjoying a simple meal became difficult. The chemotherapy treatments brought too much nausea, and destroyed any appetite to eat. Eventually it came to the place that we cooked simple meals for ourselves, because we had to eat. The joy of sharing a meal together as a family disappeared.

The reality of what Dad was going through became blatant, and controlled any kind of life that we once thought of as normal. There were ongoing daily struggles of the affects the disease was having on Dad's body. The increasing pain that robbed him of even being able to enjoy a quiet time of watching his favorite TV programs or taking a short walk. Mother suffered along with him. We did what we could to give her a break.

When I was there I'd take her shopping or a ride in the country. We would stop for a small meal together. It gave her a chance to talk, and let out her thoughts and feelings. Many times I felt unsure, not knowing what to say or do. Over time however, I came to realize it didn't really matter what I said or did. She just needed somebody to care. I did, and she came to know this. It was a connection that lasted throughout our life and would become a significant bond between us in years to come.

Toward the end of August Lynn went with me for a weekend visit to see Dad. It proved to be one God would use to bring a prick of conviction to Lynn's life and cause him to face the realities of mortality. His reactions to seeing Dads weakened condition and the pain he was enduring showed me Lynn was now being made to consider his own death, and he wasn't ready for it.

When we arrived we found he had been admitted to a hospital in Albany New York. When we got there we had to go several floors up to his room. When we found him the door was open, and he was alone. There was no water available for him, or any other evidence of recent care. We didn't know how long he'd been in this state. His eyes were shut but he was not asleep. He was in pain. Mother sat next to him and spoke a quiet greeting. Him turned to her and said;

"Mother glad to see you". His voice was very weak. "I need a drink".

We found a nurse out in the hall and asked for a pitcher of water. She nodded and walked away. We looked at each other but said nothing.

When Lynn saw Dad unable to even raise his head, and knowing he was neglected; walked to a closet, leaned against it, letting himself down and sat on the floor with his head in his hands. I could see the turmoil and awkwardness in him. He felt helpless, not knowing what to do.

A long time went by, no one came with water. I went to a nurse sitting at a desk.

"Excuse me my father needs some water. There's none in his room. We asked for some a while ago, but still have none."

"Oh,....sorry. We'll see to it." She never looked up, just continued writing.

I looked around and into some of the small utility rooms as I went back to Dad's room. I found one that had medical supplies, pitchers, and cups. I took a small pitcher and a cup, filled it with water and took it to Dad. Mother put the cup to Dad's mouth so he could drink. He only managed small sips. "Thank you", he whispered.

About an hour later a young woman came in with a meal tray. Her demeanor was abrupt, and cold. She set the tray down on the stand next to the bed but left it too far away for Dad to be able to reach it. She walked out the door, not offering to help him eat.

I looked at Mother, furious, but held my voice in check.

"Does this go on all the time?"

"Most of the time, I tried to let it be known how I feel, but no one seems to care. If you say anything it seems to get worse."

Lynn was still on the floor against the closet door. His response was simple, and to the point,

"I'd be giving these #@@#!! a kick in the #%@ after the first time I found this goin' on. I'd never put up with it."

Wiping Dads mouth with a napkin, my Mother kept her attention on helping him try to eat, but replied;

"If I had the energy anymore, I'd try to do something. But just doing what I can for him is all the strength I have now."

Lynn shook his head in disgust at the situation, glaring out into the hall. I knew he had reached the limit of his patience. But we all knew we were helpless to do anything about it. Mother was right, we had to focus on doing what we could for my father.

This was the last time Lynn came with me to visit Dad. I asked him again a couple of times after this, but he would say no, that there was a lot that needed to be done on the house. I knew it was really because he couldn't face watching Dad continue to decline. It was too awkward for him and caused too much turmoil inside dealing with his own mortality. He was in the prime of his life, and full of his own strength. Seeing it disappear in another man was hitting him hard inside. One day he knew it would be him. He couldn't deal with it.

My other sisters and brother's all dealt with Dads situation differently. The two oldest avoided the issue, and rarely saw him. A younger brother had moved to Texas and came once to see him, during one of the last times Dad was in the hospital. Another younger brother lived with our parents, and was a great support to them throughout the situation. During this time, I watched in silence the reactions of each of them. I kept my thoughts to myself. I had learned how different each one of us were, and knew there was no point in passing judgment on what they chose to do. I didn't agree with it many times. But nothing is accomplished by ongoing strife if it can be avoided. Each of us had learned to cope with our differences this way. There were disputes and arguments, but we tried to keep it to a minimum.

As fall came on, during another visit to help Mother, she relayed an event that happened during Dads stay in another hospital that proved to be an intervention by God, for the rescue and redemption of my Father.

Growing up, Mother had gotten up the courage several times, and tried to talk to Dad about his soul, and his need to let God in his life. She'd tell him he needed to admit he needed a Savior, and ask Jesus in his heart. He would either look at her in disgust and walk out and leave for a while in the car. Or, if he had been drinking he'd verbally abuse her with a barrage of cursing, ridicule, and laughing. He'd make her life miserable for days and accuse her of being crazy for believing in any god. Several times when he was drunk, I heard him say, "When they bury me, they can just dig a hole and put me in it. That's the end of it."

Sometimes Mother would get in the car and take a drive for hours when this went on, just to get some peace. But her simple attempt to bring Dad to salvation wasn't in vain. God uses any means necessary to get through to some people. Father was a hard-nosed atheist, and the only thing that finally reached him was a five year long stretch of suffering, misery, severe pain, and the ongoing reality that he was facing his death, and there was nothing he could do about it. He found he was not god. He didn't have control over his own life anymore. The daily realization that his body was failing gnawed at him. God used all of this to finally get him to the point that he was willing to listen to somebody. One day laying in a hospital, a minister came to his door and asked if he could talk to him.

According to Mother, Dad was awake when the minister showed up. He let him in. He asked Dad if he had a favorite scripture he'd like to have read to him. Dad was honest and said he didn't know anything from the Bible. So the minister knew he had to start at the beginning.

"If you died today are you sure you'd go to heaven?" he asked.

"No".

"Do you want to have that assurance, and pray with me to ask Jesus to forgive you of your sins and be your Savior and Lord?"

"Yes, I'd like to pray with you."

Father prayed that simple prayer. Then the minister read some scriptures to him, gave him a couple of tracts, and encouraged him to pray to the Lord and tell him his feelings, and needs, and ask him to help him face his situation, and be ready to go to heaven.

From that time there was a marked difference in Dads attitude, and there was a peace about him, even when he was in pain. We all could see the difference.

At this same time late in the fall, I was still working at the mill every day, which meant standing on hard floors for eight to nine hours all day. It was hard work. In late September I began to have symptoms of being pregnant. I went to the doctor. Yes, I was expecting. Lynn was full of joy. I was also. We talked sometimes all night, looking forward to having a child between us, and giving Carrie a sister or brother. I should have stopped working, and taken time off. But I was young, in my twenties, and felt the responsibility of wanting to help financially as much as possible. So I kept working, and still went to New York at least twice a month, and kept up a full workload at home at the same time. It proved to be too much.

On our first anniversary, we made arrangements to eat at a very nice restaurant. Carrie stayed with a neighbor for the evening. I felt cramping earlier in the day, but didn't think it was serious, and went to dinner as we planned. As we drove the cramping continued to worsen, but I didn't want to say anything to Lynn. I hoped what I began to fear, was not really happening. When we arrived we were seated, ordered our meal, and I tried to enjoy the evening. But Lynn could see I wasn't well.

"Are you ok?"

"I started having cramps earlier today, but didn't want to say anything. I hoped it would pass. It has gotten worse and I'm bleeding."

Our order came. We started to eat, but now the cramping was becoming worse. "Lynn, I'm so sorry, but I can't stay any longer, we'll have to stop and go home."

We made it back home and he called the doctor at the clinic in town. The doctor said she was willing to see me there. It was only a ten minute drive. She was at the door when we arrived.

After a brief exam. She told Lynn it would be best to take me to the hospital and she would meet us and oversee my care there.

Lynn was very quiet driving to the hospital. I could sense something going on with him that I'd never seen before. Avoidance, and cold impartiality. I thought I knew him, but was now witnessing a side of him I'd never known.

When we arrived, there was a nurse with a wheelchair waiting for us at the door. She wheeled me to an examination room, and Lynn was taken to a waiting room.

I was given medication to ease the pain. Doctors came in and talked among themselves and conferred together on what my condition was and left. I was given something to help me sleep. Lynn came in, and looked down at me. I could see he was the same as when he had visited my father, very awkward. He asked if the medications were helping me and if I needed anything. Then, took my hand. "I'm going now. I'll go get Carrie and make sure she's taken care of at home."

I nodded, watching him go out the door. I fell asleep, not knowing for how long. I awoke again to find two nurses on each side of me, raising the sheets to examine me. One said to the other "We'll have to get new bedding and clean her up. She's lost the baby."

I laid silently while they cleaned me and changed the bedding.

Thoughts of the abortion came to me. This was the consequence of having it, I thought. I had no one to blame but myself. I knew this. I thought of Lynn and what this was doing to him. I understood what I was sensing earlier in him. He had now lost a child also and didn't know how to deal with it. We were both in realms of pain we'd never known before, and had to find our way through it. Each in our own way.

He came the next morning and we rode home in silence. There was no more talk about it for now. There wasn't anything to say. Life and work would go on. It was just one more thing to deal with. Lynn went back to work. I took a few days off, then went back to work also.

By December Father was gravely ill. We knew he didn't have much time left. He was in and out of the hospital. When he was home it was now full bedridden care. When I was there several of us sisters and my brother helped, working in shifts. He could only keep down liquefied foods. Most of the time he had no appetite. Dad let us know he didn't want to die in the hospital. We agreed. We didn't want to deal with the anxiety of thoughts he would possibly lay in bed alone and neglected for long periods of time. We let him know we would take him home when the doctor's told us he was ready to die.

When family members go through long sessions of caring for someone like this they become numb. Going about the routine care, but emotions are shut down. We were in this place now. Medications, meals, personal hygiene and all that goes with caring for someone bedridden becomes a routine and done in a mechanical fashion. Not from not caring, but out of emotional exhaustion. You do the right thing because it must be done, and tell your body to keep going, when it's telling you it can't. You order it to obey, no matter what your body wants to do.

We made plans to spend Christmas with Mother and help her with Dad, if he was still with us. Lynn, Carrie and I made it on Friday night getting there after dark. Dad was in their bedroom. As I came in he greeted me, "I'm glad you made it."

"I love you Dad. I wish I could do something for you". These are things you say, when you don't know what to say.

"You don't understand Lorna. One day you will."

"No, I don't understand, I admit it."

We talked a few more minutes, then I went out and my brother came in. It was his turn to watch over Dad till morning.

I got up late in the night a few times to see if my brother needed me to help him. We worked together taking care of Dad's needs. We could see a great loss of strength. Dad was not just sleeping now, he was failing. He didn't have much time left.

Morning came, Mother was up. She decided to make an eggnog for Dad, and try to get him to take it. She went in and stayed a long time with him, talking to him, trying to get him to take a sip. Finally she stopped. He was too weak. He woke enough to say just above a whisper, "I'm sorry, I just can't".

Coming back into the kitchen, she looked at me. I could see the truth of his condition was hitting her, and embraced her. We just held each other for a while, saying nothing. There were no words that could describe what we were feeling and dealing with. Our hearts did the talking.

All of the family were not there Christmas day, but the house was full. Those of us who were there did what we could to give the children a sense of family and fun. Though Mother was saved, she had not grown as a Christian, and during our years growing up, didn't make the Lord's birth the main focus. We, like most people, celebrated it mainly for the kids. It was the gift giving, toys, candy, and the special dinner we centered attention on. So this morning we focused on making it a special day for them.

The Christmas meal was prepared and the table set. The food was just about ready to be served. The turkey was out of the oven and setting out, cooling to be carved. Then my sister opened the bedroom door.

"We've got to call the ambulance, Dad is dying." She continued down the hall looking for Mother.

My brother, Lynn, three brother in laws, and the rest of the family went in.
He was gone.

My sister took me out. "Let us care for him. Take care of the small kids."

I stood in the living room alone, and put my face in my hands. "Why".

Without warning a presence surrounded me. I sensed someone right in front of me. A strong person, and someone else behind him; my Father! I heard him clearly say "Lorna, it's alright. Everything is alright."
Then quickly, they were gone. After I was saved, the Lord made

known to me it was a very brief farewell from my Father and his angel. It was a blessing the Lord allowed my Father to give me. The assurance of one day meeting him again in heaven.

That evening we sat in my Mother's living room, mostly silent, numb with grief. We had stood with him to the end. Now we were exhausted physically, emotionally and in our souls.

Dad's life was to affect us all in different ways. God uses death to speak to people about their own lives, and their own death, to try to bring them to himself. Dad's death did that, for me in particular.

My Father's birthday was New Years day 1918, his death Christmas day 1977. His burial was only a few days before his 60th birthday 1978. His life had unique significance, in many ways.

Several times during his siege with cancer, he would talk about regrets he had, and things he wished he'd done differently, or not at all. He also had opportunity to go to some people and apologize for things he knew he needed to make amends with. Sometimes God gives us these chances to make things right if we can, before we leave this world. He apologized to my Mother for the many things he did and said that hurt her. She readily forgave him. She had never stopped loving him. The bond remained between them until death.

One of the things he regretted a great deal and spoke of more than once was smoking. He admitted to us that smoking and drinking had caused a great deal of heartache between him and my Mother, and affected all of us kids.

They both smoked and she didn't hold it against him. None of us did. But in his last years he stopped, and said more than once wished he'd never started doing it. It cost him years of misery, suffering, and eventually his life. He knew I didn't smoke and told me I was smarter for not ever doing it. He said to me, "If you ever have a chance to get someone to change their mind, tell them about me, tell them what it did to me, maybe it will cause them to think and stop before it kills them".

I do not grieve for my parents now. They are young again and free from pain and sorrow; enjoying heaven together. They made mistakes and many wrong choices. But they did the best they could with the situations they were born into, and the trials and temptations they endured.

We have no say in where we will be born, who our parents will be, or what social status we are born into. We grow, make mistakes, and choices in the places we find ourselves. In God's infinite wisdom, he takes every detail of our lives into account. His judgment is given with His perfect wisdom, knowing all of what we've had to deal with. When someone repents and tries to live a righteous life, He takes all of this into account.

After Father's death, there were members of my family who continued to smoke, including my Mother and Lynn. In the years to come it would again bring much heartache, suffering, and eventually be a major cause of death of both of them. They and those who loved them suffered along with them.

So, as I leave this I'll say to all who may read this, for my Father:

"Please, don't smoke. If you do, please stop".

> 1Co 6:20 For ye are bought with a price:
> therefore glorify God in your body, and
> in your spirit, which are God's.

SIX
BORN AGAIN

After the funeral service was over we spent a few days staying with Mother, helping get matters settled concerning insurances, and cleaning their bedroom out. We helped Mom purchase a new bedroom set and replaced it for her. Then we went back home to our own responsibilities.

I continued to work. Work was a good thing right now, along with taking care of Carrie and responsibilities at home. It kept the mind and body busy and pushed grief and memories away until night came. Exhaustion brought sleep and some relief.

Lynn also worked long hours at his job and many unfinished projects at home that kept him busy as well. We both drank and weekends revolved around that, along with cooking meals and working on projects. We never spent very much time brooding or thinking about what we had gone through with my parents. We weren't that kind of people. We knew what we had to do at the time, and did the best we could for them. Now it was time to move on. The things we both experienced changed our lives individually, but kept it to ourselves. But it definitely had a great effect on how we handled similar issues in our lives in years to come.

We spent time on weekends taking Carrie to events and doing things with her to give her some happiness and joy in her life, and shield her as much as we could from the realities of these kinds of hardships. We made mistakes bringing her up, as all parents do. But we made every effort to make sure she had many things kids love to do, and things we knew she enjoyed, to let her know we loved her, and help her expand her interests and opportunities. There many trips to museums, local events, and getting together with our families for meals and activities. We were always busy together.

However, in the long hours Lynn worked, he began to spend more time with people he had known before he met me. Men in the area that he'd been drinking buddies with. It proved to be a source of lasting trouble in our relationship. It was an open door Satan used to almost destroy our marriage. During the times he'd get together with these slandering, gossiping people, they would put accusations in his ear that I was unfaithful to him. As weeks went by, I began to sense a distance and sullenness between us. I waited to see if this was due to still getting over Dads death. It became clear it was something else, and began to look for a time alone with him on a weekend night, and asked him.

"Have I done something to upset you, there seems to be a distance with you, I've not known before."

"Ok, I'll tell you, have you been seeing anybody else since we've been married?"

I couldn't believe what I was hearing, I looked directly into his eyes;

"There has never been anyone else, ever. Why are you asking me this?"

He didn't look at me, but gazed out the glass doors at the pond in front of our house "Last year you spent a lot of time in New York, I know you were with your family helping take care of your Father and Mother, but there was plenty of time to do other things too."

"Where is this coming from? Or should I say; from whom?"

"You can't blame me for the question. I don't want to suspect you, but it's a reasonable one."

"Well Lynn, you can go to my family, and ask them if I was with them and what I did when I was there. But as far as the time it took to drive back here, and what I did during those times, I guess you'll just have to choose to believe me; or not. If you don't trust me, why did you marry me. I was very honest with you about my life, and the marriage with my first husband.

You knew when you married me, what kind of woman I was, and we talked many times before we ever married. You told me of the women you were involved with before you met me, and the ones in Vietnam, who you had sex with. You were honest about not even being sure you may have kids over there. You have to live with that gnawing at your mind every day. Even knowing this about you, I married you anyway. I forgave you and thought you had done the same for me. You said you did. This tells me apparently you haven't. I can look you in the eyes, as I am now, and tell you there is no other man, and never will be. You will have to choose to believe me, or not; it's up to you."

He had lifted his eyes and gazed into mine, he knew I meant what I said. He didn't answer, but got up and walked out the door. I watched him get in his truck and go out the driveway. He didn't return for a long time.

I made no attempt to find him. I was dealing with the realization that other people's slander had brought distrust, suspicion and instability into our lives. It would be a spiritual war I'd have to face the rest of our married life. I wasn't saved yet and the possibility of this marriage being destroyed became real in my mind. I kept it to myself. I made up my mind if this was going to happen, it would be him who destroyed it, not me.

I started drinking more again. It was a crutch now, a painkiller and substitute for sleeping pills. This and hard work kept the mind and body going on auto-pilot.

March came, and mud season again. A full year since Dads last visit. I sat in a chair looking out the window onto our pond remembering that time, and thinking of Mother now. I decided to call her. She picked up the phone, her voice was low, and sad.

"I'm sitting here thinking of you and Dad. How are you doing?"

"I don't know how to answer that. I'm here, that's all I can say".

"I'd rather know the truth. Would you like to come for a visit?"

"No, thanks for asking. But it's best if I don't right now. If I did there's no guarantee I'd stay very long. I'm glad you called, but right now, getting through a day is all I can manage. I'll talk again soon, take care".

I sat there looking out onto the water. The ache in Mother's heart was in mine also. It was a learning experience, watching her walk through the valley of grief and loss of a lifelong partner. She was saying things that many would think were signs of someone mentally ill or unstable. I didn't see her that way at all. I was watching someone being completely honest and daring to be. She put on no fronts and said several times that she had no strength to put on an act for people. If they couldn't handle what she was going through, they could leave her alone. I learned how to deal with my own paths of loss and grief by watching her. I respected her inner strength and individuality.

It took almost five years before Mother could enjoy a day, and do things together and laugh, without the sense of underlying grief.

On a Monday just about the first day of spring, I woke and went through the usual routine of getting ready for work, and Carrie off to school. Neighbors next to me had agreed to let her get off the school bus at their home with their daughters and stay with them until I got off work and could pick her up there. I did not know they were Christians, but soon would realize God had placed them in our life, and would use them in both Carrie's and my salvation. They had been witnessing to Carrie, and she received salvation in January, just a few months before me. They had been praying for me since then.

On this morning, after I knew she was on her way to school, I started down the regular route to work. It was still before dawn, and the headlights needed to be on. As I drove along the river to my right there was a deep embankment, and the road curved sharply in and out of high rock ledges, I saw headlights coming at me before the vehicle actually made the curve. I got over as far as I could and slowed down. It was a livestock truck, it was in my lane, and I had nowhere to go. I closed my eyes waiting for the impact. I heard a slight crack to my left, opened my eyes and saw the truck just going past me, and taking my side mirror off as it went. I looked out my rear view mirror to see it continue down the road behind me. I knew who it was, he lived right in the town I was going to. He never stopped to see if I was alright, he kept on going. I started driving. It began to sink in, just how close I came to being killed; again. As I kept driving, the other times I'd come close to death went through my mind. This time the thought came to me "Why is God allowing this, and what does He want me to do?"

When I reached the mill I went upstairs to the supervisor's office, told him what had happened, and that I needed to go home. He nodded, "Sure, see you tomorrow."

When I got home I went to the living room, took a book my sister had given me the last time she visited me, laid it on the stand next to me, and just sat looking out on the water for a long time.

Then I started reading the book. It was a paperback, and I was able to read most of it quickly. For the first time it explained to me in terms I could easily understand, why Jesus had to come into this world, die on the cross, and what it meant to me. It explained the great love God the Father has for all people. How Adam and Eve's sin separated them from God, and that their sin passed down to all of us, to this day. It explained clearly we are all born in sin because of their rebellion. Jesus came into this world to redeem us from the sin of Adam and Eve, and his sacrifice paid the sin debt for every one of us. And, that He would have come and died the same death, even if there was only one. When he rose from the grave, he conquered sin and death. Anyone who repents, asks for forgiveness and for Jesus to come into their heart and life, He will come in, and redeem them from the fall of our first parents. Then Christ would come into our lives, and help us live for Him. We can have a personal relationship with Him as a child of God. This it explained, was what being "born again" meant.

I closed the book. Tears were streaming down my face. I rarely cried. As I sat there in silence, I began to sense a Presence that filled the house. I waited and it became stronger. I knew I was not alone in the house. A tremendous surge from my soul rose up, and I spoke to this Presence "Lord, I've done so many things wrong, so many sins, please forgive me. I believe in you Jesus, that you died for me, and I ask for you to come into my heart and life, and help me live for you."

The Presence remained in silence. An overwhelming sense of peace covered me. I looked at the clock, it was almost 11:30 in the morning. I fell asleep.

My eyes opened and again I looked at the clock, it was past 3:30 p.m. The first thing I did was say another simple prayer "Lord, one thing I ask, would you please help me to want to keep on going. Please give me a reason to stay here, or take me home now. I'm so tired, and ready to go. If you don't need me here."

As soon as I finished this prayer, I looked out the living room window, to see Carrie coming up the driveway, dragging her book bag along behind her. I knew that prayer had been answered.

My usual routine each night had been to fix myself a drink, then start dinner and help Carrie with her homework, if she had any.

I helped her with her school work, and cooked our meal. Lynn came home and we enjoyed the night together. Lynn and Carrie went out to the barn to get the chores done, then we watched some television together. It came to the end of the night. Carrie needed to get to bed for school the next day. As I started up the stairs to her room I realized for the first time in years, I had not taken a drink, or even thought of one. I knew, deep inside, I was free. The same Presence hovered over me, and in my heart heard "Let your first step of obedience to Me be destroying the alcohol and pouring it out."

I went to the refrigerator. There was sherry and several whiskey's. I took all of them to the sink, and poured the contents down the drain.

The next morning I felt a strong sense I should stay home again, so called work and asked for another day off. They said there would be no problem.

I had a Bible. It was a black one I'd bought years ago, while still married to my first husband, but never read. I found it upstairs in a drawer and brought it downstairs. As soon as I had the basic cleaning and morning dishes done, I got in the chair next to the glass doors and started reading. I didn't start at the beginning, or the gospels. I went right to the back to the book of Revelation. I wanted to know the end of all of this. What was the bottom line, and purpose of this sin sick world.

I began at chapter one, and read straight through it to the end. Being a new believer in Christ, and not knowing any religious types who might try to discourage me, I let my heart tell me what to read. I've learned this is the best way to be. Let the Holy Spirit be your guide, not the religious crowd, who may sway you with their unbelief.

There were times as I read along, I'd have to stop. My eyes were full of tears, my heart aching for what God was telling me was going to come on this world someday, and it was because of our own rebellion. Even as a brand new believer, I knew this.

I got up after reading it to the end the first time, and took a break. I took a walk, had lunch, then read it AGAIN, all the way through.

Again I was in tears several times. My heart and soul was overwhelmed with the sense of God's presence. The scriptures were alive to me. It was as if I was there, seeing the scenes in reality. In my spirit, I was there. After the second reading it was close to the time of Carrie coming home. I started the evening meal, greeted her when she came in, helped her with her homework, and we ate. Lynn was gone this day, driving over the road.

When the kitchen was cleaned up, I played a little while with Carrie, then when she was ready for bed, we went upstairs together. I took the Bible with me to bed also, and read Revelation again, for the third time in this same day.

At the end of this third reading, I laid there looking at the ceiling. My heart was exploding. I didn't fully understand what was consuming me about this, but one thing I felt absolutely sure of; God was showing me in graphic terms in His word, we are in the days John was describing. I knew this with my whole being.

Tears were in my eyes again. I didn't know what to do with the weight that seemed to grip my soul. All I knew was what God was speaking to me, and showing me. I was absorbed in the immensity of what my spirit was being shown. As I laid there, I wouldn't have been surprised, if the Lord had returned that very night. This is how real He had made this event to me. Finally I prayed "Why am I feeling this way, and what do I do now?" I did not expect an answer but received one.

"You are living in and will witness events unfolding that have been described in your reading."

I did not hear an audible voice, it came from my spirit. I was a brand new Christian, but questioned "Who are you, I do not want to be deceived".

"The Lord Jesus Christ. I'm glad you question, it is a good thing to discern the spirits."

Note: In time to come, as I continued to study His word, confirmation came that this was indeed the Lord, when I found these verses:

> 1Jn 4:1 Beloved, believe not every spirit, but try the spirits whether they are of God: because many false prophets are gone out into the world.
>
> 1Jn 4:2 Hereby know ye the Spirit of God: Every spirit that confesseth that Jesus Christ is come in the flesh is of God:
>
> 1Jn 4:3 And every spirit that confesseth not that Jesus Christ is come in the flesh is not of God: and this is that spirit of antichrist, whereof ye have heard that it should come; and even now already is it in the world.

"Why are you letting me know these things? Why do you speak to me, a simple woman, a sinner, only recently saved."

"You are a servant, and my daughter. In time to come, you will be shown greater service, but not now. But as time unfolds, and you're ready to receive it."

My heart was bursting with love for this Savior. For his unbelievable mercy to me and His great love to me. He called me a servant and a daughter. I fell asleep, in the peace of His presence.

From this time, every waking moment I had that was free, I took my Bible, went to the chair looking out over the water of our pond, and studied the scriptures. I went back to the beginning in Genesis, and read it as a book, cross referencing as I went. The people and their stories were alive to me.

My spirit fed on His word, I consumed them like a sponge. The more I read, the more I wanted to read. I was like a starving child, and His word was truly manna to my soul.

After a couple of weeks, I began to feel an uneasiness at work I didn't understand. Something was different. I didn't know if it was me, or if something was going on with the job, but my heart was telling me there would be changes coming. I was right. After another month, I knew for sure the Lord was prompting me to leave. I gave my notice and let Lynn know I'd be looking for something different. He always let me have the freedom of my choices in these matters, and said I'd probably find something better.

Growing up during the time I was involved in the occult, witchcraft, sorcery, and other demonic activity, I had accumulated a great deal of reading material, books, articles, tapes, and occult objects. I also collected a lot of rock music, and had an entire trunk full of comic books from my early childhood of Marvel superheroes such as Spiderman, Captain America, Batman, and other's.

A couple of weeks after my salvation, after finishing the morning dishes, I poured another cup of coffee, took my Bible and headed for my favorite chair to study. I set my coffee down on the stand by the chair and went back to the kitchen to get a pad and pencil for taking notes. As I stepped back into the living room, the Presence I'd come to know from the first day I was saved came into the house again, and again, silence.

I stopped in between the rooms. I knew it was the Lord. Then I heard, "You have many books and materials that are Satanic and of the occult on your shelves. You need to destroy them. They are an abomination to Me."

I looked over at the bookcase at the other end of the room. I knew He was right.

"What do you want me to do with them?"

"Open your stove and burn them."

I looked at the wood stove. It was burning steady, and full of hot coals. I went to the bookcase and took arms full to the floor next to the stove, opened the door, and began throwing them in, a couple at a time. Needless to say, the house became so hot I had to open several windows, and even the door a couple of times to cool the house down. But by the end of the day, they and all the occult objects were gone.

When this was done, the Lord spoke again to me and said "Now, speak to the demons of witchcraft, sorcery, all necromancy, horoscopes, the occult, and wizardry, one at a time and command them to leave in My Name, and break their hold over your life. Take authority over them, and tell them to leave you and never come back, in My Name. Then ask for forgiveness, and renounce all activity in these things, and ask for healing and cleansing from all of it".

"Where is this in your word, that I must do this"?

"Go to Luke chapter 10:17-19, Mark 16:17, Mark 3:14,15, Acts 16:18"

I knew nothing about these verses and had to take the time to look them up and read them. When I did, they confirmed what the Lord had said to me:

> Luk 10:17 And the seventy returned again with joy, saying, Lord, even the devils are subject unto us through thy name.

> Luk 10:18 And he said unto them, I beheld Satan as lightning fall from heaven.

> Luk 10:19 Behold, I give unto you power to tread on serpents and scorpions, and over all the power of the enemy: and nothing shall by any means hurt you.

> Mar 16:17 And these signs shall follow them that believe; In my name shall they cast out devils; they shall speak with new tongues;

> Luk 9:1 Then he called his twelve disciples together, and gave them power and authority over all devils, and to cure diseases.

> Mar 3:14 And he ordained twelve, that they should be with him, and that he might send them forth to preach,

> Mar 3:15 And to have power to heal sicknesses, and to cast out devils:

> Act 16:18 And this did she many days. But Paul, being grieved, turned and said to the spirit, I command thee in the name of Jesus Christ to come out of her. And he

came out the same hour.

The next day, the Lord prompted me to get rid of the rock music and comic books as well. This was difficult for me and I had to ask for help to be obedient. My flesh liked many of the favorites I'd collected over the years and I enjoyed the rock beat. Satan knows this. Rock music is his music. He created it for one reason, to destroy the young people. He's done a very good job. The comic books were hard to destroy because not only were they a link to my young childhood, but the superheroes were what the Lord wanted gone, and the demonic bondage's. Every superhero is a demon, brought to life.

Note: When the Holy Spirit spoke to me of the need to get rid of the comic books, and ask for forgiveness, and break demonic bondage's from them, it made perfect sense to me. I had vivid memories of things that happened when I was a kid that were linked to having these superhero's in my life. Being a new believer, I had no interactions yet with other people who called themselves Christians, but would not give up their idols and pagan worship. I wanted to be free from every bondage, and was willing to listen to the Lord's instruction and correction. I was to quickly learn that a great many people, including those who say they are Christians, *won't* let go of the things they enjoy, even if it's shown to them from scripture that what they are doing is wrong, and they should get rid of it. They consciously rebel, just like so many shown in the Bible, and hang on to the demonic images, and live out the consequences. Their lives and the choices they make reveal how much they are truly surrendered to the Lord, or how much they stay bound by sin, and rebellion.

Lastly, concerning superheroes and masks; the Lord prompted me to study the demonic side of wearing masks. It's a long study, that you could take years to go into. If you want to know the real dangers in wearing masks, I encourage you to spend some time do so. Many cultures of people wear them in their spiritual rituals. A Christian should never wear a mask and if they ever have in their life; they should repent and renounce doing it; and ask for the cleansing blood of Christ to break every demonic bondage.

This country, and the world system, is completely demonic now. Satanism, the occult and witchcraft is right out in the open today, and people watch it put out in their faces during Superbowl halftimes shows, and multitudes of other media sources every day. The world now is saturated with wickedness and evil. it is ready for judgment. We are now living in the days Jesus describes would be the sign of the last days, the days of Noah. The closer a believer gets to the Lord, and the deeper your walk with Him, the less you will fit in with this world. Our level of love and commitment to Him will be tested our entire life. But the other side of this is, the greater the surrender, the greater the sense of His presence and ability to be of greater service to the Lord, in the spiritual realm.

When these items were destroyed the Lord let me know I needed to repent specifically for allowing these things in my life and renounce them as well by name. I obeyed, and simply asked the Lord to replace the bondage's with His forgiveness, mercy and heal my soul and spirit. I was shown demonic bondage's attached to these things, and I had to call them out by name, and cast them out. They left. There was no great manifestations, but there was some coughing, sneezing, and sweating. I was determined to be free, and they didn't put up much resistance.

My spirit felt the release. Now free, I became aware of the level of darkness I had been in, when these acts of obedience opened the door for the light and power of the Lord's presence to come into my soul.

In the weeks to come during times of study and prayer, the Lord would speak to me of other areas that needed specific attention in my life, and repentance and healing. The years I was married to my first husband, and the sin in our life, my promiscuity, adultery, sexual sins. I needed to openly forgive my Mother, and the uncle who Satan used to get me involved with the man who molested me. And yes, the man who molested me and used me. I was shown the importance for my own soul to forgive them, break bondage's off my life from all involvement with them, and for a complete healing from the sins involved with them.

Now, for the first time at 25 years of age, I was totally free from every bondage, and saved for eternity in Christ-born again. As the scripture describes:

> 2Co 5:17 Therefore if any man be in Christ, he is a new creature: old things are passed away; behold, all things are become new.

At this point I want to emphasize several points about this time in my life. I believe it matters, because it will destroy many wrong conceptions people have today about God's interactions with us.

After salvation, healing, whether it be physical or spiritual, and deliverance, often takes time, and allowing the Lord to take us through stages of healing. It's the same with spiritual warfare. People can't truly be delivered until they *want* to be. Many deliverance sessions end in failure, because the person doesn't really want to be free, and aren't willing to pay the price by obedience to the word of God. Or the person's spirit hasn't been enlightened enough to understand where they need the deliverance and haven't come to the place of cooperation with the Holy Spirit. We have to learn how God moves in a person to bring them out of bondage. It may take years of prayer and coming against the powers of darkness in the person's life before we see the victory. If the person continues in their sin and won't budge and their heart becomes completely hardened, he/she may die in their sins, and end up in hell. The battle is to the death. Our adversary the devil is out to do just that, kill, steal and destroy. I am much more aware now, how much prayer it took by many, and how powerfully God moved in my life, to get me to salvation and freedom. I'll only know the extent of it in heaven.

Some significant points to this story are:

1. His intervention in my life at this time was completely *His* doing, it had nothing to do with me being anyone special, having any kind of status in life, or of any reputation. This was in *His* mind only-I could never have conceived of such a thing on my own.

2. His divine interaction in my salvation, to set me free and delivered was to me, nothing short of a miracle. I did not know any pastors, any religious people, or Christians, other than the neighbors Carrie stayed with next door, and I do believe God used them and their prayers to help bring me to salvation and this deliverance.

3. These events were a crash course in teaching me to know His leading's, His voice, and in teaching me to discern the spirits, and try them; to see if they were indeed of God, or of Satan. As a brand new believer God used these profound events to cement sound biblical foundations of faith in me, and to learn to hear and discern truth from error, and it's held me well, over these many years. Every event since these first years, has been building blocks to ground me in my walk with God.

4. The Lord clearly showed me by these events that He will confirm whatever He speaks to us, and direct us to His word for confirmation. He showed me this by example during this time, and nothing else could have taught me better. There is no doubt in my mind that He is true to His word, and His word is power. The devils heed it because he has placed His word above His name.

Psalm 138:2 I will worship toward thy
holy temple, and praise thy name for
thy lovingkindness and for thy truth: for
thou hast magnified thy word above all
thy name.

In months to come, the Lord prompted me to get rid of other objects and materials that had satanic bondage to them. He opened the door for me to find reputable teachings on the subject of intercession and spiritual warfare. I will leave a list at the end of this book of those who God has put into my hands to read, study and learn the ways of God in prayer, for a reference for those who may be reading this, and have a call of God on your life, and desire to join this journey in the service of prayer and spiritual warfare.

SEVEN
BAPTISM IN THE SPIRIT

In the next several months the Lord led me to become involved in a Friday night prayer meeting my neighbors held each week, and meet other believer's in the area. I wanted to learn as much of scripture as possible, and decided to go. Much of the time was spent reading and discussing what we were learning. Everyone who desired to, had an opportunity to ask questions, bring out scriptures that brought the subject into better context, and before each meeting we prayed for the guidance and assistance of the Holy Spirit to help us in what we were reading. Each week was unique, and the presence of God was there. We were experiencing the same powerful direction and moving of the Holy Spirit that we were reading about in the book of Acts. Our spirits were being fed with the word of God, bringing light to our understanding each time we met together.

The leader of the meeting began asking me if I'd be interested in going to a women's fellowship that took place monthly in Montpelier. I hesitated. I had always avoided women's groups. I wanted no part of a coffee clutch group, sitting around gossiping time away. To me this was a waste of time and very distasteful to me. I told her this, and I could see she understood what I was saying.

"I don't blame you for feeling this way, but if you pray about it, and would be willing to give it a try once, you may find there are some women who truly love the Lord, and the focus for them is on God, as it is for us."

I listened, but told her I would pray about it, and left it at that. I wasn't ready to go any further with this right now. She could see this was the case and didn't ask again. But, I knew there was a lot of prayer going up about this from her and several others in the group.

Every waking opportunity I'd take my Bible, notebook, and sit in the chair next to the glass doors, and study, pray, and write down the things the Holy Spirit was teaching me in His word. Many times I'd sit and weep, when reading the accounts of Moses, trying to bring the Jews out of Egypt. The misunderstandings and turmoil Moses had to deal with. The people going back into sin, blaming Moses for their own disobedience; the blindness and rebellion was crushing to read about because as I read it I saw this world as God see's it now, and I saw my own rebellion and disobedience. Each story brought a new sense of the reality of God's intervention in these people's lives and the consequences they lived out, because of their choices. God used every detail of their lives, to bring specific results, some for good, but also for correction, chastisement, and judgment. I saw in each story the justice, mercy, and long suffering of God. How much he puts up with us, before he allows our own sins to catch up with us. Over the years as I read through the Bible each time, new insights and truths come up. The Bible is called the living word, because it is. The Lord uses it to bring better understanding each time we study it.

Many times as I studied the first several years, specific sins and things I had said or done to family members or people in my life, God would bring to my mind, and let me know I needed to ask for forgiveness for how I treated them. I did, and if possible went to them personally and asked for forgiveness. Doing this opens the door for the Lord to bring healing, and restoration. There are times we may be shown we've done something to someone who's passed away. in this case we can only ask the Lord's forgiveness, and healing where it's possible now, and leave the rest at the foot of the cross.

As spring came, my neighbor asked if I'd reconsider, and go with her and a couple of women from our prayer group to a women's meeting being held in Burlington in May. I had the definite feeling these women weren't going to stop trying to get me to go. I told her I'd talk to the Lord about it and let her know at the next prayer meeting. She smiled and said "Great".

The next several days, my heart was torn. My mind was bombarded with arguments for and against going. I really disliked women's groups. This was the biggest hurdle for me, to be willing to be in a room full of women. I had memories of how my Mother was treated by women when she got involved with a Bible study when I was a kid. I remembered how she never went to another one again because of the things they did and said about her. I had similar memories of being torn apart by women in work situations. This was why the war was going on in my heart. I prayed and said to the Lord "If you want me to go to this meeting help me be willing to go. You know the fight going on in my mind and how I feel about being involved with gossiping women. If you want me to do this, You'll have to help me, and change my mind."

The night before the prayer meeting I was getting ready for bed, planning to read some scripture before going to sleep. I still hadn't made up my mind about what to tell the woman who invited me. As I laid in bed reading and praying, the still small voice of the Lord spoke to me, "There would be no harm in going this once. If you will be willing to go, I'll be there with you; trust Me in this."

The Lord knew that putting it to me this way, I'd agree to go. The next night at the prayer meeting I let them know I'd go. They smiled and said they felt I'd made the right decision and that I'd have a good time. I said nothing, just agreeing to go was enough to deal with.

During the next several weeks before this meeting, the leaders of the prayer group had picked a subject in the Bible I'd never heard of before and it brought more questions and struggle within my heart, as to whether what they were teaching was really from God, or not. That was the baptism in the Holy Spirit and the gifts of the Spirit in operation in believer's today. They started in the gospels, then to the book of Acts and then into the epistles of Paul. They linked the scripture's, teaching that Jesus always intended for believer's to have the same infilling of the Holy Spirit in us today as they did in the days of the first disciple's.

As they continued on through the meetings each week, they'd ask that anyone who wanted this infilling of the baptism of the Holy Spirit to just go forward and the leaders would pray for them to receive. They would encourage them to pray in tongues, if they began to hear their prayer language within their spirits. I watched this very suspiciously, but remained quiet. Over these weeks several went forward, and were prayed with quietly, and I had to admit as I watched; there was a significant event taking place, and they did begin to speak with tongues, and give the Lord Jesus greater praise. As I continued to watch these people, I witnessed changes in them. A boldness to witness, a greater hunger for the word of God, and of the presence of God in their lives. An atmosphere of love, and the bond of fellowship grew between us and the power of God in prayer increased greatly, we all knew it. We began to experience the unity of fellowship spoken of in the Bible when His body comes together. We also began to experience many manifestations of the gifts of the Spirit during our worship time and the Bible study. The word of God became even more alive. In our prayer time when we prayed for the salvation of members of our families, we began to see God work miraculously in bringing many of them to salvation, and the fellowship grew.

I watched all of this, but still wasn't willing to be one of those who went forward to receive this baptism of the Holy Spirit. I didn't want to be deceived. I had come out of great darkness. I knew the ways of the devil from my past involvement with witchcraft, sorcery, and the occult. I didn't want to get involved with anything that was in error, even if Christians were doing it. I needed for the Lord to show me beyond doubt that this was truly from Him, and not the devil.

The day of the meeting, I went to the neighbor's that morning, and went in their car, riding as a passenger. I listened in silence to the women share with each other. Several times I thought within myself, "I hope I heard the Lord on this, and haven't made a mistake". If I had, well, I'd just let it be a learning experience, and not do it again.

When we arrived at the hotel where it was being held we were directed to the conference room, where many women were already in attendance. The room could hold about eight hundred people. The room filled, and the meeting was about to begin. It looked as if about six hundred were there. We were led to our table close to the front, and we were seated about in the middle, which held twenty on each side. As I sat down another woman came up and sat at my right side next to me. We briefly greeted each other, and shared where we were from. She said she was from New York City, and was visiting people she knew in Burlington. An announcer began to ask for all to be seated. We stopped speaking and prepared to hear the beginning of the session. The minister directed us to small baskets on our table. He said they were for anyone who had a prayer request. They could put them in the basket, and they'd be brought to the leaders up front and they would be prayed over first, before anything else was done. I wrote on a small piece of paper "Lord, if the baptism in the Holy Spirit is really of You, please fill me with the Holy Spirit before this meeting is over". I placed it in the basket and it was taken to the front. All the leaders prayed over them, along with all of us in the room.

After announcements and a brief introduction of the speakers for the day, they said there would be a time of worship and prayer before our lunch was served. A group came up with instruments, began with prayer, then we stood and joined the worship. I decided to stand and just listen to the music. Then I noticed the woman from New York City was singing in a language I'd never heard before. As I stood in silence and listened, suddenly I felt the same Presence hovering over me, that I'd felt the first day of my salvation in my house. My entire body became tremendously warm and God's presence filled me to overflowing. As this took place, I began to receive in my spirit the interpretation in English, what the woman was singing in the strange language. As this continued, my body became so hot, I started perspiring and sat down. The leader of our prayer group had been standing next to me on my left and could see something was going on, and asked me if I was ok. I told her very quietly that I'd received the baptism in the Holy Spirit while standing there during the worship time. She grinned from ear to ear, and gave me a tremendous hug.

As the meeting continued many other confirmations of the Holy Spirit's indwelling me in this new wonderful way took place. But this is enough to relay concerning this day. I'll just share some scripture on the subject of the baptism in the Holy Spirit for all who read this and give a challenge to you.

I don't blame you if you have questions, doubts, and reservations. I had many and it took the Lord Himself to help me come to the place of being willing to take Him at His word, and step out in faith and dare to believe him about what the scripture teaches on this. But read the verses on this subject, pray, and take your questions and doubts to God and ask Him to reveal the truth to you. Be willing to allow Him to lead you and open the truth to you. This is not a full list of verses, but will give you enough to do a thorough study. If you have a good study Bible, take the time to cross reference them. As you do, pray and ask God to open your understanding and help you know the truth of them:

> Mat 3:11 I indeed baptize you with wa-
> ter unto repentance: but he that cometh
> after me is mightier than I, whose shoes

I am not worthy to bear: he shall baptize you with the Holy Ghost, and with fire: See also Luke 3:16, John 1:31,

Act 1:4 And, being assembled together with them, commanded them that they should not depart from Jerusalem, but wait for the promise of the Father, which, saith he, ye have heard of me.

Act 1:5 For John truly baptized with water; but ye shall be baptized with the Holy Ghost not many days hence.

The Coming of the Holy Spirit

Act 2:1 And when the day of Pentecost was fully come, they were all with one accord in one place.

Act 2:2 And suddenly there came a sound from heaven as of a rushing mighty wind, and it filled all the house where they were sitting.

Act 2:3 And there appeared unto them cloven tongues like as of fire, and it sat upon each of them.

Act 2:4 And they were all filled with the Holy Ghost, and began to speak with other tongues, as the Spirit gave them utterance.

Act 2:5 And there were dwelling at Jerusalem Jews, devout men, out of every nation under heaven.

Act 2:6 Now when this was noised abroad, the multitude came together, and were confounded, because that every man heard them speak in his own language.

Act 2:7 And they were all amazed and marveled, saying one to another, Behold, are not all these which speak Galileans?

Act 2:8 And how hear we every man in our own tongue, wherein we were born?

The Holy Spirit Falls on the Gentiles

Act 10:44 While Peter yet spake these words, the Holy Ghost fell on all them which heard the word.

Act 10:45 And they of the circumcision which believed were astonished, as many as came with Peter, because that on the Gentiles also was poured out the gift of the Holy Ghost.

Act 10:46 For they heard them speak with tongues, and magnify God. Then answered Peter,

Act 10:47 Can any man forbid water, that these should not be baptized, which have received the Holy Ghost as well as we?

Act 11:12 And the Spirit bade me go with them, nothing doubting. Moreover these six brethren accompanied me, and we entered into the man's house:

Act 11:13 And he shewed us how he had seen an angel in his house, which stood and said unto him, Send men to Joppa, and call for Simon, whose surname is Peter;

Act 11:14 Who shall tell thee words, whereby thou and all thy house shall be saved.

Act 11:15 And as I began to speak, the Holy Ghost fell on them, as on us at the beginning.

Act 11:16 Then remembered I the word of the Lord, how that he said, John indeed baptized with water; but ye shall be baptized with the Holy Ghost.

Act 11:17 Forasmuch then as God gave them the like gift as he did unto us, who believed on the Lord Jesus Christ; what was I, that I could withstand God?

Paul in Ephesus

Act 19:1 And it came to pass, that, while Apollos was at Corinth, Paul having passed through the upper coasts came to Ephesus: and finding certain disciples,

Act 19:2 He said unto them, Have ye received the Holy Ghost since ye believed? And they said unto him, We have not so much as heard whether there be any Holy Ghost.

Act 19:3 And he said unto them, Unto what then were ye baptized? And they said, Unto John's baptism.

Act 19:4 Then said Paul, John verily baptized with the baptism of repentance, saying unto the people, that they should believe on him which should come after him, that is, on Christ Jesus.

Act 19:5 When they heard this, they were baptized in the name of the Lord Jesus.

Act 19:6 And when Paul had laid his hands upon them, the Holy Ghost came on them; and they spake with tongues, and prophesied.

1Co 12:28 And God hath set some in the church, first apostles, secondarily prophets, thirdly teachers, after that miracles, then gifts of healings, helps, governments, diversities of tongues.

1Co 12:29 Are all apostles? are all prophets? are all teachers? are all workers of miracles?

1Co 12:30 Have all the gifts of healing? do all speak with tongues? do all interpret?

1Co 12:31 But covet earnestly the best gifts: and yet shew I unto you a more

excellent way.

I will also encourage a complete study of First Corinthians chapter fourteen which gives instruction on the proper use of the gifts of the Holy Spirit and orderly worship.

The baptism in the Holy Spirit is real, and it is for anyone who will open their hearts to Him, and allow the Lord to fill you with this blessing and the gifts of the Holy Spirit. The purpose of this is to give his people the power to be witnesses for Him. To give the boldness to stand against the attacks of the enemy and the world. The gifts of the Holy Spirit are meant always to be used to bring glory to Jesus Christ and help us in our service to Him. They are not given to glorify, or bring attention to ourselves. This is very important to remind ourselves of often. The biggest problems we will face is becoming prideful and misusing the gifts for our own benefit, and becoming deceived. It's very easy to let this happen. Our egos always want to rise to the top. Our own souls need to be constantly watched over and ask the Lord to keep us in humility and teachable. If we won't humble ourselves, He will humble us.

After this day even more time was spent studying and praying. I wanted to know this Holy Spirit, the third Person of the Godhead. I wanted to be able to understand His role in my life and His purposes in connection with Jesus Christ. I have to say, in all these years, I've not come to the end of studying and continuing to learn more of Him, and His ways.

One night, shortly after being filled with the Spirit, at one of our prayer meetings, God moved in my life in a way that would be part of my walk with the Lord from then on, and increased as years went by.

We met this time at a camp at a nearby pond and recreation area that one of the elders owned. When the meeting began the room was full. Some sat on the floor, other's stood, as they felt led. We had a time of prayer, and study in scripture, but after this spent most of the time giving testimonies, and worshiping the Lord. The presence of God began to fill the room, and there was much praise among us. I was in the back of the room, where I usually went during meetings, listening and praying more than anything else. God's presence began to come down upon me heavily, and I became very hot. For some reason, I had a tremendous urge to open my mouth and start to speak. This was not my own desire, it was coming from the Lord, but I didn't know what to do with it. Finally, after several minutes of this, I gave in. I felt like I was going to explode. I knew somehow it would be better to wait until the room was quiet, and the music stopped. I said a silent prayer for God's help, and spoke out:

"Behold, I come quickly, are you ready?"

The room filled with praise, prayer, and proclamations; "Yes, come Lord Jesus". The group leaders thanked me for being obedient, but I told them I had no idea what I had done, or if it was the right thing to do. If it wasn't, I apologize and wouldn't do it again.

They smiled, and said I'd done the right thing, and they knew for some time that the Lord would use me in this fashion and that what had happened was described in Corinthians as the gift of prophecy. They suggested I spend more time in prayer and ask the Lord to help me learn more about it, and how it should be used among the believer's in a meeting. They added it was an important gift but should be guarded against deception carefully. I took note of what was said and did spend a great deal of time studying and praying over this. In time to come the Lord revealed the greater extent of my service to him in this realm. Our walk and service to God deepens and the Holy Spirit will take us into greater knowledge, if we want to pay the prices and continue to surrender in that service. It's always our choice.

However, I've also learned over the years the upheaval this causes in churches and groups, when the leadership either doesn't believe this gift is for today, the people don't want to hear what's said, and contentions develop from unbelief, jealousy, pride, or outright rebellion. Most churches today won't touch this area of service because it's too controversial. They'd rather avoid it completely. The Lord has let me know his view of most churches today, that they are in unbelief. We are in the <u>Laodicean</u> age of lukewarmness, and apostasy. Many who obey the Lord and have given unwanted prophecies have found themselves thrown out. I'm among one of them.

Lynn began to see the changes taking place in me and the ways of salvation was transforming my life. He didn't say much, but it caused him to start talking about it to his family. This brought a lot of trouble into our lives from this point on. He began to take note that I wasn't drinking with him on weekends anymore and my way of dressing changed. The Lord started to deal with me about not wearing tight clothes, revealing tops cut too low, and not wearing a lot of makeup. He didn't know what to make of the changes, but some of it was beginning to convict him. I could see he didn't like it. The Lord was dealing with his heart, as he watched me turning from a woman molded by sin, into a woman led by God.

When families are living in unbelief and don't desire a walk with the Lord; a committed Christian will be seen as a fanatic and accused of having mental problems, along with other things. This began to be the case for me. It proved to be an ongoing source of trouble in our relationship from then on. I would soon come to the place of having to make choices that would be one of the greatest tests of my faith, and one of the greatest attacks from Satan to destroy both of our lives.

During this time I also was still looking for another job. I wasn't sure which direction to take and started looking into going back to school. There was a desire in me now to do something of value and purpose and I was praying for the Lord's leading in this. An answer came soon, in a way I could not have imagined.

One day one of the women who went to the prayer meetings called me, and asked if I'd like to ride with her to a job interview she had in a local city, and get a bite to eat along the way. I was alone for the day, so said sure and went in her car. Carrie was in school this day, and we made sure we could be back before she came home. It was a beautiful midsummer day and we enjoyed the fellowship together along the way. She had applied for a part time job at a nursing home and we were going there first. I asked her if she had ever done this kind of work before. She said no, but they said they trained the people who they hired.

When we walked in she was directed to the office of the people she needed to see. I went along, just to be with her for support. The nurse came out and began to ask her questions, but looked at me also several times, as if she wanted to speak to me as well. I didn't say anything. To me, this was out of my element.

After the nurse finished questioning my friend, she looked at me again and said "Have you ever done nursing of any kind before"?

"No, actually I've never thought of it."

"Would you be interested in a position, if it were given you"?

"I have no training at all and wouldn't know where to begin. What would I be doing"?

"We need nursing assistants. You would be caring for the residents; feeding, bathing, medical procedures for some of them who need ongoing medical treatments and personal care. Responsibilities will increase in time. We will train you and give continued ongoing training during your employment, with opportunities for advancements as you go along".

I was completely taken by surprise at this offer. But while she was talking, I could feel the presence of the Lord and a very strong sense within my heart, that this was God's will for me. So, surprised at my own response, I gave my answer:

"Well, when would you want me to start"?

"If you're willing to start an evening shift we could use you right away. We could use you the first of next week and give you several nights training. If it's alright with you, we'd start you on the evening shift 3:00 to midnight. If you would desire a day shift you could certainly put your name in and we'd give you a day shift when an opening became available. But they are hard to come by, because most people want the days."

She had no way of knowing this, but the evening shift was what I desired anyway. Carrie would not be alone at home if I worked evenings. Lynn would be there for her while I worked. For me, this was perfect. I knew this was God's will for me, and agreed to start when she wanted me. I looked over at my friend and saw the look of surprise, and sadness on her face. She had not gotten the job, and watched as I was hired without even applying for one. I couldn't blame her for how she felt.

Driving back home, I looked at her and said "I'm sorry, I had no idea this was going to happen. I hope you don't hold it against me, but I don't blame you for being disappointed. I'd feel the same way if it was me".

"No, I'm not angry with you, but yes, it does prick my heart. I guess the Lord has other plans for me, I hope".

We prayed together about her still needing a job, asking that something would come her way that she was more suited for. It wasn't long after this, she found work at a local plant doing work she said she liked and it was not being on her feet all night. She was middle aged now and had felt being on her feet all night on a shift might be too much for her. This was a better solution for her. The Lord knows what we can handle and how to open doors for opportunities that are best suited for us.

When I told Lynn of this opportunity, he was pleased and said he'd make sure Carrie was with him whenever I worked, and not to worry. I went shopping and found nursing outfits and good nursing walking shoes. This change in my life was to be for a lifetime, with many ups and downs. Through every job in this field during my working years, I learned new things; about life, people, myself, and the Lord. Some of the things learned will be shared in this book, but only what I believe God wants to be. He uses everything for His glory, and to speak to hearts we may never meet. He's let me know it will be the case with this book.

The first night on the new job I was assigned to a nurse who would be training me. I knew nothing about policies, procedures, or where to start. This first night was to be an eye opening experience, on many levels.

I followed her to each room we were assigned to for that night and the residents we'd be caring for. Everyone was unique, with different levels of medical care needed. She explained to me the personal preferences of each one and whether they needed help when the evening meal was brought to them, which ones would be scheduled for a bath and what my role in helping them would be. Some were incontinent, needing personal care with changing adult diapers. Some of the men needed help with using urinals, were completely bedridden, and seemed to not know their surroundings at all. My heart became heavier and heavier as my eyes were opened to the levels of human suffering, that is for the most part, completely invisible to the outside world. I became very aware that God was giving me a crash course in seeing the *real* world, as He saw it. The degrees of pain, human frailty, effects of disease, people's own wrong choices that caught up with them; the whole gamut of people's human conditions. And, a very important point God was bringing home to me; the reality of the breaking down and destruction of the body and human mortality; death. It had been less than a year since watching my Father's battle with cancer, and the deterioration of his body, and the deeper levels of pain he endured, until death took him.

Now, I was realizing as I followed her from room to room; I had walked into a job that would make me face the same levels of pain and suffering my Father endured, multiple times over, and every night I worked. I thought about how I might get out of this, and just tell God, I'm sorry, but I just can't do this. Even while I was trying to find a way to quit, I was hearing in my spirit "This is my will for you". I was faced with two things; either obey God, and learn to do this job, which I knew I didn't want now. Or, walk out and never come back, knowing I was disobeying Him. To me, this was a no win situation.

I was a young Christian, and walking in obedience was to be an ongoing test in many different situations, just like this one. Each time I knew I had the freedom to obey, or not; but would live with the consequences of disobedience if I rebelled. God was going to use this job to teach me many things. If I decided to obey; gain spiritual wisdom and the purposes of God in these life lessons many never deal with. But I also had the free choice to say "thanks, but no thanks", and walk away. This night was a defining moment for me, for these reasons. Don't let anybody ever tell you it gets easier to obey God as time goes on, they don't know what they are talking about. But, I've also learned making the decision to obey Him opens the door for God's blessings, guidance, protection and the covering of His presence. After many years of trusting Him, this is priceless and worth the hardships and difficulties that may come. When we are standing in right relationship with Him, we see His hand of blessing, and situations change, by prayer. When we are first saved, it's just the start. From then on, it's an ongoing process of God's hands molding, shaping and transforming us into His image and it's the stuff of life, He uses to do it.

By the end of the third and final night of my training with the nurse, I was feeling the brunt of the truth; without God's help, I could not do this. I came to see the importance of praying before I left the house for work each afternoon, asking the Lord for His strength and guidance to get through the night, and to get there and back safely.

Each night I worked there were four to six of us assigned to each wing of the nursing home. We were supposed to have only six to eight residents assigned to us. But many nights we'd have more, because of those who would call in sick, leaving a shortage. It was not uncommon to care for over a dozen in a night. I'd feel frustration, anger, and helplessness, as I'd work at a walk/run to take care of each one's needs; knowing some of them needed extra care, and I couldn't give it to them. Some of the one's who were wheelchair bound would be waiting silently, sometimes sleeping in the hallway, without complaining. They had long ago learned it didn't do any good. I prayed a lot those nights, while in the midst of this, asking for more strength, and help to forgive those who didn't seem to care.

There were many caring, loving nurses who worked tirelessly, and truly loved the residents. I watched some of them as they'd bathe, play music for some who were bedridden, feed those who needed to be with special kindness and love. I asked the Lord to help me develop this in me toward these frail, forgotten people. Yes, many were forgotten, by family, and the world. We had become their family, and they depended on us for everything. There were nights I'd go home, and cry in bed, trying to be quiet. Sometimes Lynn would wake up and hear me, and just take me in his arms. At these times, God's love through him, was what helped me keep going back and not quit. His silent understanding, gave needed strength.

However, not all who worked there were doing it because of their care for the elderly, they had their own agenda's. The money of course, some of them couldn't get any other jobs. Some of them wanted to work nights in order to have their days free to do other things. Some of them resented the work, and the residents, and if they were having a bad day, or felt like taking out their resentment, the residents would be treated with either neglect, or cruelty. These people were smart enough to try to hide what they did, but more than once, I witnessed cruelty and reported it. This got me labeled a troublemaker, which caused me to remember my attempts of helping the littler kids in the playground growing up; which got me labeled the same thing then. I took these situations to the Lord in prayer and asked Him how to handle it. He was always faithful to show what would be the best way to deal with it. I was learning to trust and lean on Him each day, in every situation and *look* for His answers. Many times, the answers to my prayers at work would come within minutes.

But, there were times I'd walk into situations that were out of my control and watched as residents were treated with unbelievable cruelty. I'm glad God allowed me to see it, but each time I witnessed these things, it affected me for life. I live with the realization that every day in these nursing homes and retirement homes, where elderly folks are trying to live out the rest of their lives; somebody may be mistreating them and doing serious bodily harm to them. It grips my heart to this day, when I think of it.

I discerned that some of these residents had learned to become as silent, and invisible as possible, to keep from being abused. Some of them would feign being deaf and wouldn't answer some of the sarcastic remarks, or rough questions thrown at them. They'd sit in silence, as if they hadn't heard; but I picked up the truth, that this was a learned tactic to get the abuser's to leave them alone. I didn't blame them and after a while some of them softened and opened up to me, when they saw I wasn't the same as the abuser's. These experiences have caused me to make up my mind, if I have any say in it, I'll never go to one of these places. I'd rather die alone at home. I've prayed God would let it be so.

One night on my shift, I had to work with one of the women who I knew was caught mistreating residents and would keep watch of her. When most of the residents were in bed, the evening meals and baths were done. A few wheelchair bound folks in the hall were waiting to be taken care of. This woman decided to take one them. She was in her late eighties, small framed, weighing less than a hundred pounds. She was strapped into the wheelchair, making it impossible to get out on her own. The woman started talking to her, joking and laughing as she grabbed the wheelchair handles, "How about we have some fun on the way to bed, and take a bumper car ride".

As she said this she started pushing the wheelchair, running faster and faster until she was about halfway down the hall, then let go of the chair. She stood still laughing, watching it go on its own, scraping the rail as it crashed into the wall and continued on, with the woman strapped helplessly in it, not able to do anything about it. If her legs or arms had been extended out beyond the arm of the chair, she would no doubt have had a broken limb.

I came around the corner just as she was running with this woman in the chair, and saw how fast she was going. I stopped, so stunned I couldn't believe what I was seeing. My feet were frozen. I watched helplessly as the woman's chair collided into the wall and continued scraping down the hall for about twelve more feet. The woman was slumped over in the chair, not moving. My stomach was sick, the anger was rising into my face to the point I felt I would explode. I turned to the woman, who stood laughing like a mad woman, "What in God's name are you doing!"

"Oh don't worry, she's fine, we're just having a little bumper car ride." The grin on her face gave me chills down my back.

"You are a monster. I'm reporting you to the nurses at the desk. What in the world is wrong with you, don't you know you could kill this woman? She is too frail to take this kind of treatment." "Go ahead, you'll regret it. This woman is gonna die anyway, she might as well have some fun before she goes."

I couldn't say anything more. I couldn't believe what I had seen, and heard from this woman. This was a kind of callous cruelty I had never seen before. I wish I could say it was my last. It was to be only one, of many others over the years.

She was right, I didn't get any compassion or support for reporting her. But, I didn't regret doing it. I'd do it again. In years to come, I'd have occasion to have to intervene numerous times, for the same kinds of neglect, cruelty, and mistreatment of residents and elders. I learned to develop a backbone of steal, to be able to deal with it.

That night in prayer, the Lord spoke to my heart, to look up some specific verses when I got home, and use them as my guide in my work from this point on:

Mat 25:34 Then shall the King say unto them on his right hand, Come, ye blessed

of my Father, inherit the kingdom prepared for you from the foundation of the
world:

Mat 25:35 For I was an hungred, and ye
gave me meat: I was thirsty, and ye gave
me drink: I was a stranger, and ye took
me in:

Mat 25:36 Naked, and ye clothed me: I
was sick, and ye visited me: I was in prison, and ye came unto me.

Mat 25:37 Then shall the righteous answer him, saying, Lord, when saw we
thee an hungred, and fed thee? or thirsty,
and gave thee drink?

Mat 25:38 When saw we thee a stranger,
and took thee in? or naked, and clothed
thee?

Mat 25:39 Or when saw we thee sick, or
in prison, and came unto thee?

Mat 25:40 And the King shall answer
and say unto them, Verily I say unto you,
Inasmuch as ye have done it unto one of
the least of these my brethren, ye have
done it unto me.

If you are in a nursing home, retirement home, disabled, living
alone and family members gone; though you may feel the world
has forgotten you, God has not. His eyes are on you and He cares
for you. Talk to Him, tell him your feelings, your needs. He's only
a prayer away.

As summer came to an end and fall began, I again noticed changes
in Lynn's demeanor. A quiet distance, and being gone more on the
weekends. It brought memories of living with my first husband.

My heart became heavier as this grew worse. I wasn't surprised when one night he began a conversation I'd hoped wouldn't come up. Sitting in the living room alone together, he asked "Are you intending to keep going to those Friday night meetings at the neighbors? I'm not happy about it. I'm seeing changes in you I don't think I like. Is this a cult your involved with?"

"No, they are simply born again believers in the Lord Jesus Christ. We meet together to study the Bible, pray, and sing and worship the Lord together. There's no secret oaths, nothing is done in the dark, I've asked you to come, and pray you may be willing to someday. But I know you have to make up your own mind about it."

"My family is concerned about what you're doing, and people around here are talking too. Are you connected to any regular church"?
"If you asking if we are part of any specific denomination, no we're not. If you read the Bible, there are no denominations we need to belong to; we are instructed to follow Christ, and the scriptures in the New Testament. Our faith is in Jesus Christ, not an organization, or denomination. It's Christ alone that gives us salvation and we're instructed to fellowship with likeminded believer's. I don't blame you for being skeptical, but if you would come with me sometime, you'd see they are very open, and honest in their walk with the Lord, and they'd love to see you."

"You don't come with me anymore to visit my friends or party with us, I know you don't want to drink, but you could come and be a part of the group, and stay involved."

"It's hard to explain this, but, since my salvation I know now I have to make the decision to either follow Jesus, or go back to the life I lived before. I've decided to give my life completely to Jesus, with no compromise. If I go with you to these parties and get-togethers, the temptation to go back to drinking could cause me to stumble, and fall away from my walk with the Lord. I can't do that Lynn. I'm sorry for how you feel, but this is a lifelong commitment I've made, and there's no turning back for me. He has shown me He is real, and He's forgiven my sins, and delivered me from drinking and many other things. I'm not willing to open those doors again, not even for you."

He sat listening, looked me in the eyes, and could see I was completely serious. Standing up, he looked out the window at the pond for several minutes, then back to me.

"I can see you mean what you're saying. I'm going to go and do some more thinking about this. But right now, the way I feel is this; if you aren't willing to come back, and be a part of my family involvements, and gatherings with my friends, and won't come back to what we were before you made this change; I'll have to put it to you this way. It's either Jesus, or me. You know I've always let you live your life with a lot of freedom, but I don't like what this change has done to our lives. I don't claim to understand it all, but I don't like it. I mean what I'm saying too. When I come back, I'll let you know if I still feel this way. You may as well know and think about what you'll do, if I haven't changed my mind.

A couple of hours later, he returned. His answer was brief and to the point. He hadn't changed his mind. It was either Jesus, or him. I'd have to either stop living as a Christian and go back to what we were before my salvation, or I'd have to leave. I listened and said nothing. He walked back out the door and headed for the barn. I was not surprised and I knew there was no point in trying to make any argument with him, we were both very serious minded people. We didn't mince words with one another.

Now, after only a short time, the devil had succeeded in destroying the foundation of my marriage. He knew I'd never turn back, I'd never reject Jesus to stay with Lynn, even though I loved him. I had to make a choice, did I love Jesus more. For me there was no other choice. He had made Himself known to me in undeniable ways and had delivered me and set me free. I wasn't willing to go back into bondage, even for Lynn.

With a very heavy heart, I began to plan what I needed to do. My heart was breaking, not only for my own life, but for Carrie's. This was going to bring the same instability and chaos back into her little life, as when we were with her father and cause her to have to leave her school and the friendships she had developed. This was crushing me as I went about packing and putting our belongings in my car. The only thing I knew to do was go back to New York to my family, and start over again.

When the car was loaded, Lynn came back to the house, his shoulders were drooped. I could see he was miserable. He looked at us, with his arm out in a gesture, hoping I'd take his hand.

"Lorna, you know I love you, you don't have to leave. Take some more time, and think about this."

"I need just one answer, does the ultimatum still stand with you? Is it Jesus or you, if that's still the way it is, you've given me no choice. I'll not forsake my faith in Christ for anyone, not even you."

"Yes, it's still the way I feel".

"Then there's nothing more to be said".

His countenance was completely fallen, but he said nothing more.

I picked up the last of the suitcases, asked Carrie to come along with me, and we got in the car and started down the driveway, and the three hour trip back to New York, and an uncertain future.

As I drove the familiar route back to New York, the verse Jesus spoke came to my mind:

Mat 8:20 And Jesus saith unto him, The

foxes have holes, and the birds of the air
have nests; but the Son of man hath not
where to lay his head.

This seemed to be my state of life, again. My mind went back
over the years and the many times I'd found myself driving down a
road, leaving everything behind me. It was becoming a very weary
pattern, I thought I'd never see again. I put some music on, to
focus on something else. I had to find a way to get through this;
for my daughters sake.

EIGHT
AN ULTIMATUM

It was early evening when I pulled into my Mother's driveway. It had been a long, silent ride, except for listening to Christian music along the way. Carrie and I both sang some of the tunes together, it helped shorten the trip.

When I opened the door and stepped into the kitchen, Mother was at her stove cooking dinner. Her table was set, I could see there was a place for Carrie and I. She turned to greet me and gave Carrie a hug. Grief was   etched in her face, she was still missing Dad. I gave her a hug, and went back to the car to unload the rest of what I had brought. She had fixed a spare bedroom for us and it was big enough to hold all the suitcases. There were two small beds ready for Carrie and I.

I helped Mother with dinner, and we visited while we ate. I asked her about what was going on and if there was anything I could do to help while I was here. She mentioned her garden and some things in the house that could use some repair. I said she could show me and we'd see about doing them together in the next few days. We had come to visit her often in the last several years, so this was just another visit to Carrie, she was right at home. It was important to make sure she felt the love and support of family, in this time of turmoil.

As we busied ourselves in the next several days helping get the needed repairs done for Mom, we also visited other members of the family. I had an older sister and brother in law who lived a few miles away, and they came for a visit one evening. They cautiously asked what the situation was with Lynn and I. Without going into long details, I gave the simple answer that he was not happy with the changes he saw in me, now that I had become a Christian and had given me a choice; either the Lord, or him. I quietly but firmly looked them in the eyes, and told them that to me, this left no other choice. I had to choose the Lord, and that's what I did. They listened in silence. I didn't expect them to fully understand, but they let me know they supported me and loved me, no matter what the problems were with Lynn. They said if there was anything they could do to help, let them know. Before they left, they said they'd love it if I came sometime for dinner at their place. I said that would be great, and they left.

A younger sister was living in Charleston South Carolina at the time, with her husband who was a naval officer. They had gone together several years in their high school years, and married soon after he enlisted. They traveled several times to different military bases since their marriage and were both busy people. One evening she called while I was still at Mother's, and asked to speak to me. She asked if I'd consider coming to visit her and perhaps look for work there. I may be able to start a new life in the south in her area. This was a surprise to me, something I had not thought of. I thanked her for the offer and said I'd think about it and talk to her in a few days to let her know what I decided. I hung up, knowing I needed some time to talk to the Lord about this. I needed to know His guidance. I didn't want to do something out of His will now. My concern was for Carrie and her well-being.

As I prayed about this, I decided to tell Mother and my older sister about this too. I wanted them to weigh in on this and see how they felt about it. We met together at Mom's at her table over some coffee and talked it out. I gave my concerns about traveling that far with Carrie, she was only eight at the time. I felt this was too much turmoil and physical stress to put her through. They agreed, but also thought it may be a good opportunity for me to find a job in a completely different area and a new life, with my other sister and her husband there to help me get started.

Then my older sister looked at me and said "If you want, you could let Carrie stay with us. I'd be glad to take care of her for you while you went down on your own first, and had a chance to look for work and see if you could find a place for you both. If you did find something, we'd bring her down to you, and you'd be able to move into the new place and be set up when we brought her down. It would make it easier for you both."

This brought a sense of relief to me, and lifted a lot of worry from my heart. But, I asked "Are you sure you want to do this, your kids may not want another kid in the house every day."

"We wouldn't want it any other way. We're family. If you want to go down and see if you can get a fresh start there, this way you could do it and not put Carrie through all that."

"I want to thank you both. I hope I can repay you both for this one day."

"Don't even think about that, it doesn't matter at all. We'll get a room set for her and you can bring her things over when you're ready, and call back down and let them know you're coming, and when. Sounds like a plan to me." She lifted her cup and took a sip, with a twinkle in her eyes. I could see she knew the decision had been made.

Within a few days Carrie was settled with my sister and her family. The morning I planned to leave, I said farewell first to Mother. We had breakfast together, talked about not worrying, staying safe, the things families always say, that binds them with love. I felt torn and wondered if it would have been better to stay with Mother and help her. Her life was not easy now. She worked part time, but couldn't handle anything more. She only received a small veterans pension from when Dad was in the army during the war. It helped, but she had nothing left over each month. I mentioned to her that I could change my mind and stay and help her.

"No, you need to do this. You'd never be at ease, thinking you may have made a mistake and should have gone. Once you're down there it won't be long and you'll know if you belong there or not. Either way, it will give you a chance to think things through and ask the Lord to help you make the right decisions along the way. If it doesn't work out down there, come back here. You'll have a place waiting if it doesn't."

We embraced. Her wisdom, and bond of love was glue between us.

As I pulled out onto the interstate heading south, I made sure the map I had traced out the routes to my sister's home was on the front seat next to me, in easy reach. I had never driven this far alone. I prayed as I went, asking for the Lords protection, guidance, and help in staying on the right routes, and not get lost.

Only a couple of times I had to stop, go over the map, and backtrack a few miles to get on the right route. I was relieved to find the sign at the entrance to the apartment complex they lived in, and found their number on the door.

I had only brought a couple of suitcases and when I rang their bell, they both came out, greeted me warmly, and we each took what I had and made it into their apartment. They had dinner ready. We talked and shared about our lives and events. Before we knew it, it had become quite late. They showed me my room, and parted for the night. After putting my things away, I laid in bed praying, asking the Lord for His guidance in this trip, to help me find employment, and a home suitable for Carrie and I, if it was His will for me to be here. But, the last thing on my mind before exhausted sleep took me, was Lynn. My heart was aching, missing him. The love was still there, as strong as ever.

For a few days, after breakfast each morning, my sister would take me with her on the errands she would tend to. I'd ride along as she drove and listen to her tell of the events that went on in the community, her job, her husband's position in the navy, and their future plans. I was happy for them, but my mind went back to my own life and the home I thought I had with Lynn, now gone. We had worked so hard, put so much of ourselves into that place. We both loved our home. We were bound to it with chords of love, and devotion. I knew this chaos we were in was an attack from Satan, to destroy our lives and our love for one another. As I listened to my sister relay their plans and hopes, I knew it would be best for me to say as little as possible. I couldn't muster false hopes right now. The thought of starting over again, alone, was a long dark road to me. But right now, I couldn't see any light at the end of this tunnel.

After about a week of riding with her to the various places of her daily routine, I began to get the confidence to take my own car and do some exploring short distances. I began searching for work, picking up newspapers, going to local nursing homes, and looking at the housing situation. I decided to start going job hunting almost every day, at least in the mornings and be back at the apartment for dinner with them in the evenings.

During a day when my sister was home, we visited quite a while and she asked me about the situation with Lynn and I. When I explained his ultimatum to me about my faith in Christ, she looked puzzled and serious. I knew she wasn't saved, and understood the concern in her eyes.

She asked: "Isn't being a Christian supposed to mean love and forgiveness"?

"Yes, I agree with you about that, but he wasn't giving the ultimatum because of anything I was doing. It was because I stopped going with him to drinking parties with people he knows, and stopped drinking with him on weekends like we used to. When I asked

Jesus to forgive me, and received His salvation, He delivered me from alcoholism and I know I can't go back. He's also worried I'm involved in a cult. It's hard to explain to him that I'm not, because he knows nothing about the Bible. I've read some verses to him, to explain what being saved means, but he doesn't understand yet. I've been praying for his salvation since I got saved, but there is a very hard battle going on in his heart and soul. The devil doesn't want to let him go."

She listened, seriously considering what I was saying.

"I don't know if I really understand what you're saying, but I can see the dilemma you're in. I can't say I blame you for not being willing to go back to drinking. I'm glad you quit. Maybe he'll change his mind. We can hope, anyway."

"I haven't given up, but I know I can't sit and do nothing. I have to think of Carrie and try to keep on going. In the meantime, I intend to keep on praying for him and asking God to change his heart and if it's His will, bring us back together. I still love him, and I believe he still loves me. This is a spiritual battle and right now, it looks like the devil is winning. I'm just hanging on to Jesus, and asking for him to intervene."

"I don't blame you, don't give up."

Then she changed the subject, and brought up something in our childhood, I hadn't thought of for years; the dark mirror my older sister had given to me, and I brought home. She relayed how it scared the daylights out of all of us, and the horrible dream I had.

She continued on, also bringing up a health problem that she was dealing with, severe allergies. She explained that they started several years ago, when she was in her late teens, and continued to get worse each year.

Now she was in her early twenties, and they were so bad she couldn't use regular cleaning detergents, dish soap, or anything with strong chemicals. She was also now allergic to almost all foods and had to eat a special diet. if she didn't, she would become seriously ill. The symptoms ranged from nausea, to violent cramps, skin rashes, her throat would swell up and her esophagus would close up entirely to the point she couldn't swallow anything. She explained she had gone to many doctor's trying to recover from this and get rid of it, and that two of them had said they felt she would never be able to have kids because of it. I could see the anxiety and fear in her eyes over this.

While I listened to her, I heard the Lord speak to my heart "This is a spiritual problem, not a health problem. She is being attacked by demonic powers, and yes, they are linked to the mirror. Remember the drowned woman in the pool in the dream you had; that it was your sister. Satan's demons entered her as a child, and has been tormenting her in various ways since that time and are trying to kill her."

As she continued talking with me, I silently questioned the Lord; "If this is true, why are you telling me this and what do you want me to do about it"?

"I want you to witness salvation to her, and then leave it alone and simply pray for her to open her heart to be saved. Then begin to pray that I will help her see she needs to be delivered from the demons that are causing the allergies in her body. You will need to fast and pray for this, it will take time."

I didn't say anything to her while we visited that day. I decided to pray and wait for the opportunity to share the gospel with her, and trust God in this. He was beginning to open my spiritual eyes to a realm of service I'd never known before. There was a sense of expectancy and faith rising in my spirit about this. My soul was hungering for a deeper understanding of walking in the ways of

God and He was beginning to open these doors now, by giving insights into the spiritual connections of the allergies and the demonic bondage's in my sister.

This was to be an ongoing matter of prayer and fasting that went on for more than a year, before a complete deliverance happened for her. But, this was the beginning and her situation was a main focus of prayer until it was completed. Further along, this will be continued. As I listened to her, and the Lord's direction going on within me, it became much clearer to me why I had to come down here. I began to realize, it may not have had anything to do with staying here permanently. It may have been to get the ball rolling to get my sister saved, and set free from these horrible demons trying to kill her. As this scenario unfolded in my mind, I could feel the confirmation deep in my spirit. The Lord was letting me know I had put the pieces of the puzzle together correctly, and He'd direct me along the way, to get her saved and free.

In the next couple of weeks when the occasion became available, I did sit and share the gospel with her and we shared back and forth about her questions, and reservations. I asked her if she'd like to pray to receive salvation and surrender her life to the Lord and be ready for heaven, whenever she died. She was honest and said she needed some time to think about it. I didn't try to force her, I remembered the Lords mercy to me when I was being convicted for many months before I finally opened my heart to Him. I knew it was best to just pray, and let the Lord convict her, and draw her to Himself. I felt in my heart she would come to Him, I'd already heard the assurance of it. I just had to stand in faith, and keep praying.

In the meantime, I continued to look for work. It was beginning to look as if finding one would not be easy. Each job I applied for was either already taken, or it didn't have enough hours to it. I was looking for something full time with benefits if possible. Looking for a place to live was also proving to be unsuccessful. I began to wonder if I'd have to expand my search to other parts of the state, even though I didn't want to. I prayed and asked the Lord to please open a door for me in the area, and continued searching.

One night the phone rang while I was alone in the apartment. My sister was out, so I picked it up.

"Hello, I'm glad it's you. It's me, Lynn. I hope you'll talk to me. I've missed you and Carrie. Is there any way we can settle this problem between us?"

My heart was beating out of my chest, my throat was dry, I didn't know what to say, nothing would come out of my mouth.

"Are you there?"

"Lynn, I'm here, but I'm so surprised. I don't know what to say, except you know the only solution is, just let me come back and accept me as a Christian woman. It's that simple. I will never try to force you to become one, but I'll admit, I'll keep praying that you will get saved".

"I thought you'd say that. You know how stubborn I am sometimes and I know I've let people influence my mind. I love you, and that's not changed. I want to come down. We need to talk. If you're willing to see me, we can go over this again, and come to some understanding. I want you and Carrie back with me, if you're willing to give this another try."

"Lynn, are you willing to let this be between you and I alone, without the influence of your drinking buddies and your family? This is the biggest problem between us, you listen to other people too much and believe the accusations against me from them. Ask yourself, have I done anything to you or been dishonest in any way to you, to deserve this treatment? If you're honest, you have to say no. I love you, that hasn't changed, but this intrusion on our lives

132

by these people is destroying us and you don't have to let it. My being a Christian isn't going to harm you in any way, it hasn't to this point. My faith in the Lord only increases my love for you, I wish you'd understand this."

"You're right, but you know, it's hard for me to admit it. If you're open to it, I'll be down by day after tomorrow. Then we can spend time getting these problems hashed out and taken care of. I want our lives back the way they were, before all this happened".

"I'll never shut the door to you Lynn, the only one who will ever destroy this love and bond between us, is you, if you let it. You come, I'll be waiting and praying. You may as well hear it and know the truth; if you take me back it will be as a Christian woman. Think about that, while you're coming and if you can accept this; that is the whole point to this problem."

"I'll be there, as soon as I can, bye".

I sat there in my sister's living room, looking out at the inner courtyard of the apartment complex, numb from the realization of what just happened. I didn't know what to do with the emotions running rampant in my soul. I loved that man. Sometimes I felt like smacking him upside the head, because yes, he was stubborn, and foolish for continuing to listen to troublemakers and people who didn't care in the least for him. He just didn't realize the war we were in and it wouldn't make any difference right now to try to explain it to him. But, I saw in this phone call, the direction God wanted me to go. This marriage wasn't over. Satan had not won. I intended to be prayed up and ready, when Lynn got here. This relationship was going to be restored.

The call came in the evening, just as he said. He was waiting at a restaurant parking lot and would follow us back to my sister's place. We found him and brought him back with us. It was late, so he had a meal of leftover's and we all said goodnight, retiring for the night.

The next several days we spent going to local places, gardens and events; mostly to talk. The presence of God was very strong between us. When I had prayed before he arrived, the Lord had let me know the best thing to do was let him do most of the talking; and simply be honest.

Lynn was never one to make long speeches. We had long ago become accustomed to just enjoying each other's company, without a lot of useless talking. As we drove to the different places, I let him be the one to open up and express his concerns. I just made it plain again that if I came back home with him, I'd not hide my faith in the Lord, nor would I stop going to services or end fellowship with other believer's. He'd have to come to terms with this and be willing to accept this part of my life, and Carrie's as well. I left it at that and let him think about it.

After a few days of this, we went to a public garden nearby where we could finish this talk. It was early spring and in South Carolina, the flowers were in full bloom now. We sat at a bench, with blooming azalea, rhododendron, daffodils, and tulips everywhere. Overlooking the bench there was a pond, with lilies in bloom at the water's edge. In my mind, I sensed the blessings of God, in allowing us this opportunity and that He had set this up for us.

Our conversation lasted several hours. We went back over our first meeting, the many months of work and what we had accomplished together at the house. The last year of seeing my Mother and Dad go through his battle with cancer, his funeral, and how it changed our lives. It brought back the reality that we had built a solid foundation in our lives of love and responsibility. We needed to find a way to restore that foundation, and shut the door to outside forces trying to destroy it. We both agreed to that.

It was late afternoon when we finally left that garden, with a new commitment between us to start again and close doors of outside forces. He voiced his agreement that he needed to start minding his own business, and not hang out with men he used to spend time with. His life was changed, marriage brings responsibilities. He needed to be willing to take them seriously.

I did make the statement to him once that I thought he needed to hear, that when I married him, it didn't include drinking buddies, or his families intrusions. I didn't mind him seeing his family, but didn't really want our lives and our decisions hinged on their opinions. I didn't marry them, I married Lynn. He understood what I meant.

By the time we went back to my sister's place, we had settled much of what was in our hearts and minds. He had rented a car and planned for me to follow him back to the place he got it and then take over driving my car back to pick up Carrie and my belongings at Mother's, then go back to Vermont. We felt we'd be back home within four days.

As we started out, Lynn decided to take me back through the Shenandoah valley. This was a blessing from the Lord, a gift. Many times we don't realize the love and care the Lord has for each of us and how he arranges these blessings, knowing our specific likes and what gives us pleasure.

The entire trip through this valley was met with rows of blooming bushes, meadows in full bloom, and the weather was warm and sunny. We took our time and ate at small local places along the way.

We stayed only one night at Mother's when we arrived back in New York, we wanted to return home. Lynn needed to get back to his job and I wanted to put the house back in order and clean it up. I could imagine in my mind, what needed to be done.

During all this, I was also concerned for Carrie. This was not the kind of turmoil an eight year old should be going through. I watched her to see if she seemed upset, sad, or too quiet. On the way back to Vermont we stopped at places we knew she liked, and let her have her favorite meal, cheeseburgers and fries; and of course, ice cream. She did seem quiet at first, but as we ate, she started opening up and chatted most of the way from then on. I made sure in the days ahead, to spend time talking to her, asking questions and doing things I knew she liked. I wanted to bring activities into our family life and bring back her sense of belonging. Lynn picked up on this and nodded to me that he could see what I was doing.

I opened the kitchen door and walked in; looking into the living room. It felt as if I'd been on a very long journey and came back as if a stranger. Could this house be a home again. It depended on the choices we would make along the way, there was no way of knowing right now. We'd have to take one step, and one day at a time.

The first thing Carrie looked for was the cat. When she found him, all was well for her, for the rest of the night. We unloaded the car. Lynn went to the barn and took care of the animals. Then we went upstairs to bed. I prayed a simple silent prayer "Thank you Lord. Please, help us mend this family together again."

Our lives went back into the routine of hard work on our jobs and work in, and around the house on weekends. I started going to the Friday night prayer meetings again. Carrie was put back into school and we took her with us everywhere we went, especially on weekends. There was always something to do and we visited his parents on these weekend jaunts to keep in touch with them and make sure they were doing ok. Though they were retired, they stayed very active with gardens in the summer. His Mother still canned many vegetables and picked berries and preserved them. His father kept busy with community activities and building projects. He had built several houses in his life and liked the process of doing it. He had several guys who he knew for a long time, that would help him. He was often in the middle of working on a house when we'd stop to see them.

However, Lynn also got involved with the house building projects with them at times and would spend a lot of hours helping build a house for his father, who didn't need one, while ours was still unfinished; when the time should have been spent getting our own done. I spoke about it sometimes, but quickly saw he was not going to heed me, so I just let it go. It wasn't worth it to say anything.

There were also times Lynn would get involved in business deals, or make a decision to purchase something and not tell me until he had to, or somebody else would tell me. This happened enough times that it caused problems and tension throughout our marriage, because it was a clear sign to me that he didn't consider me an equal partner in this relationship. As the years went on with us, we became married separates; both having our own accounts, car payments, insurance payments and doctors and medical needs cared for separately. These are the things that develop many times, when there's not equality; in order to salvage the marriage.

One day in the early summer, shortly after we reconciled, he decided to purchase a new pickup truck, without letting me know about it until after he did it. When he brought it home I warned him I didn't think we could afford the extra payments right now, that it would stretch us too much and we could get behind on the payments. He didn't seem concerned, so again, I let it go. He was making the payments. If he found he couldn't keep them up, he may have to lose it. I decided not to worry about it anymore and asked the Lord to help me trust Him in this.

It wasn't very long, and I found he had gotten behind and we were in trouble.

This is a true story, taken from my journal. It was a learning experience from the school of the Holy Ghost.

Meeting the Deadline

Our truck was repossessed because of being behind on payments several times, and was now again one month behind. I had been unaware of this, and had to ask the Lord to help me forgive Lynn for keeping this from me.

We went to the bank and talked to them to try to negotiate and reclaim the truck back. However, they refused and advised we try to get a loan at another bank. We knew the chances were slim for us to be able to get another loan anywhere because Lynn had been late in keeping up the payments because he had been laid off.

That night, I prayed alone and asked the Lord to help us save the truck, but it looked impossible. The men from the bank had come and taken the truck, and said we would have to come up with the entire amount of the loan to get it back. They also gave a deadline; tomorrow at 3:00 p.m.

During the night, as I was praying about this mess, the Lord spoke to my heart, "The president of the bank will try to convince you to take out a mortgage to release your truck. Do not do let them talk you into it." I said out loud in the dark, "What do we do?" An answer came "Trust ME, I will take care of this."

The next morning we were on the way to our bank and as we drove I spoke to Lynn about the implication that perhaps the bank would bring up taking a mortgage out on our house, and told him I would not agree to it if they did. Lynn, simply said "I don't think they will do that, but we'll see what they say." I didn't say anything more, but I've made up my mind; we own our house, and that isn't going to change.

We arrived and sat in the president's office, and she started talking about options. Then she said "One way to take care of this entire problem is to take out a mortgage on your home, and refinance the truck into it. This would consolidate both loans into one, and make it much easier to keep your payments up." Lynn looked at me and said nothing, but I knew what he was thinking, "How did you know she would do this?" was in his eyes. He got up from his chair, and I started for the door, "No, we will look for another solution to this". She smiled grimly and said "You have until 3:00 p.m.

The amount still owed on the truck was $5,800.00. We went to a bank in Lebanon, but they were very reluctant and said they would review our credit. Lynn went in to speak with the head of the bank. While he was in the office, I sat alone and prayed in the spirit, centering my soul on the Lord.

On hearing our story, he said he had no reason to grant our request but that he knew Lynn was telling the truth in admitting he was partly to blame. "If you had not told the truth, I would have known it, and your request would have been denied." he said.

After an hour of negotiations with the head office of the bank, we were granted a loan for the full amount. I was beginning to get anxious; I looked at the clock, it was a little after 1:00 p.m., we only had a few hours left.

Papers were signed, we were issued a check to the bank we owed the money to, and we headed up the interstate. We arrived at the bank at 2:55, five minutes before the deadline was up. There was an employee at the front door, locking the bank for the day. As we walked up the steps to him he said, "Come in, you just made it, I was closing five minutes early, because it was so slow this afternoon."

God rescued us; just in time.

The Holy Spirit has taught me much about His ways in this experience. I am still learning from it to this day. Some profound things I learned were:

1. God's omniscience, He is all-knowing. None of the events that took place were a surprise to Him. He already knew the future of what was in the mind of the president of the bank who tried to persuade us to take out a mortgage and gave specific instructions to me that helped us to gain the victory in this situation. Paul describes this as the gift of the word of knowledge, and the word of wisdom, as he taught it in Corinthians. God has directed me many times in other situations over the years.

2. Our honesty, or the lack of it, is vitally important in the outcome

of our trials. If Lynn had lied to the bank president about why he needed the loan, the results would not have been a success, but failure. We would have not gotten the loan.

3. God will answer a prayer in such a way that it gives total glory to Him; which it must.

Several other significant things happened during this summer. The leaders of the prayer group began planning a baptism for those who had started coming and received salvation. Many had expressed the desire to be baptized in water. We had a nice pond in front of our house that gradually went to twelve feet in depth. One night at the meeting I offered to have it at our house and perhaps a picnic outside, if the weather permitted. It was early July, and we could improvise if it rained and gather in the house. The leaders and the people all agreed. The date was set for July twelfth. The men talked about bringing a barbecue grill to cook outside. I spoke to Lynn about it when I got home. He seemed pleased and offered to help get the picnic area set up outside.

I prayed quite a bit before this took place. My desire of course, was that watching the believer's gathering in fellowship and getting to meet some of the men there would be opportunity for them to start a conversation and that the Lord could use the situation to be a witness to Lynn. Often I'd have thoughts of us serving the Lord together and what a powerful witness for God he could be, and the work we could do together as a team for the Lord. Listening to the other members, especially the men during the meetings, my heart would long to see my husband openly being a strong witness for God, among the men he knew and our families together. I had no way of knowing the road we'd be traveling in our future; and it was best I didn't.

The day of the baptism Lynn made sure the yard was neatly mowed and picnic tables set up at the front of the pond. There was a lot of people expected to be here. We estimated close to a hundred family members. Thirteen of us were scheduled to be baptized. We were prepared if anybody in the crowd decided they wanted to get saved and baptized at the same time. We had prayed about this as a group for quite a while and the presence of the Lord was there in a significant way, all day.

One lady, a friend of mine, had an unsaved husband also and we'd been praying for him for a long time. We could see the conviction going on inside him at times and the spiritual warfare. She told us of times he'd be drinking, come home angry and bring on an argument, trying to get her to deny her faith. We prayed harder. She told us he planned to be there this day, to watch her get baptized. When she arrived she was with one of her kids, but her husband changed his mind. We prayed a simple prayer for him again, that God would deal with his heart and get him to come, if it was the Lord's will.

He showed up an hour later, not looking very happy. He stayed away from the crowd of people, but watched his wife when she went in the water and the elders helped her go under and back up. There was a look of happiness for her on his face, in spite of himself.

I was among the ones being baptized, but waited till all the others were done first. When I walked down to the elders waiting, in the corner of my eye, I saw Lynn, leaning against one of our huge trees at the water's edge. He was smiling, not saying anything. The elders quoted the verses of baptism in the name of the Father, Son, and Holy Ghost, and gently put me backwards into the water. I went down and came up, signifying my sins washed away, and giving witness to my faith in the risen Jesus Christ.

The gathering afterward was full of happy conversation. Everyone wanted to help with the meal. Several had brought instruments, and gathered to play and sing afterwards. The afternoon went by quickly and soon we were aware the sun was setting. Some slowly began to leave. My friends husband had left much earlier. His countenance was sullen, she said she expected him to not be happy when she got home. We prayed together and came against the demonic attacks trying to keep him from the Lord. I could see she wasn't looking forward to going home. I prayed silently for her, for strength to deal with her situation in her home. We both knew what it was like and could see how the devil used everything he could to deceive and stumble the unsaved men. It was a cycle of drinking, sometimes drugs, beer buddies always trying to bring accusation and trouble. Kids who weren't saved and the difficulties of trying to keep a home together in the midst of all of this; and keep praying for their souls. Our prayer meetings and the times we shared and prayed together, was what helped us keep going, and kept us in our faith. We battled discouragement and weariness all the time, because the battles in these areas seemed to be never-ending. We also saw many powerful answers to prayer and watched some of these hard men go to their knees and get saved and delivered. When this happened, it was fuel to our souls to keep going, keep praying, keep believing. The Holy Spirit was moving in a mighty way at this time, in the late seventies, in the surrounding area.

For the next several weeks during the prayer meetings, we'd especially bring up this lady's husband in prayer for his salvation. By mid-August, one Friday night, he came with her. We were amazed and thrilled. The presence of God was all over him as soon as he walked in the door. His face was red and he had a hard time saying anything. He mumbled something about not knowing why he was here. We knew instantly to say as little as possible and just keep praying under our breath during the meeting. We greeted him warmly, but didn't swarm over him. He needed space and shown love and kindness, without smothering him. He sat and listened to the message, the sharing, and interactions of questions answered. When worship began, he sat silently, but we could see him becoming quite emotional and having a hard time hiding it. This was a very rugged man, his wife had told us she felt it would be a huge miracle for God to get through to him.

Toward the end of the meeting, the leaders began to play and sing again, but just quietly. The elder started sharing the gospel slowly, and in a way that brought the love of the Lord out in the open. He invited anyone who would like to give their life to the Lord, to just raise their hand, and the leaders would be glad to pray with them to receive salvation. The expectancy in the room was like electricity. We knew this man was burning up, we could see it.

He finally raised a hand "I want Jesus, I don't know what to say, but I know I need forgiveness".

Two of the men who were elders quietly moved toward him together, put their hands on his shoulders, and asked him to just repeat with them as they prayed. He began with them, and they led him to the Lord.

God's presence powerfully enveloped him; we could see and feel the change come over him, before our eyes. He began to weep. I looked at his wife, she was in tears. The people in the room continued to pray and the leaders continued playing and singing softly, as the Holy Spirit brought this rough man to salvation and into the kingdom of God. He went on to be water baptized a month later and became a strong witness for the Lord in his community and both of them served the Lord together from this point on, as the Lord opened doors for them.

As powerful and profound as these events were as they unfolded, the attacks from the devil increased too. I've learned to expect this, Jesus teaches us it will be this way. Every open door he can find, he will use to bring trouble, hardship, turmoil and destruction if he can.

Early in the year I had found several part time jobs in the area taking care of seniors in their homes. It was work I preferred rather than nursing homes. I could give these folks the care they needed, make nutritious meals for them, do things to help with repairs in their home, get to know them; and their preferences. It was a slower, more rewarding work. In many ways it was a ministry. The hours were set up in such a way that I didn't have to worry about a babysitter for Carrie and there was some flexibility if a situation came up, that I may need to be with her.

As fall began, once again a change developed in Lynn. I recognized the signs, because they were the same as before. He started staying gone Friday nights, this meant he was with his drinking buddies. The weekend drinking got worse and he spent more time at his parents, helping his father with his building projects. On a Friday night before I was to go to a prayer meeting he came home, and he'd been drinking. I was getting Carrie ready and set my Bible on the table as he sat in the living room, sullen and quiet. He watched me as I walked through, to get something upstairs.

I sensed he wanted to start an argument, it was written on his face. I prayed silently for the self-control not to let it happen.

"I don't get what you find is so great about going to that meeting with those fanatics."

I'd heard this before and was ready. I gave a quiet answer "I go there to honor the Lord and learn about the Bible. That's my main focus and the people who go feel the same way. We love the Lord, it's that simple."

"I'm getting tired of spending Friday nights alone, we could be doing things together, but instead, you're wasting time with people who could care less about you."

"I've invited you to come many times, but I'm not going to force you. As for me wasting time there, I'll just repeat what I said; I'm going there because I love God and want to know Him more. We've been over this before and you agreed to allow me to be a Christian;

this is part of being one."

"I'm beginning to change my mind again. We were happy before you started all this. Those people are a bad influence on our lives. I wish you could see that."

"That's funny Lynn, I feel the same way about your drinking buddies. I know this is where this is coming from. You've been talking and listening to what their putting in your ears again and you come home and take it out on me. Before I came back here with you, we talked about this for a long time. As far as I'm concerned, there's nothing more to say about it. I'm going and you'll have to accept this. It's only for a couple of hours."

"You can go, but I don't have to like it, or accept it. I'm feeling like I may have made a mistake and we should have stayed apart."

I looked him in the face "Lynn, I'm going, I'll be back in a while".

That night everybody could see from my face, that things were not well in my home. I didn't say very much, only briefly explained the situation. Everyone prayed with me, for the Lord to intervene and change Lynn's heart. I didn't stay as long as usual, as soon as the service was over, I went home. My heart was again heavy for Carrie. She was old enough to see and know when this tension was going on. I hated this ongoing turmoil, but would not cave in to threats from him. I knew where it was coming from. I had to stand in my faith. if I wavered now, he would never allow me to serve the Lord, or walk as a Christian. I wasn't going to let this happen for anyone, and he had to know it.

When I came through the door, he was still in the same chair. He'd been drinking more, and the TV was on, but he was looking out at the pond. I could sense tension and turmoil in the room. He had been brooding while we were gone. He looked at me and began "I've been doing some thinking while you were gone. I'm sorry to have to say this, but I have made a mistake. I should have let you stay in South Carolina. I'm going to put it to you again, and you can do what you want. You'll either have to give up on this Jesus and go back to being with me as we were when we first married, or you'll have to leave. It's either Jesus, or me".

I wasn't surprised at what I was hearing, but there wasn't any need as far as I was concerned, to spend any time thinking about this. I was ready to answer him right then, and did.

"You've picked the wrong person to give another ultimatum to. When you came to South Carolina, we spent several days talking. I asked you many times to search your heart and make very sure you were willing to let me be a Christian and live as one. You gave your agreement and your word, that this would not happen again. But, here we are again back to this point. My mind is made up. I love you, but I love Jesus more. I will never, and I mean *never* deny him for you, my own family, or anyone else in this world. I know the drinking buddies you hang out with have had a hand in this, but you don't have to listen to them, you know they are liars. Your family has also put the thought in your mind that I'm mentally ill, because they don't know the Lord themselves and never read the Bible either. Of course nothing they see me do would make sense to them. The scriptures tell us unbeliever's cannot understand us. They and you, are living in darkness, and sin, and cannot see how the devil is using them to destroy us. I want this marriage to work and I still love you, but my answer hasn't changed. So, what do you want me to do?"

His eyes were piercing with anger "Get out".

I gazed steadily at him, "You mean this and are ready to tear apart this family and send Carrie into turmoil again"?

For a brief moment there was a tinge of regret in his eyes, but then "I hate to do this to her and you; but you could change your mind you know. It seems to me, you're the one being stubborn".

"You don't understand now Lynn, but what you're demanding me to do, is to deny my faith in Christ. If I do that, I've lost my soul, in order to let you have your way. I'm not willing to spend eternity in hell for you, or anybody. It's not a matter of being stubborn, it's a matter of hanging on to my faith in God Almighty. So, I'll get our things together and we will go, but know this; this time, forget it, there will be no next time".

"Yeah, I know, you'll tell everybody it's my fault, like before".

"I never spoke to anyone about what we went through, you did the talking, just like you are now. There's nothing more to say. This must stop".

I went upstairs, Carrie was in her room. I held her for a few moments, then told her we would be going to New York. She'd need to put her things in her suitcase. She had heard our arguments. She sat huddled on her pillows, and just nodded her head. I didn't know what to do with the emotions going on in my heart. I forced them to shut down; the only thing of any importance now was Carrie and making sure I gave her support and love.

We gathered our suitcases and toys for the trip and put them in the car. I changed into jeans and a sweater, to drive in comfort.

Lynn didn't get up. He'd been drinking a lot while we were gone. I could see he wasn't in any shape to do much. But, he was already regretting his rash ultimatum.

"Can't you bring yourself to admit I may be right".

"No Lynn, because you're not right and if you were honest with yourself, you'd admit it. This is not a game Lynn, if you give ultimatums, you're playing with our lives. I'm not playing a game, my life is a walk of faith now with God. It could include you, if you'd let it. God loves you, but you refuse to let Him in, even an inch. Now, is it still either you, or Jesus? I need to hear it one last time, before I stay, or go".

"Yes, it's either Him, or me".

"Goodbye Lynn, I hope you have a good life".

This time the journey began in the dark. It was just as well. I had put a pillow in the back seat so Carrie could lay down and sleep, while I drove. It had been a long day and she was tired even though she was also very sad. She began to doze soon after we began. I put on some music and let it play softly to help her, and my own troubled soul. I didn't know what to say or how to pray about this. I could hardly believe this was happening again; I only knew to pray in the Spirit and let Him do the interceding.

It was past midnight when I pulled into Mother's driveway. Her lights were out. I knew she would probably be asleep. I hated to wake her. Leaving Carrie asleep in the back, I went quietly to the door and went in. Mom had heard me and was in the hallway when I came through the door.

"Are you alright? I'm glad you're here, but something must be wrong for you to come at this hour".

"I don't know how to say this, except to just blurt it out; Lynn told me again to either deny the Lord, or leave. I told him more than once that this time he better make sure this is what he wants; and he did. I don't know what to think or do anymore. But Mom, you know I can't deny my faith in the Lord".

"No, you can't. You go get Carrie, I'll get the room ready for you and we can talk more in the morning. I know this is a nightmare for you. I can't believe he's done this again. You can't keep going through this, it has to come to an end".

I got Carrie settled in bed and finally laid my head on Mother's pillow. My mind was swimming with the reality of what had happened to us. Once again being thrown into what seemed to be a never ending mess; our lives again torn apart.

For the first time since my deliverance from drinking, the thought came, that if I could have just one, it would give some relief from this pain in my heart and soul. But I immediately knew the source of this, and rebuked the familiar spirit of alcoholism and commanded it to leave and not come back. As I laid there, the presence of the Lord enveloped me and the mercy of needed sleep came.

The next morning we took our time over breakfast and talked about what the next step was. I had already decided going south again was not for me. Whatever happened now, it would be either back in Vermont, or here in Mother's area. She suggested taking a few days and just visiting with her and letting Carrie visit with some of her cousins and we could go see Mother's sister in the Adirondacks. It would give me a chance to calm down and think things through before making a serious decision. It made sense, so the next week was spent doing just that. It brought home to me; life does have storms, chaos and troubles, but after the storm there are seasons of calm. I've learned that when I'm in the middle of the storm, keep my eyes focused out in front of me, to the calm on the other side.

Toward the end of the week I told Mom I needed to do some thinking and would be gone for a while, and asked if Carrie could stay with her while I was gone. She said sure.

I took my Bible and drove to a place along the Hudson river, where we went sometimes during the summer, picnicking and swimming. There was a place that had flat sloping rocks that went down to the water. People would gather there at times to swim. It was the middle of the week and most people would be working now. I found the place empty, parked my car and took my Bible with me, to sit for a while quietly and talk to the Lord. My heart was heavy, my mind torn in many directions. I wasn't sure what the right thing to do was. My life to this point had been one set of problems after another. I knew much of it was my own doing before I was saved. But the last couple of years, with the Lord now in my life, and trying to do the right things. I hoped and prayed that our life would continue to improve, our home would be finished and we were still hoping for more children. Now it looked as if all of our dreams and hopes were never going to be a reality. I was tired inside, though I was in my twenties, I felt old and weary in my soul. I didn't know if I had the strength to keep going anymore. Discouragement was just about overwhelming me.

As I sat on one of the flat rocks under a pine branch for shade, I looked out on the water watching the waterfowl as they played over the surface, flying just over the top, then diving under with mighty splashes. After some time, in the peace of the atmosphere over me, I began asking the Lord some questions.

"Lord, you already know what's been going through my mind sitting here, but I need to ask You, is everything Lynn and I worked together for over the last couple of years been for nothing? Is the devil going to win and tear our lives apart, and Carries life be possibly harmed forever? What can I do differently to turn this around; or can it be? I've prayed for Lynn's salvation, since the day I got saved. But he just seems to get worse. Is this the end? I need you to show me and speak to me in some way. I know I'm not supposed to expect to hear Your voice all the time, but guide me in Your word and give me some clear direction on what to do, or I'm probably going to make a wrong decision. I need to know what You want."

In my heart I just heard a quiet instruction, "Go to Matthew Ch. 19:29". I picked up my Bible and found the verse, and read:

Mat 19:29 And every one that hath for-

saken houses, or brethren, or sisters, or
father, or mother, or wife, or children, or
lands, for my name's sake, shall receive a
hundredfold, and shall inherit everlasting
life.

"If you're telling me that all this will turn around and I'll receive a hundredfold, I have to admit, right now, I can't believe it. He's thrown us out twice, and I have almost nothing now. I have to watch every penny and as you've put it in your word, when You were here; I have "no place to lay my head", it seems."

There was no more guidance given, but the peace remained. I was sitting with my knees up, with my arms resting on them; looking like a frog, I just put my face in my hands and said "Lord, whatever you intend for my life-I surrender it to you. I don't know what else to do. Just help me get through each day, walking in your will, that will be enough."

I sat there a while longer watching the sun get low in the sky. Evening was coming, it was time to get back to Mom's house and help her with dinner. The verse in Matthew came to me when Jesus spoke in the Sermon on the Mount, "Don't worry about tomorrow; sufficient for the day, is the evil thereof". For me, this was the best advice to take; deal with today, that was enough.
I decided to let Carrie stay with Mother while I went back to Vermont and look for an apartment in the area I had lived in. It would make it possible to keep Carrie in the same school, find a job, and work toward getting a home of our own. I wanted to go to nursing school and improve my ability to get a better job. I shared this with Mom and she was glad to let Carrie stay with her and said she thought this was the best idea for us.

I went to the leaders of the prayer group, and shared with them what had happened and what I was planning to do. They gathered around and prayed with me. Several of my friends mentioned apartments I might be interested in in the area. One lady offered to take me to one and also offered to help me move, if I chose it. I was glad to hear of these opportunities, I didn't want to live in limbo. I wanted to get going in a firm direction and put the past behind me.

I got in her car, and she drove to the village she lived in, where the apartment was. It was an upstairs two bedroom apartment on the third floor. It was affordable, in the middle of town and within walking distance to most things. I decided to take it and paid the landlord the sum he asked for. Then we went to her place for lunch and planned how to go about my moving in. I called Mother from her place, and told her I'd found an apartment and would take the next few days to get all the rest of my belongings from our house in East Corinth, set it up, then come back to New York for Carrie. Mother was glad to hear the news and said to not worry, and take as long as needed before coming for her. It set my mind at ease knowing she was in good hands.

It took only two days. I was glad Carrie didn't have to be there to go through the stress of taking our belongings out of the house and the process of moving to another village. It was hard enough going through it alone. I just kept praying as I worked and asked the Lord to help me focus on what I had to do, and numb my emotions. It's the only way I could get it done. I made sure I went to get my things when Lynn was working, so we didn't have to meet. He didn't know what I was doing, and frankly, I didn't want him to. At this point he was the last person I wanted to see right now. He had thrown us out twice. For me this was the end.

When the apartment was ready, I went back for Carrie. I spent only that day with Mom. We had dinner together and talked a long time. I told her she was very welcome to come sometime and visit with us, when she had the time. She said she probably would when she knew I was really settled in, to let her know by giving her a call now and then. We agreed, hugged in the driveway, and Carrie and I headed back to Vermont.

I had talked to her, and in simple terms let her know what Lynn had decided and that we now were on our own with the Lord. There was sadness and it wasn't easy relaying the truth of what we were facing, but I wasn't the type to put false hopes, or create fantasies about our situation. She needed to know I was being truthful with her, in good times, and the bad.

We arrived at the apartment in mid-afternoon. It gave me time to get Carrie adjusted to her new room, show her the small back yard she could play in, and the surroundings in the village. The friend who helped me get the apartment was within walking distance and we saw each other almost every day. We would share meals together, prayed about many things and saw answers come in many situations. She and her daughter were a great source of support, friendship and love during this time. Several other people from the prayer group also lived in this village and we often would go to the meetings together. We also went to Christian events in the area during the time I lived there. God used these people to be an extended family, in a time when mine seemed to be falling apart. I've asked the Lord to bless them and grant them their rewards for their love and acts of kindness. Many of them are now in heaven. One day I look forward to meeting them again, on that better shore.

We lived in this village for a little over a year. In that time God used it to teach many more things about walking with God in the valley. Deciding to obey His word, even when I didn't understand why. And, more lessons were learned about hearing his voice. He used all of us in the prayer group just about every day in some fashion, to witness for him. More people were saved, healed, and Jesus was lifted up; even in the midst of the troubles we were facing in our own lives. This interaction between us, and the power of the Holy Spirit bonded us together with strong spiritual chords. When Jesus is first in a person, group, or church; He honors those who love him, and are not ashamed to call Him Lord.

NINE
DIVORCE AND BACK

Early in the spring of 1980 a couple who were elders in our group brought up to us that they were planning to go to Washington D.C. at the end of April, to a rally called Washington for Jesus. They gave a brief explanation of what it was going to be about, and if anybody in the group wanted to go, let them know. They'd help us reserve a place on the bus they were going down in, with other church groups in the area. They said there was a set fee for the three day event, and if we gave it to them they'd get our seats on the bus and the hotel room for us. Several in the group expressed an interest in going and started making plans. I wanted to go, but didn't see how I could. I had to watch every penny, and couldn't justify spending money on something like this.

But, one of the elders who was going looked at me, and said "We really think the Lord would want you to be there. If you say yes, we'll take care of getting you reserved on the bus, and the hotel. You can pay us when you can."

As they were talking, I sensed the Lord's presence in this, and knew it was what He wanted.

"Ok, but it bothers me to have you do this. As soon as I'm able, you will be repaid."

"Don't worry about it, we're glad you're coming. We know you'll be blessed; and we think there's reasons you should go."

As the years have gone by, I've watched and prayed over the

conditions of this nation, and realize the truth of what they said to me that day. It was to be a significant part of my service to God, throughout my life.

The emphasis of the rally was put in a pamphlet given to us by a local church. We received our reservations in the mail, along with our hotel reservations. The rally was to be held from April twenty-eighth, through the twenty-ninth. It gave a brief overview of the rally, how to get to it, the speakers who would be there, and the main thrust of the meetings in general.

The main theme of it was to be:

1. "The United States has gone off course spiritually and is consequently facing serious crises,"
2. Repentance and the need for divine intervention to bring the nation back to God.
3. The need for intercessors - people who know how to pray, and come before God for the nation, and bring restoration.
A four point message was to be brought consistently:
1) we are in bad straits;
2) we must seek God;
3) we should repent
4) then righteousness shall return.

Also mentioned, that would be major topics were, denouncing homosexuality in our nation, abortion, excessive government spending, and that "our government has aided our enemies and destroyed our friends, and our poor have become perpetual wards of the state."

The statement also asserted that the nation's elected officials "are servants of God, then servants of the people."
These points were a matter of prayer in our group during the meetings, until we made it to Washington.

Note: As I look back on this event, and the memories of what we prayed and marched for then; how much more the emphasis of what we were there for- apply to us today in this country. We are now drowning in government corruption. Sadly, my heart tells me we've gone too far, and will never turn back to God as a nation again. If I'm wrong, I'll be the first to admit it. But, I don't think I am wrong. Today, I'm praying for the Lord's return, and looking for it; as Paul did.

There were about ten from our prayer group going, and when the morning arrived to board the bus, we all drove in just a couple of cars, filling them as much as we could. We were full of excitement, and had brought plenty in our bags to snack on along the way. We knew the bus was scheduled to stop for a break so people could eat twice on the way down, but we all decided to stick to a tight budget and not get tempted to waste money on needless things. Before we knew it, the bus was very full. We squeezed together to give room to passengers still coming on. In those days, there were no seat belt rules, you just used common sense, and moved over to make room for someone else if you could. We should go back to those days.

Two elders from our group got into a conversation with the driver, and this kept up the whole way down. Mingled in, there were many giving testimonies, singing, and praying every time we came into another village; for the people to open their hearts and let Jesus in their town. We were having revival meeting, on the bus.
When we arrived in Washington, it was getting toward night. We found our hotel and our rooms, and separated; planning to meet in the morning over breakfast and coffee.

The bus picked us up again, and took us to the drop off destination for the rally. Ours was at a subway, which was supposed to connect us to Fourteenth street, and we were told on the map to follow it to Constitution and Independence avenues, where the rally was to be held.

When we arrived at the subway, it was already crowded, and we were underground. The driver told us we'd see a set of stairs, and take them up, to where it connected onto Fourteenth street. As we gathered our group together, we started following our elders, and found the stairs. When we got to the street above, we stood there, not quite sure which direction to take, and looking for sign that would guide us.

Suddenly, behind us a deep man's voice spoke to us, and we turned to see a very tall, heavy built man carrying a briefcase, in a suit and overcoat "You folks look like you may need some help, are you looking for the gathering for Washington for Jesus?"
The elder did the replying "Yes, would you know which direction we should take?"

"Yes, surely, you are on Fourteenth street, the place you should be. Now, follow it all the way to the end. It will take you right to where the gathering is getting started. As you go, do you see these buildings along the way? We nodded yes.

"This street is a devils playground of prostitution, and pornography is made here, and every kind of wickedness goes on every day, all day. As you are walking down through, please take the time to pray as you go, for God to intervene in this wickedness, and bring some out of bondage's of sin and perversion. It would give the Lord great pleasure, and he'd surely heed the prayer."

We listened totally engaged in what he was saying. His voice was very serious, and grave. Then, without warning, he turned, and before our eyes - he vanished. He didn't just turn around and leave, he was instantly gone. We gasped, we couldn't believe what our eyes had seen. The elder, after a few minutes, when he could talk, said "My word, that had to have been an angel". All of us nodded in agreement. There was no other explanation that made any sense. We did as we were asked, and found the center of activity between the two avenues, and the area we were assigned for our group. It was just beginning, and all day, approximately thirteen hours; people continued to pour into the area, until it was full to overflowing. There were many speakers, giving messages at different locations. We were free to go to the ones we felt led of the Lord to attend. There was also much prayer going up from gatherings all over the area.

At midday, a huge line gathered of people from every state to represent where they came from. It went far into the distance; and we marched and prayed as we went. We saw policemen, ambulance drivers, and people of every walk of life, lift their hands to Jesus Christ, and many gave their lives to Him that day. The atmosphere was drenched in the presence of God, and everybody there knew it. The call to repentance was the main focal point throughout the rally, and each speaker brought out the verse that was chosen to represent our call as a body:

> 2Ch 7:14 If my people, which are called by my name, shall humble themselves, and pray, and seek my face, and turn from their wicked ways; then will I hear from heaven, and will forgive their sin, and will heal their land.

God's call to restoration for a people, and a nation is simple. But today, many years after this powerful meeting to restore this country, it seems people would rather have chaos, rebellion and the wicked rule over them. The continuing deterioration of this society, is evidence of this.

Later, when we listened to the news reports, more than one of them commented on the fact that the area was left cleaner than when the people in the rally gathered. The people hired to do cleanup said there was really nothing to do, except take care of the porta potty's, and they just made sure the area was mowed, and everything was tidy. When I'm driving along highways today, the sides of the roads are littered with trash of every kind; cans, bottles, and various kinds of garbage, another sign of a gluttonous, rebellious society. An ungrateful, unthankful people run this land now, and it shows.

If anyone looks this event up now on the internet, the articles will give a number of about two hundred thousand in attendance, but those of us who were there know the truth. The media lied then, like they do now; and the numbers are what we call "fake news". When we first got home afterwards, the news gave accurate numbers of over a million, close to a million and a half. But soon we couldn't find the accurate news articles anymore, they disappeared, and the propagandists took over. But the most important thing to us, was we got to see a monumental move of God, at a time when the atheists were trying to take over everything, and we saw things our eyes were meant to see, and take back home, to tell others.

On the way home, we got the same bus driver. The elders sat right behind him again, talking the whole way back. The driver was asking questions, and we could tell, God was getting through to him. By the time we got to the New York City line, he was ready to accept Jesus as his Savior. When he pulled over at a diner for a break, to let people off to get a bite to eat, the elders stayed on the bus, and led him to the Lord. As we started on the rest of the trip home, the driver was singing and praising God, along with the rest of us.

These kinds of events were moves of God that brought fuel to our faith, and every soul saved gave increased purpose to our service for the Lord. No one talked about money, that was only an afterthought. If God showed us he wanted us to go somewhere, or do something specific, we prayed and believed Him for the needed funds. We always got it, plus extra. It was during these days of powerful moves of God, we learned how He worked, how to follow His lead, and what was important to Him. It was always the same-souls.

We learned to move with God, expect miracles, and look for His hands in our work, without a dollar sign in front of it.

Learning the ways of God during this time, has brought a discernment for truth and error, that I couldn't have learned any other way. Now, when I've watched major ministries become like businesses, with money at the forefront, and what they have to do to stay afloat, I know much of what they are doing is of the flesh. But they cannot see it; and if anybody tried to tell them, they'd be rejected.

I have nothing against those who do have larger ministries, I know some of them do love the Lord, and are working for Him. I do not envy them, and there's no jealousy about what they achieve.

But, I'd rather remain as Paul, a prisoner for Christ, and keep the center of my ministry on souls, and what's on God's mind, than on the next meeting and how much money it will bring in. The next book, or a famous celebrity to have to pay, to entertain the people in the pews. My feeling is, if they are getting anybody saved, delivered, and healed, God bless them. But, I've been taught a different approach to working in His kingdom, and prefer it.

After getting back from the rally, I took note of Carrie. She needed some attention. We went to a picnic area, took a lunch, our fishing poles, and had some quality time together, just for the fun of it. I asked her about school, how things were going for her, and if she was doing something she liked in classes. She seemed to not really want to talk about it, becoming quiet, just sitting chewing on her sandwich.

"Is something going on I need to know about?."

"Sometimes it's hard on the bus. Some kids are always looking for trouble."

I could see the problem.

"You're getting bullied, aren't you."

"Yeah. But, I'm not the only one. A couple of other's are too."

"It's hard to put up with, I went through it too. There's no easy answers to it. Do I need to go to the school and talk to somebody to get it to stop?"

"No, if you do, it will just get worse. I've seen it with other kids parents who tried it. It don't make it any better."

"Yes, I know what you're saying. But if it gets too out of hand, I can, and will. I just want you to know that."

"Thanks Mom. I may talk about it again, but it's better off this way."

"Ok, I wish there was something else I could do. But at least you know I'm here for you, don't keep it bottled up. If you're having a bad time, talk to me about it, and get it out; I want to know about it."

"Ok, well, I'm done Mom. How about we go fishing now, and see what we can catch."

We took our poles and went to the water's edge. I helped cast hers out as far as I could get it to go for her, then cast mine out, and we sat on the ground; watching the water ripples.

I wasn't surprised at what she had told me, I had suspected it. My heart was heavy for her. Why was there such cruelty, such selfishness in this world. No matter how old I got, it made no sense to me.

Yes, now I knew the truth that Satan was the god of this world, and ran it with his demon hordes. Knowing this didn't make dealing with the cruelties of life any easier. I wanted to protect her, as my parents wanted to protect me, when I was a kid dealing with the same thing. I just lifted a silent prayer, that God would help me be there for her, and give the love and support she needed; and that she'd know it. I had known my parents love and strength through the tough times growing up. I wanted the same for her.

Early summer came on, and a change took place, that again proved to be a learning experience for me. Watching the interactions of other Christian leaders, they're reactions, and behavior towards each other, while trying to serve in their capacities as pastors, and teachers. It was a sad observation, but one God put in front of me, to teach me several lessons.

A middle aged pastor and his wife from another town, began a midweek Bible study and prayer time at a woman's house, that we had recently met. They invited us to attend, and be a part of the group. I decided to go, and bring Carrie so she could be a part of it too. It was just a short ten minute walk from our apartment.

This man was a serious believer, very devoted to serving the Lord, and had a church of his own where he lived. He and his wife decided to do this after they had prayed about it. They believed the Lord spoke to their hearts that this area needed a Bible study. He was an excellent teacher, and I made a point to be there every week, after hearing his first teaching. He stayed strictly with the scriptures, and taught them with wisdom, and accuracy. I was looking forward to gaining much in my walk with the Lord, from sitting under this man's anointing.

Soon, however, several members of the prayer group I had been going to for a long time, heard of this. They knew of him and his wife; and began a campaign of gossip and slander against them. I had never seen these people do this to anyone else before, and it took me by surprise. I couldn't understand what they had against this man. I asked if they knew of any direct sin, or anything he had done specifically to warrant this attack on him. I also asked if he didn't have proper credentials, or was part of a cult. No, they said, there was no problems of that kind. They were not happy that he had decided to start a meeting in what they considered "they're" area, without coming to them, and sitting under their group first. "Oh, now I get it" I thought. These people felt this pastor should have asked for their "permission" to go ahead and start this meeting. Instead, he just obeyed the Lord's voice, and calling, without consulting them.

For the first time, I was beginning to see the infiltration of deadly religion, and inflated egos, creeping into this fellowship, that had started out with such love, and freedom in Christ.

I couldn't keep quiet, I felt so upset in my heart. I decided to put my two cents in "Am I detecting a hint of jealousy here, or am I wrong; I hope I'm wrong."

"We're not jealous, but there are verses that talk about not getting into another ministries territory, we just think they should have come to us first and talked and prayed about it first with us."

"I don't agree. There's certainly plenty of souls in this area, that no one needs to be worried about stepping over anybody's boundary lines. If he's right, and the Lord directed him here; and I feel He did, then we should be willing to give him the freedom to do what God's given him to do, and leave him alone."

They looked at me, and could see I was not going to go along with them "If you continue to go there, we think it could cause problems among us."

"Well, I'm sorry you feel this way, but I am going to keep going. All I've seen from this pastor is love, and a solid foundation of faith in Christ and knowledge of the word of God. I want this in my life right now, and intend to continue."

From this point on, an increasing separation and tension developed among us. Eventually this, and several other things that crept in, destroyed the fellowship entirely.

As the years went by for this pastor, the attacks against him only increased. This was a kind, serious man of God, who's only desire was to serve the Lord, and teach the word of God to those who were hungry to know it. I was one of those who wanted it. He was met with adversity everywhere he turned, and I watched with sadness, as some of those I had looked up to, were a part of tearing this man to pieces with their mouths. Finally, hoodlums in the town he had his church, burnt it to the ground. This broke his heart, and his spirit. It finished him as a minister.

I've watched this same scenario take place with other serious servants of God. The onslaught of attacks from the gossips within the churches, and persecution from unbeliever's, converge on them all at once; and wear them down, and break them, until they give up. My heart goes out to them, and pray for them. Satan knows his job very well, and those whom he can get to do his bidding. Sadly, many of his best workers are churchgoers, and "upstanding members of the community".

During this time, I continued to look for work. A friend brought a small pamphlet to me one day, it was about a writer's guild, from Atlanta Georgia. It spoke of an offer of a correspondence course, for those interested in a career in writing. It gave information and the address to look into it further. I decided to see what it was about, and called for more information. When it arrived in the mail, I read it over. I liked what it offered, and as I prayed, my heart felt a peace, that this could be a good opportunity for me to change directions.

I worked on the courses throughout the rest of the time I lived in this village, about a year. When I completed them, I received their graduating certificate. It proved to be the right decision, a job that came my way, ten years later in writing, editing, and proofreading. Also at this time, I received divorce papers in the mail from Lynn's lawyer. It gave the proposed reasons for the divorce, and the date it would become final, if it was not contested. I wasn't going to contest it. If he wanted a divorce, I'd just let the time go by, and let it become finalized; and it was.

But, toward the end of the year, still no employment opened for me. I felt it was time for me to face having to leave, and move again. I decided to take a few days and visit Mother, and think it through before making another change.

Mom was glad to see us, and we spent most of the time catching up on what was going on with both of us. Carrie was glad to have time to see her cousins, and play with them. When Mom asked about whether I'd found a job, I was honest, and said no. And that I was thinking of moving again. I didn't want to, but couldn't stay idle, and let more time be wasted.

"You've been there long enough, if there was anything for you, you'd know it by now. Would you consider coming back here again, and see if you can find work? There's good job opportunities where I am now, and if you took their test, and applied for work there, you'd have a good chance of getting a well-paying job, with benefits."

My Mother worked part time at a local residence for the mentally deficient and disabled. It was a government run agency, and the employees were well trained. The salary and benefits were very good. I could see her point, and thought "At this point there was nothing to lose, maybe this was the route I should take". I said I'd think about it, and we went out for the day, to just have some fun. Along the way, we stopped for lunch, and Carrie was in her element, cheeseburgers and fries, and ice cream.

That night, I laid in bed looking at the ceiling, thinking about what Mom had said. It made sense to come back, and go through the process of getting work where she was. The place was only a little over a mile away, and close to everything. I lifted a prayer, and asked the Lord to help me make the right decision, and left it at His feet. Whatever happened, my life was in His hands.

When I got back to my apartment, events took place that helped me make the decision to move back to New York. The details aren't important, but God used several things that made it very clear. Yes, He wanted me to make this change. Winter was coming on now, and going through the process of packing, and making this move, was going to have to be done taking the weather into consideration. I called my family in New York, and let them know my intentions. My older sister said to let them know when I was done packing, and they would come over with their van, and bring my belongings back too.

At the end of December I called, and they came, helped pack everything into their van, and my car; and we headed back to New York.

It was January, snow covered the ground. But the day we moved, the weather stayed sunny, and relatively warm for our region. When we arrived at their place, most of what I brought was stored in their basement, until I found a place of my own.

About a week later, one evening my niece asked if I'd like to go with her to town, and so some shopping. I did need a few things, so said "Sure". We got in her mother's car and started the familiar route to a nearby mall, just a couple of miles away. It was dark outside, and we drove onto a two lane road that had intersections coming onto it from both sides. I briefly noticed a cars headlights ahead of us, coming very fast, from the right, onto our road, but thought surely they would slow down and stop before getting to the intersection. My niece was talking to me, continuing on. She also assumed it would stop before getting to us. But it didn't. Just as we reached the intersection, the other car hit us head on; the last thing I remember, was hearing my niece yelling "No!".

The car hit us going over forty five miles an hour, in a twenty mile zone. It hit the passenger side where I was sitting, just in front of the door, sending us both off the road to the left, out into an open area about fifteen feet off the road. Our car was totaled. My knees had gone up under the dashboard, making the glove compartment open. My head went forward, hitting the rear view mirror, knocking me unconscious.

My niece says it was several minutes before I woke up, and answered her "Are you Ok?"

When I awoke, I mumbled yes. But I felt the pain in my knees, as I laid slumped in a heap in the seat. I felt something running down the left side of my face, and reached up to wipe it off. In the dark, I couldn't see that it was blood.

In a daze, I sat there not knowing what to do, and started hearing voices outside. People from neighboring houses had heard and seen what happened, and some of them came to help.

Then a man came up to my side of the car, and started asking if I was ok. I looked at him but didn't say anything. Again he asked "Are you ok? I'm so sorry, I'm the one who did this, it's my fault." It was the man who hit us.

Someone had called the police, and an officer offered to take us back to my sister's house. We got out of the wreck, and the officer helped into his cruiser. It only took a few minutes, and we were there, and he helped us get back into the house.

The man who said he'd hit us also came with us, and again, admitted he had done it. He explained to my sister and brother in law what had happened, and where the car was. My brother in law went with the officer back to the car, to get it towed to a garage.

Once in the house, my sister came around the corner and said "Oh my word, you're bleeding. Sit down, and I'll call the hospital, and take you there to get some help." The man who hit us again admitted to her that he was the one who did it, and was so sorry. The blood that I had unknowingly wiped away from my face, was now covering my jacket, my hands, and the entire left side of my face. No one knew how bad the damage was, and didn't want to take a chance of making anything worse. The man who hit us came close and said, "I'm an eye doctor, and it looks like you've got some damage close to the eye, and the bridge of your nose is bleeding. You definitely need medical care, to see what may need to be done to repair the damage."

As he was talking, he was close enough to me, that I could smell alcohol on his breath. He was drunk.

My sister drove me to the hospital alone. I sat quietly, feeling badly that this had happened to them, feeling responsible somehow. "I'm sorry Sis, you didn't need this to happen."

"Don't worry about that now, it's not your fault. We need to get your face taken care of, everything will be fine."

She stayed with me a while, until they admitted me, and took me to a room; then she went home till morning.

I was given a sedative, and other medications, and fell asleep, not waking until late the next morning. A doctor came in and spoke of my left temple area needing stitches, and the bridge of my nose being badly bruised. He said to expect both of my eyes to be blackened, and that I was very fortunate that it wasn't much worse. He gave a prescription for pain, and said I'd need to see him again, to watch the temple area to see if it would heal properly, and to see if I had a concussion in the next day or so. He released me to go home, telling me to call immediately if headaches persisted. He also said it was, to him, a miracle my knees weren't broken. Because the impact of them going up under the dashboard, destroyed the glove compartment. They were severely bruised, and black and blue, taking several weeks to heal. But, when I saw what the car looked like when I was taken to see it; I only had praise and thanksgiving to God that I was still alive. It looked like it had been hit by a tractor trailer. The entire front, from my door forward, was torn to pieces.

Once again, the devil had schemed to kill me, and if he could, my niece as well. Once again. God's hand intervened. I am convinced that those who belong to God, will not leave the earth, until it's His time for us to go. I won't say we won't go through many trials and troubles; I've had my share. But, I believe there's no devil in hell, that can kill us, until our intended days are up. God is in control of our lives, and we can trust Him.

The older I grow, I've come to have this attitude; if I die, and this body is destroyed, I win. The verses below give good counsel, wisdom, and guidance. I go to them often, when adversity comes, it sets everything in right order, and it makes facing daily obstacles easier to bear.

Psa 90:12 So teach us to number our days, that we may apply our hearts unto wisdom.

Psa 39:4 LORD, make me to know mine end, and the measure of my days, what it is; that I may know how frail I am.

Job 14:13 O that thou wouldest hide me in the grave, that thou wouldest keep me secret, until thy wrath be past, that thou wouldest appoint me a set time, and remember me!

The verses above teach us we have a number of days, set times. If we are surrendered to God, He keeps watch over those days, to perform them. In the verse of Jeremiah below it tells us God's thoughts toward us are of peace, not evil, and to give us an expected end.

> Jer 29:11 For I know the thoughts that I think toward you, saith the LORD, thoughts of peace, and not of evil, to give you an expected end.

When our time comes to die, Paul describes for us, the state we will enter eternity-incorruptible, immortal, we've entered heavens gates; in victory.

> 1Co 15:53 For this corruptible must put on incorruption, and this mortal must put on immortality.
>
> 1Co 15:54 So when this corruptible shall have put on incorruption, and this mortal shall have put on immortality, then shall be brought to pass the saying that is written, Death is swallowed up in victory.
>
> 1Co 15:55 O death, where is thy sting? O grave, where is thy victory?
>
> 1Co 15:56 The sting of death is sin; and the strength of sin is the law.
>
> 1Co 15:57 But thanks be to God, which giveth us the victory through our Lord

Jesus Christ.

A commentary by F.B. Meyer adds some excellent insight into victory over death.

VICTORY OVER SIN AND DEATH

Corinthians 15:53-58

Life on the other side will be as real and as earnest as here. We shall not dissolve into thin mist or flit as bodiless ghosts. We shall each be provided with a body like that which our Lord had after, He arose from the dead. It will be a spiritual body, able to go and come at a wish or a thought; a body that will be perfectly adapted to its spiritual world environment. The last Adam, our Lord, will effect this for us. But we must in the meanwhile be content to make the best use of the discipline of mortality, keeping our body pure and sweet as the temple and vehicle of the Holy Spirit until we are born into the next stage of existence. Always the physical before the psychical and the psychical before the spiritual.

What triumph rings through those last four verses! As generations of Christians have stood around the mortal remains of their beloved, they have uttered these words of immortal hope. The trumpet's notes will call those who have died and the saints that are still alive on the earth, into one mighty host of transfigured and redeemed humanity. Oh, happy day! Then we shall be manifested, rewarded, and glorified with Christ. All mysteries solved, all questions answered! Till then let us abound always in the work of the Lord."

Now, do some people die before their time? Yes, these verses give some clarity:

> Ecc 7:13 Consider the work of God: for who can make that straight, which he hath made crooked?

> Ecc 7:14 In the day of prosperity be joyful, but in the day of adversity consider: God also hath set the one over against the other, to the end that man should find nothing after him.

> Ecc 7:15 All things have I seen in the days of my vanity: there is a just man that perisheth in his righteousness, and there is a wicked man that prolongeth his life in his wickedness.

> Ecc 7:16 Be not righteous over much; neither make thyself over wise: why shouldest thou destroy thyself?

> Ecc 7:17 Be not over much wicked, neither be thou foolish: why shouldest thou die before thy time?

This infers that we can hasten, and even cause our own premature death, by our disobedience and wrong decisions. Those who are called by God can be rescued by His interventions, if He chooses, to accomplish His will in that person, even if they've rebelled. The story of Samson is a good example; and a lot can be learned by studying his life. We must remember God is sovereign, and can choose to save someone or allow them to be taken from this world, by His own discretion. He is God, we are not.

After a couple of weeks, my wounds were healing. In the meantime, I'd been continuing to search for a place of our own. I learned of a small mobile home in the same park as my Mother, that was available. It was just a short walk from her, cross lots on another lane. It was something I could afford, so I took it. I could see the benefits of being there for Carrie, she would be able to see her grandmother every day.

It was only ten feet wide by thirty feet, with one bedroom, and a small space in the middle of it, that was used as a second bedroom. In this tiny space there was a small washer/dryer unit, which I was very happy about. No need to have to go to a laundromat. The kitchen and living area in the front was combined, and so small, there was only room for a two seat kitchen table, a love seat sofa bed, and one chair. I had to put a TV on a shelf over the refrigerator, there was no room for it anywhere else. But, I cleaned it up, put pretty curtains on the windows, and we called it home.

It was early spring, and one day I went with Mother to the place she worked and started the process of trying to get employment there. Many people in the area worked there, because of the good benefits, and it was an excellent work environment. It was not uncommon to have to wait over a year to get hired, there was a long waiting list, and there were many levels of care for the residents, and those who wanted to improve their positions, were expected to go through much training, counseling, and pass tests to qualify. I was ready to go through whatever was needed. This was an opportunity I didn't want to pass up. So, this morning was the first of many applications, and conversations I had over the next several months, to secure a place sometime in the future.

In the meantime, with the free time I had at home, and was alone, I'd spend as much time as possible in the scriptures again, studying various subjects. God began to direct me deeper into the realm of intercession and prayer. He was also prompting me to learn more about the power of fasting and prayer together, and how to go about it. Books were put into my hands about people who centered their lives on prayer and intercession; Rees Howells, Madam Guyan, Watchman Nee, Joy Dawson, and other's.

I would spend many hours in the afternoons, and evenings after Carrie was in bed, studying, and talking to the Lord, and asking questions. The Holy Spirit would direct me to verses in the Bible, that answered those questions.

These times were invaluable. I learned the importance of seeking God's face, asking for His answers, and every time, He'd direct me to verses that gave them. It increased my foundation of faith in knowing Him, for who He is. The more you do this, the less you will fit in with people. As years have gone by, doing this has changed me to the point of finding myself in direct opposition with many people, Christians and unbeliever's alike. Why? Because I don't question God's reality, or His deity. I know Him, not as much as I desire to; but I know He is real, and no one could ever change that in me now. For me, it was too late, I wanted to know God, and His ways; not someone's opinion of Him. Through these many hours of seeking, and through every answered prayer, I've found Him.

One night, going toward 3:00 a.m., my eyes opened from a sound sleep.

Looking at the ceiling, I laid still, wondering if a burglar was trying to get in. Everything was quiet, then I sensed the presence of the Lord. A few minutes went by, and I decided to ask "Lord, what's on your mind?"

"You've been led for several years to learn the deeper walk of faith in prayer, intercession and fasting, it's time to begin to put the knowledge to use."

"In what area Lord?"

"Your marriage."

"What!?" I'm divorced. It's over, Lynn has made it clear he will not have me if I'm a Christian. I can't see any way to change this."

"No, in the natural, there isn't any way. But, your marriage to him was My doing, and what God has joined together, let no man put asunder."

"I'm sorry Lord, but I just don't have the faith to believe this can change; and I'm not sure I even want it to anymore."

"Will you take one step in obedience to prove Me in this?"

"What would that be?"

"Take three days, and do a Daniel fast, of no pleasant bread, and nothing solid until after 3:00 p.m., only one small meal a day with your daughter. During that three days, along with the fast, intercede that Lynn's heart would begin to change, and that my conviction would move him to begin to want to restore the relationship with you. Say nothing to anyone, just go about your usual routine of life. This must be between you and I. Trust Me, make the decision to obey in this, and stand and see what happens."

I laid there looking at the ceiling, now in silence. He was waiting for my answer. My heart was torn to pieces, I thought this was all over. But, my mouth opened, and I said "Ok Lord, I'll set a time soon and do what You've asked. But it's hard for me to believe I'm going through this again."
No response, just a saturation of peace in the room. This was

another one of those situations, I had the free choice to obey; or not. I'd learned it was best to obey.

During the three days of fasting, the Holy Spirit led me to study the twenty one day fast in Daniel, the fast of no pleasant bread. I encourage anyone who desires to know deeper spiritual warfare in combination with fasting, to study Daniel chapter ten. I'll only add a short version of this teaching, but much more could be added. I'll let the reader go further in studying this at their own discretion.

Dan 10:2 In those days I Daniel was mourning three full weeks.

Dan 10:3 I ate no pleasant bread, neither came flesh nor wine in my mouth, neither did I anoint myself at all, till three whole weeks were fulfilled.

Dan 10:11 And he said unto me, O Daniel, a man greatly beloved, understand the words that I speak unto thee, and stand upright: for unto thee am I now sent. And when he had spoken this word unto me, I stood trembling.

Dan 10:12 Then said he unto me, Fear not, Daniel: for from the first day that thou didst set thine heart to understand, and to chasten thyself before thy God, thy words were heard, and I am come for thy words.

Dan 10:13 But the prince of the kingdom of Persia withstood me one and twenty days: but, lo, Michael, one of the chief princes, came to help me; and I remained there with the kings of Persia.

Dan 10:14 Now I am come to make thee
understand what shall befall thy people
in the latter days: for yet the vision is for
many days.

Dan 10:15 And when he had spoken such
words unto me, I set my face toward the
ground, and I became dumb.

I felt my emotions going through great turmoil in the midst of this
fast, the Lord let me know this was part of the warfare. I learned to
ask the Holy Spirit at these times, to give me the strength and peace
to not give in to emotions, to use self-control, and if necessary,
come against demonic powers and rebuke them, commanding
them to leave.

During a time of prayer one afternoon alone, I felt I had to ask the
Lord something that bothered me about this whole thing. So, I just
opened up, and began "Lord, in your word it tells us if a husband
or wife leaves, we are to just let them go. Lynn has told me to leave
twice, because of my love for You. Yet, You're telling me to believe
for a reconciliation with him again. Why?"
The still, small voice in my spirit said "I suffered, died, and rose
again for him, as well as for you. Tell me, is the value of one soul-
his soul, worth what you may have to endure for his salvation?"
For several minutes, I couldn't say anything; I had not looked at
this in those terms before. I needed to ask this question.

"I've gone to several pastor's, told them my situation, they've
advised me to begin a different life, and not return to him, even if
he came back to me and asked to start over. They said it would not
be a good idea. What do you say?"

"Go to First Corinthians chapter seven, and read it". I did, and I
was prompted to especially study the verses below:

1Co 7:8 I say therefore to the unmarried and widows, It is good for them if they abide even as I.

1Co 7:11 But and if she depart, let her remain unmarried, or be reconciled to her husband: and let not the husband put away his wife.

1Co 7:13 And the woman which hath an husband that believeth not, and if he be pleased to dwell with her, let her not leave him.

1Co 7:14 For the unbelieving husband is sanctified by the wife, and the unbelieving wife is sanctified by the husband: else were your children unclean; but now are they holy.

1Co 7:16 For what knowest thou, O wife, whether thou shalt save thy husband? or how knowest thou, O man, whether thou shalt save thy wife?

As I sat there on the couch, looking out the window, I knew what God was showing me; to believe Him for the restoration of this marriage. But, I asked aloud one more time "Lord what about what I was told by the pastor's?"

"People change, people change My word, but, My word, does not change."

I closed my Bible, and made my mind up; if we didn't reconcile, I'd remain single the rest of my life. I never wanted to marry another man again. I'd finish this fast, and watch to see what happened; if

God would bring him to my door. If he didn't, I'd live the rest of my days, as Paul described; and remain single.

One night while still in the fast, I had a dream. A small group of people were gathered in a wedding ceremony. I stood in the dream at the back, watching it, and noticed the woman was wearing a green dress; and I thought "The color isn't really that attractive", the man doing the ceremony was elderly, with white hair. Then I was behind him, looking at the two getting married, it was Lynn and I. I awoke, when the ceremony ended and the pastor said "And now I pronounce you man and wife." I told this dream to my brother, and a couple of other people in my family, and then kept it to myself.

About a month went by, and one evening, a knock came at my door. Opening it; Lynn stood, and asked if I'd be willing to let him in and talk.

I wasn't going to make it easy for him.

"No, I don't want to let you in, and can't see there's anything more to talk about."

"I don't blame you for feeling this way, but I'd like to talk. Can we go somewhere else then, wherever you want to go."
"Ok, take me to the place we've gone before, on the river. I'll send Carrie to her grandmother's, then go with you."

I called Carrie from her room. When she saw Lynn she ran to him, and jumped up into his arms. My heart was wrenched. She said she was so glad to see him, and wanted him to come in. I had to intervene.

"He and I are going to go for a while, there's something we need to do. You get some toys, and go across to your grandmother's, and we'll be back in a couple of hours. Then you can talk more with him."

She came back out with toys in hand, and we waited and watched as she walked the short distance to her grandmother's door; as she went in, she waved to us.

We got in his truck, and he drove slowly to the place we'd been several times before, the same place I'd sat alone, and prayed for us, when he told me to leave the first time. We went to the flat rock, and both sat down together, looking out over the water. Neither one of us said anything for several minutes. I wasn't going to say anything. This was going to be up to him.

Finally, still looking at the water, he began "I've done just about everything to ruin this marriage, and you've no reason to listen to me. But, again, I've finally come to realize I love you, and always will."

"Nobody in this world would believe it, if they watched you, and knew what's been done."
"Yes, you're right."

"What do you want to do?"

"I want you and Carrie to come back home."
"You mean get remarried?"

"Not yet, but I'd like us to get back together, and work on fixing our lives again."

"I'm not willing to move back in with you, without being married. I'm not interested in just living with you. It would make it even easier for you to just kick me out again, and I'd have no legal recourse if we separated again."

"My thought is, it would be easier for you too, to just leave, if you found we couldn't make this work."

"No way. If I ever came back with you, it would only be after being married again, and this time you'd better know, it would be for keeps, until one of us is dead. I'm not going through this again for anybody, not even you."

"Sounds like we're at a stalemate. You won't change your mind?"
"You should know by now, the answer is no."

Nothing more needed to be said. I got up and went back to the truck. If God wanted this marriage to be restored; a lot of work in his heart would have to happen first.

He stayed long enough to spend some time with Carrie, and we went for a meal together at a local diner. Then he went back to Vermont. He asked if he could come again. I said yes, but wasn't willing to change my mind, so he'd better realize it if he did.

Over the remainder of the year he came about once a month. The Lord prompted me to fast and pray several more times. The problem with his attitude about just living together was a major obstacle, along with his drinking.

Late in the fall, he came again to visit. I could see he'd been talking with people he knew again. He was argumentative, and angry. I went with him in his truck to a local store, and as we were driving back to my place, he said I was being stubborn for not being willing to just come back, and start over with no strings attached.

I'd had enough of this "Lynn, that's it, it's time for you to go. I've made it clear where I stand. You're very crafty about trying to turn this thing around, and make me the one to blame. I'm not going to let you get away with it. You need to go back to Vermont, and leave me and Carrie alone. I'm not going to go through this anymore." Stopping in my driveway, he looked at me "If you won't change your mind this time, I'm not coming back."

"Go Lynn, and don't come back." I shut the truck door, stood back and let him leave. My heart was torn again. I knew what God had said to me months ago, but everything I was seeing, and hearing, was telling me it would never happen. I knew it would never be God's will for me to just live with him, and I wouldn't want to anyway. The devil was having a good time, making the most of this tragedy between us.

I made myself forget the whole thing for a couple of weeks, I couldn't take anymore. I focused on Carrie again, and my Mother. We went places on weekends together, worked on projects and hobbies, on our gardens together, and planned meals at Mom's house. We'd work together in the kitchen, and put music on to enjoy while Carrie played with her toys. We listened to hymns, and Christian songs, and lifted our spirits. I wasn't going to allow our lives to be totally controlled and destroyed by this constant turmoil, and disruption.

Then during a prayer time, once again the Holy Spirit directed me to fast and pray about reconciliation with Lynn. My answer was simple and honest;

"I'm sorry Lord, but I don't have the faith to believe you for this. If you want me to do this, you're going to have to push me through; I can't do it."

"Just be willing to start, I'll carry you through."

I obeyed, but my heart was totally numb. There was no desire, no faith, no strength of my own to believe for this. Truth known; I didn't even really care anymore. I just obeyed, because I knew the voice of the Lord, and couldn't say no to Him.

This was to be a forty day Daniel fast, which would mean it would end just before Christmas. I had been attending a church in Saratoga New York, and at one Sunday evening service a special guest speaker talked on the very same subject of what I was going through in my marriage. He and his wife were separated. She was unsaved, and he was praying and believing for his wife's salvation, and their marriage to be restored. His situation was almost a mirror of mine. When he finished his message, he asked if there was anyone else in the same situation as his. If so, to come forward and the leaders would come together in agreement, and pray for God to intervene for us.

I knew I had to go forward, the Lord's presence filled the room. When I went to the front they asked me to relay my story. I gave a brief explanation. They all looked at one another, and gathered around me; and for quite a while there was powerful prayer going up, for Satan to get his hands off of my, and my daughter's life, and to open Lynn's heart and move him to do the right thing; and restore our marriage. It was a powerful night of being in the midst of some of God's people, who knew how to pray.

During the past months, I'd continued to work toward getting employment at the facility for the mentally deficient, and received a notice shortly after Christmas, that I'd been approved for a position. At the same time, another mobile home in the park was up for sale, and I felt it would be a better situation for Carrie and I.

It was bigger, newer, had a larger yard, and Carrie could go to the same school. I began looking into it, and an appointment was made to sign papers to purchase it. The woman selling it was willing to come to my oldest sister's house, who also lived in this park; and we could sign the papers and she'd give me the keys to it then.

The day the papers were to be signed, I sat waiting in my sister's living room for the woman to arrive to settle the deal; when the door opened, and Lynn came in. He looked everywhere until he found me, sitting in a low chair at the end of the room.

"Lorna, we need to talk."

My sister was not happy "Lorna, you're just getting ready to start a new life, don't get into another situation with him again, don't let this opportunity go by."

The house was full. Other members of the family turned and looked at me. I could see they were not happy either. They had watched the struggles and hardships I'd gone through from two separations. Now, as I sat here waiting to sign papers to a better home, and a job that had good benefits and a better future; and again, he comes back on the scene. They didn't say anything, but I could see the apprehension on their faces.

"Is there someplace we can talk."

My sister pointed to her room, down the hall "Don't go anywhere with him, just go to my room. When the lady comes, I'll ask her to wait till you're done. Try not to be too long. Don't let him change your mind." She glared at Lynn, as he followed me to the bedroom.

We shut the door, and sat on the bed.

"I've been a fool. You have no reason to believe me, and I don't blame you for not wanting to listen to me. But, I love you. I always will. Will you marry me, again. You were absolutely right, no woman should be willing to be used, and that's what I was expecting of you. I'm sorry. I want to marry you, if you'll take me, and this time, we'll make it work."

As I sat there listening to him, I knew in my heart, that whatever answer I gave, this time, it would be the last time. If I didn't obey what I knew God had spoken to me, and wasn't willing to remarry him; there would never be a next time. This was the last time. I would never see him again.

"Yes, I'll remarry you. But, as you said; this time, it is to the death." We embraced, there was no need for any more words.

When we came back to the living room, the lady was at my sister's table waiting to sign the papers to the home I was about the purchase. I had to apologize to her, and my family; and explain that my plans had changed. The lady said that was ok, there were several others who had shown an interest in the place, and felt it would be sold to one of them, so not to worry.

My family didn't dispute my decision, but I could see the looks of concern on their faces, and I couldn't blame them. There was no point in trying to explain to them how God had directed me over the past year about this. I'd have to put this in His hands and ask Him to help them understand.

If Lynn had come through the door just a half hour later, it would have been too late. I would have signed the papers. If that had happened, this would have shut the door to any future again with him. God's timing is always perfect.

On January 2, 1982, we were remarried at the same church in Saratoga New York, by the pastor, with several of my family members there as witnesses.

The pastor of this church was a tall, elderly man, with white hair. My sister gave me a green dress, with a short multi-colored green jacket, which helped give it a stylish appearance. I wore this at the ceremony. My sister knew nothing of the dream I'd had previously, of being remarried in a green dress.

It took a couple of days to pack our belongings from the tiny mobile home, and load them into Lynn's truck and trailer he'd brought to bring us back with. Then we went to see my Mother before we left. She sat at her kitchen table, waiting. She smiled, but I saw the sadness on her face too. Our ties had grown together, it was not going to be easy to leave her here. We talked a while, Carrie was quiet also, she knew it would mean not being able to see her every day, as she had become accustomed to.

"We love you Mom, don't stay away. Please come and see us when you can."

"I will, don't worry. You need time to get your house back in order. Give me a call when you are settled in, and I'll come for a visit."

"It won't be long. When you come, we'll go fishing, and do some berry picking this coming summer."

"Sure, we'll plan on it, and look forward to it. You be careful driving back now, and let me know when you're home. Just call so I'll know you're home safe."

Lynn answered "Will do."
Carrie and I gave her a hug. Other family members were also there to see us off. Each wished us well, and we spoke of getting together sometime soon.

I drove my car behind Lynn's truck, full of my belongings, and we headed back to Vermont. Carrie went with Lynn, running to the truck. He picked her up, putting her in the passenger side next to him. He said she talked nonstop until she fell sound asleep, as he continued down the road.

This time, it would be a one way journey. We both made a commitment this time, that would remain the rest of our lives.

Our Pond in Newbury Vermont

TEN
SPIRITUAL WARFARE ON EVERY FRONT

As soon as we returned home, we both began going to our doctor's to have tests done to determine if we needed medical help to be able to have more children. We had talked about it several times before we remarried, and felt this was a needed step.

He began a series of tests at the hospital and I made appointments with my doctor. We found out we both had medical issues that were making my being able to become pregnant difficult. His tests revealed a very low sperm count, which they felt was due to exposure to Agent Orange in Vietnam. My doctor found my uterus was damaged, and probably causing problems for us also. We both were discouraged.

I took it to the Lord, and asked for His intervention and healing. But, as I did, several things came to my heart, that I had to admit to myself. I had brought the damage to my body on myself, from having the abortion. Yes, I'd been forgiven, but sometimes, we live with the consequences of our actions. I was being shown this was the case for me. I know some people, even Christians will not agree with this. I'm not going to argue about these kinds of things. I've had women tell me they'd had several abortions, got saved, and went on to have other kids. Why? I have no idea. Only God knows, He is God, and does what he chooses. Anybody who tells me they know all of God's mind, and why he chooses to allow some things in this world, is only showing their arrogance, and foolishness.

I'm simply relaying what I believe God showed me, about my case personally, and I believe I heard Him right. There's a verse that tells us "Let everyone be persuaded in their own mind." After a great deal of prayer about this, I believe I've been shown God's answer, and have accepted it.

> **Rom 14:5 One man esteemeth one day above another: another esteemeth every day alike. Let every man be fully persuaded in his own mind.**

In Lynn's case, the doctor's came to the conclusion, his low sperm count was from exposure to Agent Orange, combined with his bad eating habits, and life choices. He drank and smoked. All of this was contributing to his body not being in good health. His ongoing unwillingness to make changes in his habits would soon bring suffering and hardship on him, and those who loved him, for the rest of his life. But we had no way of knowing this right then. Again, this was another case of the mercy of God, to not let us know our future. There's times He does, but also times he hides it; and protects us from what we're about to walk into. Sometimes, we're better off not knowing, until it happens.

While we were in this process, I received a call one day from my younger sister from Charleston South Carolina. Her husband was now a lieutenant in the Navy, and was being transferred to a base in Maine. She was letting me know where they'd be living, and wanted to see me sometime when they got up in our area.

As she was talking, the Lord's presence came upon me, and spoke to my spirit "This move is of me. When she comes back to this area, she will be saved, and delivered. Begin to pray and fast for her, before she arrives in New York."

She confirmed what I'd just heard in my heart from the Lord by saying "We are going to stop in New York first, and stay with family for a short while, then go on to Maine."

"Give me a call, and stop in to visit when you're on your way to Maine."

"Yes, we will. There's a lot I want to talk to you about. I'm still having a lot of trouble with the allergies. I'll be going to a doctor when we get to Maine, and see if I can find one who can help me. A doctor down here says he doesn't think I'll be able to have any kids, because they're so bad."

"Well, we'll see what God says about it. I'll be praying for a safe trip for you both on the way up."

So, on their way to Maine, after a few days spent with our older sister and her husband, they stopped to see us, and spent a couple of days with us. Her husband was happy to be transferred to a northern base, and they planned to buy a home nearby. We spent the first evening of their visit sharing what was going on among us, and our hopes of being able to have more children. My sister nodded in agreement, they were hoping to have children now also, and that her doctor's diagnosis would be wrong.

I didn't say anything when they first arrived, but as soon as she came through the door, I could see she had lost quite a bit of weight, and there were dark circles under her eyes. I made it a point to be praying about this. She shared that while they were in New York visiting our older sister; she had witnessed to her, and prayed with her, asking forgiveness of her sins, and for Christ to come into her life and be her Savior. She had received salvation. So, though the outward signs of the allergies were evident, at the same time, I could see a real peace, and abiding presence of the Lord in her. I knew she had truly been born again.

After they left, one morning alone in prayer the Holy Spirit prompted me to plan another fast toward the end of May that would go into the third week of June. I hesitated in even seeking further about this. I'd learned over the years to be cautious and not just listen to voices, but be waiting for further confirmation through prayer, and Bible study. The promptings persisted, and increased. So I planned what day to start; and asked the Lord for specific issues He wanted addressed during this time. Several came, two of which were Lynn, and my younger sister with the allergies. I was guided to spend a lot of time praying in the Spirit, and addressing the specific problems they both had, that needed healing and deliverance. I also knew there were other things concerning them, the Lord would not reveal to me. I'd have to trust Him as I just let the Holy Spirit do the interceding. This is an area of prayer that few delve into, because it requires enough faith to not have all the details, but willing to do the warfare anyway; and willing to wait for the full picture of what and why you're doing the intercession, until sometime in the future.

It was the end of the third week of June when this fast was over. The very next day my sister in law, my oldest brother's wife called, and asked what Lynn and I would be doing about the first weekend of July, and if we'd be able to come for a visit. My brother could use a hand repairing his roof. I said I'd talk to Lynn, then get back to her and let her know.

When he came home that night, I relayed the story. He said he'd be glad to help, and to give them a call to ask when to come, and if he'd need anything picked up on the way to help get the job done.

We planned to drive to my Mother's, and stay with her during the job, and have a barbecue the day of the roof repair, with most of the family there for the day.

There was a lot of joking, laughter, and helping with the cooking, while the men on the roof worked getting the repairs done. As evening came on, we had planned to leave to go back to Vermont that day, so Lynn could go to work the next morning. He looked very tired, so I drove. He slept at times in-between stops for gas.

In my heart, something was uneasy. I didn't know why. Something just seemed wrong; I also thought of the time of fasting and prayer I'd just come out of, and wondered if it had something to do with this.

The next morning, as he was getting ready for work, he briefly spoke of still being tired. He looked as if he hadn't slept. My spirit was heavy as I watched him go down the driveway, and prayed a silent prayer, asking the Lord to please watch over him, and bring him home safe.

That night, still looking weary, he sat at the table for dinner, and started eating, but could not finish his meal. He apologized, saying he knew it was delicious, but just couldn't finish it. I asked if he should lie down and rest. He agreed, and went to the living room couch, and tried to lay down, and watch some television. However, after about an hour, he began to speak of being in pain in his chest. No matter what he did, or how he changed his position on the couch, he couldn't get comfortable. By nine o'clock he said he was going to try to go to bed. After only a short time, he was back up, still with pain in his chest. I knew now, something had to be done. I spoke to him, and said we needed to call the doctor at the village clinic, to see if she would look at him. She said bring him right down immediately. We were there in a few minutes. After taking his blood pressure, and checking his heart beat, she knew he needed to be taken to the hospital, and called for an ambulance to transport him, he was having a heart attack.

I decided to follow the ambulance, and drive my own car, in order to be able to travel back home, if need be. My senses were starting to shut down. I became numb, but in the fog, went over in my mind what I may need to do, depending on what the doctor's found. Upon arriving, they immediately took him to ICU, and began hooking him to oxygen, and monitors for his heart. I was taken to a waiting room, where I stayed for several hours. As I sat alone, praying, a woman came in, and asked if I needed anything.

Her eyes were full of concern, and compassion. I could see the mercy of God in her as she sat with me. I said no, I didn't need anything. Then she asked an unusual question "What do you feel like doing right now?"

I looked at her. A flood of thoughts raged in my head. We'd been remarried less than a year, we had hoped and planned for more children, we were both still young; I was twenty nine, he was thirty six-why had God allowed this to happen....,"I feel like I want to scream."

She picked up my hands in both of hers, looked me in the eyes and said "Yes, I don't blame you. Go ahead, and scream."

I squeezed her hands, "Thank you for understanding, but no, not now, not like this." She reached over, and brought me to her, and embraced me, for a long time. I just held her, needing this expression of the love and compassion of God. It held me when everything in me wanted to have a complete breakdown. When she knew I was going to be able to get through, she got up and gave me a card with her name and number, letting me know that she was there for me, if I needed her. I've asked the Lord to bless her, when she came to my mind many times over the years, for her strength, and discerning love.

Several hours went by. A nurse came to the door saying I could see Lynn for a few minutes, and then I'd be able to go home, and get some rest. I followed her into the room. She quietly said if I needed her, she's be nearby. I stood silently assessing what was before me. Lynn lay on the bed, with heart monitors hooked to him, as well as oxygen, his blood pressure was extremely high. His breathing was irregular. He laid unconscious, they had induced a medicated sleep.

Then, I sensed the presence of the Lord, and in my spirit heard "This is why I asked you to do the time of fasting and prayer last month. I did not tell you the whole reason then, because it would have been too much for you to bear. His body has been damaged by a great deal of abuse he's done to himself. Drinking, smoking, and harmful eating habits. If you had not prayed and fasted in the Spirit for him; he would have died. He will not die, but he will be on medications for the rest of his life. I will raise him up, and he will return to work, in time."

I stood alone watching him for quite a long time; taking in the reality of what the Lord had spoken to me. As the years went by, what he said to me was proven out. He did go back to work, after about a year and half of recovery time, and did take medications the rest of his life; over twenty years. But, in the meantime, there was an almost two month span of time in the hospital, six weeks of it in the ICU ward.

After 3:00 a.m., I drove home, making it in the driveway at about dawn. I had taken Carrie to Lynn's parents, and made plans to pick her up the next day, after I'd had a chance to rest. I had called them briefly at the hospital and told his Mother his condition, and that he'd make it; but it would be a long recovery time.

A little over a week later, my sister from Maine called, and asked how Lynn was doing. I gave an overview of what the doctor's said, then asked her how things were going for her. "I'm not doing very good. The allergies have gotten worse, I can't go outside anymore, if I do I can't breathe. I can't hold much down trying to eat either. My doctor is concerned it may kill me; he says he believes I'll never be able to have any kids. He's the second doctor who's told me this. Do you have any suggestions of what we can do?"

"We've talked about this, and you agreed that it's a demonic problem. I'll ask you; are you willing to go through a deliverance session, with some people in my prayer group, and believe God to get you set free from these demons causing the allergies? If you are, I'll call them and see how many of them would come, and pray with you and get you set free."

"Yes, at this point, I want to do whatever it's going to take to be free. I've nothing to lose."

"Alright, I'll call you when a time is set up, and you can come then."

A group of eight were willing to do this, and I let her know they could do it a couple of weeks later, in the first week of August, in the evening. When the meeting day arrived, she came first, in the late morning. A couple of friends were already at my house, when she came through the door. Her eyes were sunken and blackened, she looked like a walking skeleton. One of my friends said she believed she discerned a spirit of Death on her. I agreed. I believe if God had no had us intervene for her when we did, she would have not lived much longer.

When the rest of the group arrived that would participate, we began with prayer, and anointed each of us with oil. There was two elder men who led the session; and began calling out specific demons they felt the Lord had spoken to them. The manifestations began in earnest. My sister's sincere desire to be free played a big part in the success of the demons having to leave. Every time one was called out by name, she also demanded them to leave. She also was shown she needed to renounce all involvement with the occult, sorcery, witchcraft, and other forms of demonic activity, as the Lord revealed it to her and those in the group calling them out.

At one point the Lord directed her to specifically repent of wearing witches garb on Halloween nights several times, as a teenager, and young woman. She also had to ask forgiveness for allowing herself to be used by Satan in this manner, and how it influenced others she knew, and her involvement in seances. It caused me to go back to my first days of salvation, and how the Lord led me in the same path of renouncing the evil activities I was involved in, repentance, and His restoration. Now I was witnessing it in my sister, at my kitchen table.

Another important point to this is, the Holy Spirit brought up to my sister her need to ask forgiveness for speaking into the scrying mirror I had brought home, which my Father had to get rid of, when we were kids.

We both were shown during this deliverance, that Satan had used this horrible mirror to bring much torment to our lives. Spirits that were in them from people doing incantations and hexes came into us as kids, because we didn't know any better. Satan doesn't care if you understand his tactics, he counts on you NOT knowing. Our ignorance often helps him bring a lot of misery into our lives. I prayed again, asking the Lord's forgiveness for being foolish, and bringing it into my parents' house, and the torment it caused us all. We both renounced all involvement with it, and asked the Lord's healing and to shut the doors to any further demonic abuse from it. We knew as soon as we were done, that we were forgiven, and our spirits felt the presence of the Holy Spirit deep within. We knew we had the victory over it.

This showed all of us in the group, how serious God takes it when we fall into such deep rebellion. It takes time, and complete sincerity to get totally free from these demons, once we've opened the door of our souls to them.

Finally, toward 2:00 a.m., the last, and we felt the strongest demon was commanded to come out. The spirit of Death. It did not want to leave. There was another round of snarling, hissing, growling, and other manifestations, that tried to get us discouraged. But my sister said she felt this was the final one, and she wasn't going to let it stay any longer, and torment her any further. I give her credit, she did all she could to work with us and the Holy Spirit, until she was indeed free. She *actively* assisted in her deliverance. This level of obedience helps tremendously. When this spirit of Death finally left, she was exhausted. She barely made it to the small bed we had set up for her in my living room. We helped her get undressed, in a nightgown, and she was asleep within minutes.

The next morning, the first thing she said was "That coffee smells terrific, I'll have some." Along with a good cup of coffee, she enjoyed a large breakfast of eggs, bacon, toast, juice, and more coffee.

After helping clean the kitchen, she looked out and saw the sun shining in our front yard, and said "I think I'll take one of your lawn recliners and go out and lay in the sun for a while." She stayed out several hours, and came back in for a good lunch. Before the deliverance session, being outside would have caused her tremendous pain, with great sores and rashes breaking out on her skin, and she would not have been able to keep any food down, she would have vomited it up. She ate breakfast and a hearty lunch, with no side effects; and never had any from then on.

I took my Bible while we were eating, and found the scripture Jesus quoted, and said we'd use this as our victory verse for the rest of the day:

> **Joh 8:36 If the Son therefore shall make you free, ye shall be free indeed.**

Many more things could be added about this story, but aren't necessary. A little over a year later, they had a son, who now has several children of his own. Again, God overrode what the devils plans were for her, and blessed them with children and grandchildren.

The main points to this event are:
1. God's compassion and care for one individual-which shows how much he cares for every person, he is no respecter of persons.

2. Those of us he used to help her get delivered were not people of any special importance. We were just everyday people, who were serving God in the capacities we were able, and standing on His word in faith.

3. We were willing to take the risk of failure. As my sister said, at that point, she had nothing to lose-and everything to gain. We chose to take God at His word, and use the verses that were given to us by the Holy Spirit, to wage this war against Satan. God honored our faith, and she was set free.

The verses the Lord gave us to use in this session were:

> Luk 10:17 And the seventy returned again with joy, saying, Lord, even the devils are subject unto us through thy name.

> Luk 10:18 And he said unto them, I beheld Satan as lightning fall from heaven.

> Luk 10:19 Behold, I give unto you power to tread on serpents and scorpions, and over all the power of the enemy: and nothing shall by any means hurt you.

> Luk 10:20 Notwithstanding in this rejoice not, that the spirits are subject unto you; but rather rejoice, because your names are written in heaven.

> Mar 16:17 And these signs shall follow them that believe; In my name shall they cast out devils; they shall speak with new tongues;

> Mar 16:18 They shall take up serpents; and if they drink any deadly thing, it

shall not hurt them; they shall lay hands on the sick, and they shall recover.

Act 5:16 There came also a multitude out of the cities round about unto Jerusalem, bringing sick folks, and them which were vexed with unclean spirits: and they were healed everyone.

Act 8:6 And the people with one accord gave heed unto those things which Philip spake, hearing and seeing the miracles which he did.

Act 8:7 For unclean spirits, crying with loud voice, came out of many that were possessed with them: and many taken with palsies, and that were lame, were healed._

Important points:

1. Jesus saw Satan fall from heaven-we were waging war against an already defeated enemy, we needed to remember this when engaged with him and commanding his demons to leave.

2. We are given authority over the demons by Jesus Christ; it's in His authority we are to command them out, they must obey the authority of that Name.
3. We are to never give any glory to anyone for the victory-except Jesus Christ. He alone gets the glory.

After going through this event, do I believe everyone with allergies is demonically oppressed? No, every situation is different. If people pray and seek the Lord for their case, He will reveal what's needed to be done. However, most depend on the medical industry, which is a money managed institution now, and it is run as a business.

Their answer to most physical manifestations is a combination of drugs and many times demonic mysticism such as Reiki and Buddhism. They end up making their medical situation worse, and don't realize it, out of ignorance, and being deceived.

Let's take a look at an example from scripture:

Return of an Unclean Spirit

Mat 12:43 When the unclean spirit is gone out of a man, he walketh through dry places, seeking rest, and findeth none.

Mat 12:44 Then he saith, I will return into my house from whence I came out; and when he is come, he findeth it empty, swept, and garnished.

Mat 12:45 Then goeth he, and taketh with himself seven other spirits more wicked than himself, and they enter in and dwell there: and the last state of that man is worse than the first. Even so shall it be also unto this wicked generation. See also Luke 11:24-26

In May of 2017, I was diagnosed with uterine cancer, and went through surgery. Afterwards I was scheduled to go through a series of chemotherapy treatments at a nearby cancer center. The account below was my experience. It clearly describes the concerns I've just spoken of, and hope it will be a warning to anybody who reads this.

From my journal:

"After surgery last year in May for uterine cancer, a series of chemotherapy treatments were set up for me in a local cancer center that was to go on for the rest of the summer and into

September of 2017.

The first visit proved to be eye opening, and disturbing. What I thought was going to be a medical treatment dealing with cancer turned out to be much more. I was taken into a room where I was interrogated, and asked very personal questions by a woman who turned out to be a Reiki master, and another woman who sat and wrote all of my responses down. I soon realized I was being carefully scrutinized. My discernment was keen and correct. Not only was I going there for chemotherapy treatments, but these people were going to try to get me to submit to Reiki practices. I was being indoctrinated, but very subtly. They were not being totally honest about what they were really doing with their questioning; and my uneasiness got worse as time went on.

I made it clear I was a Christian, and a minister. This did not help me, it just brought further interrogations. However, I decided to do as the Lord tells us, "speak the truth in love", and let the chips fall where they may. My stand in faith proved to cause each visit to become more difficult. Whenever I shared my faith in Christ I saw marked opposition and manipulation to get me to stop. However, I sat there while getting treatments, and listened while several times other patients were "laid hands on", and Reiki practices and yoga were done on these people. I found this total hypocrisy, and wondered how the medical field had become so corrupted to allow this, and promote it. I increasingly saw the danger I was really in.

Finally at the last treatment I went to, I was placed by the front desk where I could be observed and controlled. At the end of this session, I decided to not continue, and canceled the last chemotherapy appointment.

What are my greatest concerns about this?

1. I wasn't told I'd have to be involved with a Reiki master when the appointments for chemotherapy treatments were made for

me. I wasn't given a choice of whether I wanted to talk to her or not, I was controlled and guided into it without knowledge or consent.

2. The questions asked of me were very personal, which I didn't care; I answered them honestly. But, the questions had nothing to do with getting medical treatment for cancer, they were questions about my personal beliefs and practices in life; which had nothing to do with what I was supposed to be there for. I made it clear that I had no intention of allowing Reiki to be done on me.

3. When these people realized I was very serious about my faith in Christ, the atmosphere changed completely. I also saw evidence of a lot of gossip, which is to be expected in these places, but it shouldn't be there. It made me dread having to go to any more, and the pain I was enduring from the treatments should have been enough to go through.

When I look back on it now, I believe God allowed me to go through this to open my eyes to the dangerous mixture the medical field and eastern religions such as Buddhism has become in this country. America was founded on a Biblical foundation, but has been hijacked by eastern religions. Now Christianity has been undermined, and those who stand for the Bible, and its teachings are treated as if we have mental problems, and actively persecuted and shut down; unless we go along with it and condone what they are doing. In the studying I've been doing over the last several months, I found there's a lot of big name bible teachers and preachers who are going right along with this new age form of mixing eastern religion with Christianity. They have become apostate, and don't have the

discernment to even know it."

I realize this is out of sync with the flow of this story. However, it fits with   this subject, and hope the reader can see the need for it being here.

If somebody with an illness goes to a physician, and that doctor advises, or incorporates eastern religions into their medical practices, they are opening the door to the devil and his demons, and telling them to "come on in" and they do. Satan can heal; did you know that? Yes, but it doesn't last, and the person will often get worse, and other diseases come upon them. Many die from this, not knowing what they have done to themselves.

After seeing my sister off, back to Maine, my focus went back to my own situation. Lynn was still in the hospital going through a long recuperation process.

He was released at the end of August, and given a regimen of light exercise, like walking, with no lifting for at least six months. They said about one third of his lower heart had been damaged permanently, and he could expect to be taking medications the rest of his life. But he could improve his abilities and strength a great deal if he followed the doctor's orders. Coming so close to death, he made serious changes to his diet, and quit smoking. His overall health improved quickly, just by doing this. He remained on disability for a year and half, then felt he wanted to go back to work. It was not a desk job, as many may choose. He went back to driving a cement truck, and a schedule men younger than him, might find too much to deal with. It wasn't unusual for him to put in a twelve to fourteen hour day. Our lives became just as busy, and productive, as before he had the heart attack.

For the next ten years, God bestowed many blessings on us. There were also more encounters of people needing ministry, prayer and deliverance. Whenever I had the time; there would be times of seeking the Lord in deeper areas of intercession. The Lord was expanding my work in specific prayer for nations, leaders, and world events. I was told several times by the Holy Spirit to not speak of this ministry; but keep it between myself and Him, unless He specifically asked me to tell someone else. When I asked the reason for this, the answer given was;

"I reveal secrets, to those who know how to keep secrets."

> Gen 18:17 And the LORD said, Shall I hide from Abraham that thing which I do;

> Pro 11:13 A talebearer revealeth secrets: but he that is of a faithful spirit concealeth the matter.

> Psa 25:14 The secret of the LORD is with them that fear him; and he will shew them his covenant.

> Amo 3:7 Surely the Lord GOD will do nothing, but he revealeth his secret unto his servants the prophets.

There are more verses that go further, but these are enough for any serious student, to be able to research deeper into this.

This is one of the reasons it's taken almost twenty years for this book to be written, even after the meeting with Mr. Davis. I've learned the value of keeping my interactions with the Lord between myself and Him. I prefer it that way. Most people would not believe, if I shared much of what has been between God and I. I don't fear the mocking ridicule, but Jesus gave the verse "don't cast your pearls before swine", for a good reason. There's a time and place to share the things of God. But most of the time, it's best to be silent. This book has become a reality, only after a very long time of testing the spirits, to see if they be of God.

While Lynn was recovering at home, I found two part time jobs doing home health care for the elders in the area. This helped a great deal with making sure Carrie's needs were met for school, and medical care. While I was working she was able to stay home with

Lynn again.

During this time, I took an upright piano my Mother had owned when we were growing up, and had it restored. New keys were put in it, and a harpsichord installed in it. The sound that came from it after it was restored was amazing. I found a piano teacher close by her school, and for six years, she took lessons once a week; practicing her lessons at home in the evenings. It was the beginning of a permanent part of her life. She played piano and guitar for many years in local churches and ministries, and still does at times, in the area.

Another blessing that took place during these years, was a settlement I received from the car accident in New York. It took several years for the lawyers to finally come to an agreement on who was to blame (the drunk eye doctor), and what my injuries were worth. When it was finalized, I received enough to pay off several bills, and purchase a childhood dream that I thought I'd never have, an Arabian horse.

Lynn knew of an Arabian horse farm near where he worked, and said if I wanted, he'd take me with him on a Saturday when he had to go check on something at his job. So we went the next weekend.

When we pulled into the driveway of the farm, there were paddocks on both sides. In a small one next to the barn, a beautiful young filly was walking back and forth, very alert to her surroundings, neighing as we came in.

We got out, and the owner showed us his available stock. It was a difficult decision, all of them were lovely. Then he took us to the young one that looked to be black, that we saw as we came in. He explained she was actually listed as a gray on her pedigree, and as years went by, she would become almost white. It seemed hard to believe, but whatever her color, it was her intelligence and beauty that caught my eye. The owner explained she was just two years old, and they had started doing a small amount of training with her on long lines, with a bit in her mouth. But no one had saddled or rode her yet. I listened, knowing it should be another year, before her back was strong enough to support a rider, for just a half an hour. My heart leaned toward her. As I stroked her, and spoke to her; our spirits melded together.

"I'd like to take her, if she's available."

"Yes, will you be picking her up, or would you like me to deliver her to you?"

"We haven't got a trailer yet, so if you could deliver her, that would be wonderful."

"That's fine, let's go in, and I'll make out the sales agreement, and begin the transfer process of her pedigree into your name."

"Oh, does she have a name yet?"

"Yes, she is Willows Tempest". As years went by, and she was trained in several disciplines, I came to appreciate that name; it fit her perfectly.

The business transactions were completed, and the day of the delivery was set up. On the way home, we talked about getting the barn ready for her, and a supply of hay and grains.

I had ridden horses before, but didn't have the experience of fully training a young horse from the very start. With the investment in buying this quality animal, I decided to find a trainer who could give me lessons in riding and teach me to train my horse at the same time. I found a very compassionate young woman, who was well trained herself, and a good instructor. I began weekly lessons with her, which went on for quite a few years, until I'd reached the place of being able to train a horse from birth to show quality. I also attended many training seminars, and clinics throughout the years I owned horses, and used the training methods I learned; taking them back home, and improving my own horses abilities. Deciding to put in this kind of discipline and dedication paid off. We showed our horses across the state, and New Hampshire; winning state championships for several years. Willow went on to be a driving champion, English pleasure, and a wonderful school horse herself; giving a lot of kids lessons for many years.

I had also been going to a woman's fellowship meeting for a couple of years, and this year, new people were going to be appointed in leadership. During a fall meeting, God's call became clear to me. This was in 1983.

This is the account, from my journal:

"The first time I knew I was called of God was in late 1983, at a Women's fellowship meeting on a Monday night. I had been an active member for two years, and a new group of leaders were about to be voted in. As I walked to the front of the room, to take my seat, a voice in my spirit began to speak to me; "I am calling you to be the prayer chairman in this chapter, into intercession, and as a teacher. In years to come you will teach my word in many places." I thought it was the devil and under my breath in a quiet voice I said "In the Name of Jesus, I rebuke you, and command you to leave me!" As I reached my seat and began to sit down, the voice spoke again, "This is the Lord, not the devil my daughter. I am calling you to serve me in intercession and as a teacher."

I silently prayed "If this is really you Lord, I'm asking that you would confirm it to me before this night is over at least 3 times by people who do not know anything of what I've just heard." Within a very few minutes the woman who as going to be the next president of our chapter came right to me and said,

"Would you be praying tonight about taking the position of prayer chairman, I feel in my heart God has called you to it." In another half an hour, someone else came to me and said almost the exact thing. I did not answer them, but I thought "That is two, only one more to go."

The guest speaker that night gave a powerful testimony. She had been healed of stage four cancer of the stomach; a fatal disease of the intestines. At the end of the meeting she said anyone who wished to, please come forward and she would agree with them in prayer. I stood up, and said to myself I would not tell her what I wanted prayer for, but would just ask her to pray with me for guidance. When I walked toward her, she took my hand and started praying before I had a chance to say anything. In her prayer she said, "Lord, you've set this woman apart for your service. Use her for your glory, sanctify her, and protect her from the attacks she will endure. Give her strength, wisdom, and boldness to teach your word with courage and power. As she wages war in the heavenlies for you, give her the guidance and protection of your angels." (I remember every word, even though it was over thirty years ago.) I opened my eyes, and we looked at one another but said nothing, we embraced and parted. I look forward to meeting her again in heaven."

It would take another full book to relay the events, and ministry that God had in store for me in the years I served as prayer chairman. I'll only share a few. God had me believe Him for the finances for many trips across the country, to conferences, and ministry events. The needs were always supplied in abundance. I was privileged to sit in conferences which held many thousands of women and men both. The most significant ones were in Washington D.C., with over seven thousand in attendance, Knoxville Tenn., approximately three thousand, Hartford Conn., several thousand, as examples. In each of these conferences, the Holy Spirit brought out specific areas He wanted us to focus on, and important issues we needed to address in the body of Christ. They were events that God used to bring His mind and His agenda's to our attention; and these many years later, I continue to see the significance of each one of them.

Naming a few:

1. The need of ongoing individual, and national repentance-in order to maintain a healthy relationship with the Creator, and be able to receive His blessings.

2. The necessity of accountability/integrity in ministry-in order that the Holy Spirit will have the ability to use a ministry to further the gospel, without the infiltration of corruption. In this, I'm not saying we will never sin again, or fall-it means, when we do, we will do as David did-acknowledge our sin, confess it, and turn away from it.

3. The importance of the family unit to be defined as God's word describes it; one man/one woman in the marriage union.

If we look around today, sadly in many churches; we see that this is not what's being preached today. Our moral foundation is broken, and the evidence of it is shown in the sin we allow to go unaddressed. Today, those with the courage to speak up against sin, are finding it very difficult to maintain any kind of ministry. I've been sold out to Jesus for a long time, and my ministry is solely to Him.

I was asked to speak once during the time I served as prayer chairman, and give my testimony of the restoration of my marriage to Lynn. When I relayed to the leadership a sample of what the message would be, they contacted me, and asked that I *not* include the part where I spent the afternoon in the tiny trailer interceding, and what the Holy Spirit gave me in prayer, and the scriptures concerning marriage. I asked them why they wanted this taken out. They said it would upset some in the group that had already had divorces, and were remarried, or in other relationships. I asked them if they really thought God would approve of what they were asking me to do. I didn't get a straight answer, but they stood firm, and hoped I'd leave that part out. They didn't want the conviction of the Holy Spirit, on this issue.

I went to the Lord about it, and didn't hear anything directly; only a strong prompting to go back and read the scriptures again in First Corinthians, and what Paul had to say about divorce and remarriage. I went back to them that afternoon, and what God had said to me then;

"People change, people change my word. But, my word does not change."

As I remembered this, I knew I didn't need any other answer from the Lord. This was the answer. I could stick with what the word of God teaches on it, or bend to what the people wanted me to say. God was giving me another chance, to obey, or not; it was up to me.

The night I was to give the message, I sat watching and listening to the other leaders. Some of them were pensive, and careful with their words. This, I could see, was going to be a night of warfare. I'd spent a good deal of time in prayer, asking for the Lords strength and guidance to do the right thing. I was set to expect any reaction, and just stand my ground in God's word.

When announcements were over, and the worship time came to an end, I was called up to begin my testimony. I shared it as I knew the Lord wanted it, with the encounter and verses given to me that day in the little trailer. I shared that I knew I was to stand in faith for our marriage to be restored. I didn't leave out anything. As I continued speaking, several women got up, and left. I wasn't surprised, I could feel the tension and the atmosphere in the room become very somber. I continued on to the end, and sat down.

The president went to the microphone, and awkwardly closed the meeting, saying if anybody wanted prayer, to come forward. I was already seeing and experiencing the truth of what was prayed over me the night God called me into this ministry. This was the beginnings of the walking out alone, standing for the word of God, and facing the adversity, even among the brethren.

A couple of weeks later, the testimony I gave was recorded on tape, and a copy was sent to me, to check it out. As I listened, when it came to the part of the verses in First Corinthians and my discourse with the Lord in the trailer; it had been erased. The women in leadership had censored it out. The president over me called a couple of days after she knew I'd gotten it, and asked what my thoughts were. I said it was too bad that the women didn't feel they could allow the word of God to be proclaimed as it is in the Bible, regarding marriage; and that one day we will all be held accountable for not having the courage to stand for what God teaches about marriage and divorce and be willing to heed His commands. She didn't have much to say in answer to this, and hung up, saying she'd see me at the next meeting.

For me, this was the beginning of the end of my role in leadership for this Montpelier chapter. I was already beginning to experience some of the warnings in prayer given over me, when I was called into ministry. Facing adversity and having to take a stand for the word of God, was going to be a matter of course in my life.

The most difficult aspects of being a Bible teacher is dealing with:

1. Rebellion-people are rarely willing to admit they are in rebellion, and even when they do, aren't willing to pay the price of obedience to God's word. I've failed in this area myself, the only time I've come out in victory, is when I've chosen to repent, and turn around and surrender to the Lord.

2. Egos-arrogance and pride are walls of iron that cover people's

hearts and souls. It takes a miracle of God for the word of God to penetrate our selfish pride. For a great many, this never happens. The Bible is clear:

> **Pro 16:18 Pride goeth before destruction,
> and a haughty spirit before a fall.**

3. Intentionally twisting the scriptures-people are very crafty at being able to twist scripture to make it say what they want it to say. They will corrupt it in order to cover their sin, which they love, and remain living that sinful life; believing they will never answer to the One True God. One day, sadly, many fall into hell at the end of their life, still believing the lies they've created for themselves.

There's more hope for someone who knows they are a sinner, who is open about not being perfect, and know they need forgiveness. The ones I have concern for are those who cannot see their sin, and refuse to acknowledge that they need a Savior. Pride and arrogance is on wide display in this day and age. We can see the evidence of this everywhere.

I go to these verses often, to remind myself, what God requires of a teacher, and examine my heart; whether I'm being honest before Him, and with myself:

> **2Ti 4:2 Preach the word; be instant in season, out of season; reprove, rebuke, exhort with all longsuffering and doctrine.**
>
> **2Ti 4:3 For the time will come when they will not endure sound doctrine; but after their own lusts shall they heap to themselves teachers, having itching ears;**

2Ti 4:4 And they shall turn away their
ears from the truth, and shall be turned
unto fables.

2Ti 4:5 But watch thou in all things, endure afflictions, do the work of an evan-
gelist, make full proof of thy ministry._

Another sign to me, that we are coming to the end of this age,
is the great increase in the occult, and Satanism. It's everywhere,
and accepted in just about every form of media. Google censors
many Christian sites, and those who are whistleblower's. But you
can find pages and pages of information about witchcraft, sorcery,
Satanism, and oh yes, pornography-pages without number. It is
very clear who is the god of this world, and the media industries
are raking in the money, while destroying millions of lives every
day. Many of these people claim to be atheists, but they're not.
Because they'll go to a seance, promote a Satanist on a platform
making huge amounts of money, and allow just about every form
of entertainment that elevates evil. These people also put on a good
act about loving kids, but want abortion to remain legal, and will
march to demand the right to kill the baby. If you dare research
further, you'll find many of them are child abusers, pedophiles, and
participate in child sacrifices. They wear a multitude of masks, and
most of the public buy's their lies.

They believe in the devil; and if so, they also believe in God, but
have openly rejected Him, and are trying to get you to worship the
enemy of your soul too. If you've fallen into the trap of involvement
with the occult, witchcraft, Satanism; I pray you will wake up, and
reject Satan's wares, and surrender your life to Jesus. The only sin
He can't forgive, is the one we don't confess, and keep allowing to
rule over us.

I finished the term of prayer chairman, and went back to work in
home health care again; putting in long hours, especially weekends.

Our house was filled with busy enterprises. Training horses, music, going to events with Carrie, and family activities. There was always something to do, we were never bored, there was no time for boredom.

God didn't drop me from being of service to Him after my term was up with the women's fellowship group. It just went through changes, as life does. My service to Him became deeper, more involved in prayer for specific nations, and people He'd place on my heart, and how He wanted them prayed for; and to watch in the news media for the answers to come. It sometimes took years, but the answers came. Each time an increase in discernment, and knowledge in how to pray in the Spirit developed. Every answer to these intercessions increased the desire to go further. Answered prayer is fuel to our faith. I believe, as Samuel, Daniel, David, and other's; it is a lifelong service, born of a hunger to know Him. There's no bottom to the depths of God's heart, His love, and His Divine Person.

Before going further into this story, I'll add a necessary point. If anybody who's not saved picks this up, and reads the accounts of Satanic activities, demonic bondage's; and the work salvation, and of the Holy Spirit to bring deliverance-it will make no sense to you.

> 1Co 1:18 For the preaching of the cross is to them that perish foolishness; but unto us which are saved it is the power of God.
>
> 1Co 1:23 But we preach Christ crucified, unto the Jews a stumbling block, and unto the Greeks foolishness;
>
> 1Co 1:24 But unto them which are called, both Jews and Greeks, Christ the power of God, and the wisdom of God.
>
> 1Co 2:14 But the natural man receiveth

not the things of the Spirit of God: for they are foolishness unto him: neither can he know them, because they are spiritually discerned.

2Co 4:3 But if our gospel be hid, it is hid to them that are lost:

2Co 4:4 In whom the god of this world hath blinded the minds of them which believe not, lest the light of the glorious gospel of Christ, who is the image of God, should shine unto them._

For you, this is my prayer:

Act 26:18 To open their eyes, and to turn them from darkness to light, and from the power of Satan unto God, that they may receive forgiveness of sins, and inheritance among them which are sanctified by faith that is in me.

Eph 1:18 The eyes of your understanding being enlightened; that ye may know what is the hope of his calling, and what the riches of the glory of his inheritance in the saints,_

And, that you would come to understand what it means to walk in this blessed state:

Isa 61:10 I will greatly rejoice in the LORD, my soul shall be joyful in my God; for he hath clothed me with the garments of salvation, he hath covered

> me with the robe of righteousness, as a
> bridegroom decketh himself with orna-
> ments, and as a bride adorneth herself
> with her jewels.

Read the story of the Prodigal son, that Jesus taught in Luke chapter fifteen, when the wayward son came home to his father. What did the father do?

> Luk 15:22 But the father said to his ser-
> vants, Bring forth the best robe, and put
> it on him; and put a ring on his hand, and
> shoes on his feet.

This is the joy of the saved sinner. The forgiveness, mercy, and adoption into the family of God. All sins are covered in the precious blood of the Lamb, the Father opens his arms, and say's "Welcome home."

If you do not know Jesus as your Savior, it's my prayer, you'll surrender your heart to him now, and let Him cover you with His robe of righteousness.

ELEVEN
JUGGLING COMMITMENTS

During the last year I served as prayer chairman, the Lord spoke several significant things to me. I've kept to myself, and in my personal journals. He's let me know it should go in this book. It was in 1984, during times of prayer and fasting. I've watched over the years to see if what was given to me would become reality. In the last ten years especially, now they can be easily researched and found.

1. One night in a dream-I saw a man in a parked vehicle get out, walk to the back, open the hatch/trunk, and a swarm of small insect like things came out and flew in unison over his head, and he seemed to somehow direct them to do what he wanted. Then the picture changed; and I saw untold millions of these tiny things that looked like dragonflies, they covered the sky, flying in unison, and attacking people on the ground-killing them with what looked like stings. I woke up in a cold sweat, and couldn't move for quite a while. I asked God "Lord, what in the world was this? Was it just a nightmare?" In my spirit I heard "No, you will see these with your eyes one day-and they will be used during the Tribulation, and torment and kill multitudes."

Today in 2020, anyone can Google weaponized drones, and will find many Youtube videos, and articles about mini drones used in the military. Some are as small as a mosquito, and look just like one.

I will list just two here:
Future weapon used by intelligence(Mini drone)- https://youtu.

be/stHLrBs-_iE
US Military Released Micro Drone Swarm From FA 18 Super
Hornet Jet...- https://youtu.be/CGAk5gRD-t0

COMPILATION OF MINI DRONES

2. In another dream I had several times in 1984, and repeated
years after; of driving on an interstate highway, looking over at
the opposite lanes, and behind me in the rear view mirror, as far
as I could see-there were no vehicles. In the dream, I remember
saying "What is going on, is this in the entire country?" As the
dream continued, I'd be driving into a city-and the streets were
completely empty, no people or vehicles of any kind-it was eerie,
and ominous. I'd awake, looking at the ceiling, not understanding
what I was looking at, and couldn't believe I'd ever see such a thing.
Today in 2020, I've read articles and seen video footage and
photos of entire cities-with streets empty, no people or vehicles
of any kind; because of the corona virus pandemic. I've ridden on
highways and, just like in the dreams-looked as far as my eyes could

see, in the rear view mirror, and across to the opposite lanes-and no cars, trucks or any vehicles of any kind. About a month ago, I had to take a trip to a small city here in my area, and drove through it on empty streets, and no one on the sidewalks; it was like a ghost town. I do not know this as a fact, but in my heart, I believe these empty roads are a sign of the condition of the nation, and that it will not get any better as time goes by.

3. Again in dreams-I've seen people in dark military garb, with automatic weapons, running up to front doors of people's houses, and knocking the doors open by force, and taking the people out, and putting them into covered military transport trucks; to destinations unknown. I knew however, as I watched this, that these people were never going to go back to their homes. I also watched their homes being destroyed, and burned by these military invaders.

Today in 2020-I've seen the military do this as I watched news clips of people being invaded and forcefully taken, but what I saw in these dreams was a national scale; which hasn't come-yet.

The reason I believe God wants these to be shared here, is we are getting close to seeing all of what I've mentioned here, on national news. I do not know any dates, but the events happening today looks very much like we are headed for a police state for a country; and the Lord wants his people warned, and looking to Him for His strength, protection, and guidance. We need Him in order to deal with what is coming, or we're not going to be prepared.

I say this because of something that happened one evening in this same year, 1984 that pertains to this. I was out taking a walk, and talking with the Lord at the same time, about some specific situations in the country He had me praying for. I was alone, and still quite a ways from the house. I asked about the time of His coming, if He would show me the approximate time; something to look for that would give me some idea when to start "looking up".

In my spirit, I heard the still voice "When My Body, as a whole, begins to look up, and cry for Me to return; I will hear them, as I heard the children of Israel, and My servant Moses brought them out of bondage."

I've been watching and listening to the leaders of multitudes of churches, mega ministries, and TV evangelists, to see if they would begin to do this. For many years, until recently, they've continued to spew their prosperity gospel. With the lock down of this country because of the pandemic, their ministries are being hindered. I'm watching to see if they'd begin to realize how serious our situation is, and that this is the beginning of a permanent change, and not for the better.

Persecution is going to continue to get worse, and when the forced vaccines start taking place; Christians are going to have to make the decision on what they are going to do. Through this, I'm waiting to see if the Body of Christ will begin to meld together, and start seriously praying for the Lord's return, as I heard in my spirit many years ago. Because regardless of how much longer we may have, the truth before us is; we are seeing the beginning of the end, whether we like it or not. I'm praying that the Body of Christ will become unified in praying for Christ to come back, and rescue His people. This is the only answer for this planet.

Also in regards to these mega ministries; I've prayed that some of them would repent, and come out of their false teachings, and stop deceiving God's people. If they don't, my heart is heavy for their future. Some of them need to *really* get saved.

I'll relay one more incident, because I know the Lord wants me to; but have struggled with being obedient-because many church people will not be willing to hear this, but I must obey God.

During the fall of 1987, I asked a young friend of mine, who had been saved just a few years to attend a local women's conference with me in southern New England. There was going to be some speakers there, I thought she would benefit from, and get sound Bible teaching. She agreed and we went together. It was to be a three day event.

The first day went well. We attended the evening service, that went on until close to eleven at night. We made it back to our rooms, and shared our thoughts of the sessions we heard. We were both tired. We put out the lights, and were almost asleep, when we began to hear a lot of laughing, and raucous noise out in the hall. My friend said she was becoming afraid, and I could understand, the rowdy behavior kept getting worse. I prayed and asked the Lord what we should do, I felt like going to the front desk, and reporting the problem. In my heart I heard "Confront the issue, open the door and see what is going on. You need to see it." I did, I got up, opened the door-looked down the hallway, and could not believe what was before me. Many of the doors to the rooms were open, with women standing in their doorways, other's in the middle of the hall; laughing, screeching, in full party spirit. In the middle of the hall-the worship leader who sang that night was on all fours on her hands and knees, and the woman speaker of that night was on her back, riding her like a horse. I couldn't stand anymore, and spoke out "What are you people doing, don't you know what a terrible witness this is for the Lord? You are bringing shame to His Name. This is absolutely disgusting." The speaker fell off the worship leaders back, onto the floor. She got up and they both ran to their rooms and slammed their doors; along with all the women in the doorways down the hall.

The next morning we went back home, before the conference was over. I've never been back to another one.

I asked the young friend if she would continue to follow the Lord, and not let what we had seen detour her walk with God, or her faith. She said no, it wouldn't; but that she probably would not go to another one. I nodded, as I had already made the same decision.

We prayed together when we got back home, and asked the Lord to help us forgive them, and that He'd bring conviction to their hearts and get them to see the wrong of what they were doing, and asked Him to use it to be a lesson to us in our own walk with Him. After dropping her off, I silently prayed, asking that Satan would not be able to use this to damage her walk with Christ, that her spirit and soul would be healed from what she experienced.

I wrote a graphic letter to the women I knew, who had put the conference on, and told them what we saw and heard; and what I thought of it. I also relayed what I said to them in the hall; it was a terrible witness for Jesus Christ. It brought reproach to His name; and it sickened my heart. I never received any response, and didn't expect to.

I could relay several other events such as this, but this one is enough-the churches and ministries in these last several generations, have become totally corrupted, and I'll say it again-apostate. They will answer for their false teachings, and behavior one day.

Over the years people have spoken of the fact, I rarely smile. Some experiences such as I've described already is why. I'll challenge you to pray, and ask God how He sees this world, and ask with sincerity in your heart. Then, get yourself prepared for a very heavy load of truth. It will change you forever, and how you see this world. Whenever I've challenged anyone to do this, I've never received an answer, and many have chosen to avoid me from then on. I am not surprised. Let's take a look at what God's word has to say about what God sees, when He observes this world. I'll only use a few verses, which would take you weeks to research and study by cross referencing:

The condition of this world, described by Jesus:

Mat 19:17 And he said unto him, Why

callest thou me good? there is none good but one, that is, God: but if thou wilt enter into life, keep the commandments.

(note: Jesus said this in this manner, because he was living in a human body, and not yet risen-he was God in the flesh-but no flesh is good in God's sight/a paradox, he was speaking in terms of his present human condition)

Joh 3:19 And this is the condemnation, that light is come into the world, and men loved darkness rather than light, because their deeds were evil.

Joh 3:20 For every one that doeth evil hateth the light, neither cometh to the light, lest his deeds should be reproved.

Joh 7:7 The world cannot hate you; but me it hateth, because I testify of it, that the works thereof are evil.

Joh 8:43 Why do ye not understand my speech? even because ye cannot hear my word.

Joh 8:44 Ye are of your father the devil, and the lusts of your father ye will do. He was a murderer from the beginning, and abode not in the truth, because there is no truth in him. When he speaketh a lie, he speaketh of his own: for he is a liar, and the father of it.

Joh 8:45 And because I tell you the truth, ye believe me not.

Joh 8:46 Which of you convinceth me of sin? And if I say the truth, why do ye not believe me?

Joh 8:47 He that is of God heareth God's words: ye therefore hear them not, because ye are not of God.

No One Is Righteous

Rom 3:10 As it is written, There is none righteous, no, not one:

Rom 3:11 There is none that understandeth, there is none that seeketh after God.

Rom 3:12 They are all gone out of the way, they are together become unprofitable; there is none that doeth good, no, not one.

Rom 3:13 Their throat is an open sepulchre; with their tongues they have used deceit; the poison of asps is under their lips:

Rom 3:14 Whose mouth is full of cursing and bitterness:

Rom 3:15 Their feet are swift to shed blood:

Rom 3:16 Destruction and misery are in their ways:

Rom 3:17 And the way of peace have they not known:

Rom 3:18 There is no fear of God before their eyes.

Do Not Love the World

1Jn 2:15 Love not the world, neither the things that are in the world. If any man love the world, the love of the Father is not in him.

1Jn 2:16 For all that is in the world, the lust of the flesh, and the lust of the eyes, and the pride of life, is not of the Father, but is of the world.

1Jn 2:17 And the world passeth away, and the lust thereof: but he that doeth the will of God abideth forever.

Jas 4:4 Ye adulterers and adulteresses, know ye not that the friendship of the world is enmity with God? whosoever therefore will be a friend of the world is the enemy of God.

1Jn 3:13 Marvel not, my brethren, if the world hate you.

I'm looking forward to the day, when this life is swallowed up in victory, and I'm standing on heaven's shores; never to see people suffering, in pain, being tortured and killed, liars, thieves, and robbers getting away with their evil deeds. When I'm in a place where righteousness reigns-forever.

Into the late eighties, the Lord began to open doors of opportunity for me in the area of writing, computing, and editing. A job opened at a local legal publishing corporation. They published law books for the state of Vermont, and other states, and provinces of the United States. I saw that God was using the time I went through the correspondence courses in the writer's guild in Atlanta, ten years earlier, as a stepping stone for this opportunity. It was a very challenging, and rewarding job. It gave me many of the skills and abilities I've used in the websites, and writing I do now. I worked at this job almost seven years, starting as a proofreader, and moving into computer typesetting, and some editing.

During the years I worked there, I also worked part time on weekends doing home health care for the elderly, our lives were very busy. Carrie was in college, and living at the campus.

Lynn went through several minor surgeries during this time, and had a couple of episodes of heart trouble also. Several times I'd come home around midnight from work, to find all the lights on in the house, but no one there. He had driven himself to the hospital. I'd call there to see if he'd made it, and if he needed me to come down, to be with him. I never knew what I would come home to find, and prayed throughout those days and nights, for the strength and wisdom to know what to do. I clung to the Lord in my everyday trials, and learned to lean on him for everything; and do to this day.

One day one of his doctors from the hospital called and wanted to talk to me. He asked how I was doing. I was honest, and said sometimes it was all I could do to keep going; and just learned to deal with life as it came. He then asked if there was anything I might be able to say to Lynn, to persuade him to take better care of himself. He had gone back to eating a poor diet, a lot of fatty foods, and drinking again. To my dismay, he also had started using tobacco again-this time chewing it. The men he associated with didn't help him one bit-their influence was a major cause of a lot of trouble for us, throughout our entire marriage. I listened to the doctor, and replied that many times I'd tried to talk to him, to no avail. If I knew of anything to say or do; I'd surely do it. He understood my situation, and said if I ever needed somebody to talk to, give him a call, and gave me his number. This was a small bit of compassion from someone who didn't have to get involved, but did. It made a difference for me, and helped me keep going; and try to keep doing the right thing, and not give up.

Then, the owner of the publishing corporation decided to sell it to another company, and from there, it went through a series of renovations, and leadership changes, which brought on the end of this law book publishing company. I watched as those in higher leadership made decisions to bring in very expensive new computers, and a whole new system set up, costing millions of dollars. Within a very short time, we were told they had decided to move the company to another state. I, along with many others became a statistic, and given the option to either move with the company, or take a severance payment, and lose our jobs. I saw firsthand the demise of a company, by mismanagement. Whether it was intentional or not, only God knows. But, the results for most of us, was the loss of a good job, and not much prospect of being able to find another one like it. In my opinion, it was a combination of corruption, a lot of self-interests, and those in power making as much profit as they could, with tax write offs - it's my opinion, I've a right to it, and will stick with it. The last day of work was July fourteen 1994.

The next morning, after my last day, Lynn could see I was sad, and asked if I'd like to go somewhere after he returned from work that afternoon. I wished him a good day, and said I'd think about it. I sat in my chair looking out over our pond, and watched him go out the driveway. I must have fallen asleep, and began to dream. But it was not just a dream; it was a vision of my future. Below is the account of that day, July 16, 1994, from my journal:

July 16, 1994 - It is late evening, and I'm still reeling from something that happened earlier today. My mind is boggled, and my spirit is torn in many directions. I'm having a hard time believing what happened to me, and don't think anyone else would at all.

I feel I must try to put this down, but even as I start, there are no words that will do justice to what I've seen, and heard.

A Trip To Heaven

I sat in a recliner late this morning, feeling sorry for myself, and very despondent. Two days ago, I had worked my last day as a legal proofreader for a law book publishing company. I'd been there quite a few years, and along with many others were given the option of moving with the company out of state, or taking our retirement, or severance pay, and leaving. I had to leave, and now my life looked like a blank wall. Not only was I losing a good paying job, but all the benefits with it, and the fulfillment of a challenging job that I liked.

As I sat there looking out the window alone, I became drowsy, and noticed the clock on my piano said 11:35 a.m., then I must have gone into sleep.

Then, I woke up. But instead of being in my living room, I was standing in the middle of a very wide gravel road. Four or five cars could have lined up across it, and along the road were columns of huge trees, and their branches went over the road, making a canopy over it, but I noticed that sunlight still came brightly onto the road.... there was no shadows from the branches. These trees were so large, it would take perhaps 10 men reaching and touching hand to hand to circle them. (I'm trying very hard not to exaggerate)

The sun was warm, but not oppressive, there were amazing smells, aromas of flowers; like light perfume. I was so amazed at what I saw, I could hardly take it in.

To my left, thru the avenue of trees, I saw the land open up and gently slope downwards revealing a very large body of water, like a huge pond. The water was still and calm. Flowering bushes, trees, and flowers were along the banks, I could see pathways thru them and places to sit right next to the water. The water had all kinds of water fowl, ducks, geese, and swans.... which I've always loved.

The colors were brighter than anything I've ever seen, but not unpleasant. As I continued to try to take this in, I became aware that I was barefoot. I always loved being barefoot, and walking in sand. Looking down, I noticed the gravel was very fine, like gold dust, and felt wonderful between my toes. I stooped down, and picked some up, letting it go thru my fingers. It was like the finest of gold, but as it poured out of my hand, it made no cloud, or fumes in the air. It was pleasantly warm to the touch.

I stood up again, and then noticed that there was someone standing to my left, and slightly behind me. It was a man, tall, very quiet. He was serious, but with great peace. His hair was dark, as well as his eyes. He stood silently observing me, allowing me to have these moments to myself. But, as I gazed upon him, I knew he was my angel, and somehow I knew him, and that we knew each other well. I recognized his spirit, but didn't know how.

I thought to myself "what am I doing here, and where am I?" In my mind the angel answered me "This is heaven, I'm going to take you to your home." I was speechless. I looked ahead of me, and now noticed that about 100 ft. away was a carriage with two horses harnessed to it, and a silent driver waiting in the front seat, with his back to us. The horses stood in complete calmness and obedience. They were the most beautiful matched pair I'd ever seen. Their color was like a new copper penny, and their manes and tails flaxen blond, and they were exactly the same size.

The angel spoke to my mind again "they are waiting for us, we need to get in, and go with them."

We both stepped up into the carriage, and sat down behind the silent driver. The seat was beautiful deep royal blue velvet, the floor deep rich red. Golden ornaments were on the carriage but not overdone. It was magnificent.

As the driver lifted the reins, the horses started in unison. He never had to say or do anything more. They seemed to know exactly what to do, and did it with complete calmness. I looked down and noticed they had no shoes on their feet. The angel saw my expression and in my mind he said "There is no need for shoes, there will never be anything to harm them here."

Moving along the avenue I looked to my left. Between the trees I saw sloping hills, and pastures sectioned off, and animals in them. Each kind of animal was in their own area. Some like cows in one, sheep in another, and many many horses. Some of the pastures were open and vacant, with beautiful flowering bushes hedging them. The greens were so numerous it was amazing to see them flow together. I could hear and see birds of many varieties I'd never seen before flying in flocks, and playing in the air.

The hills went on as far as the eye could see, and beyond that, magnificent mountains far in the horizon. I was overwhelmed with the beauty and harmony everywhere. Everything was in perfect proportion, nothing out of place.

It seemed we drove for a long time, the road gently started to curve to the left, bordering the water and still the avenue of huge trees. Then suddenly the scene changed, we came to the end of the lines of trees and the road opened up to the panorama before us, the land to the left still sloped to the pond, but more open with lawns and well placed small gardens along its borders. The open fields to the right continued on and on. Directly in front of us, I saw a building. As we approached it, I noticed again it was in perfect proportion to its surroundings. It was a two story structure, white, a semicircular entry with columns in front of it. The steps were also semicircular, seven steps to the door. They were double doors, dark green, with gold fixtures. There were high windows on each side with green shutters. The shape of the home was rectangle, with four windows in the front (two at each side of the door) at the lower and second levels. The gravel avenue came up within just a few feet of the sloping lawn in front of the home, and a walkway of a few steps to the door.

The driver stopped at the front, and the angel got down first. As I stepped down, I noticed that now I had simple gold sandals on my feet, they fit perfectly. We went up the steps, the door opened and stepping thru..... I was speechless. The foyer was huge and open to the second floor, and was domed. The dome above me was beautifully sculpted stained glass of many colors that streamed lights of color to the entire entry. As they hit the floor they mingled in a spectacular fashion, like a kaleidoscope. But this was not irritating or extreme, it was beautiful, and was full of life.

The floor was muted milky marble, and there were muted gray marble columns bordering the circle of the foyer. Beyond this, there were two stairways bordering the walls on each side. They arched to the floor like a graceful skirt, with iron railings beautifully designed. These two stairways met at the second floor with a walkway between them and beyond I could see that there were floor to ceiling windows on the far wall which looked to the outside and the back of the home. This made the home very light and appear even larger. There were doorways on each side of the foyer on both levels, and I could see they were rooms of different kinds.

Below to the left a room like a reading, and music room combined. Beautiful furniture, a fireplace, instruments that looked like they had been used often. One, like a cello, leaned on a chair very invitingly. The walls were lined with bookcases to the ceiling, filled with volumes. The windows looked out over the country, and each scene was one of peace, and serenity. The appointments and colors were perfect.

To the right, there was a dining room. A long table with many chairs, and upholstered seats. Flowers were in the center of the table, and looked vibrant with life.

On the second floor, the rooms were like bedrooms. They each had private setting places looking out over the gardens, and the mountains beyond. The colors were soft, muted, and calming to the soul. The patterns in the fabrics complimented the styles of the rooms but there was imagination, and surprising details making the room inviting and interesting.

On the first floor, beyond the foyer it was open to the back. More windows were there looking out onto a formal garden, with stone walkways within it. Flowers, bushes, roses, birds, climbing vines with beautiful flowers framed the outside of the windows. The aromas were rich, and deep.

But, one of the most amazing things in this home was within the walls that the staircases lined. The walls themselves were huge two story aquariums! They both were full of fish of every kind, some I'd never seen before. As I looked upon them, they came up as close to the glass as they could and in my mind I heard them say to me "hey, come on in and play with us. We're glad you're here!" I could hardly believe what I heard.... but then all of a sudden I was in the water with them! But I didn't get wet, they swam around me with joy, and I swam with them enjoying every minute of it. Some of them were huge, the same size as me, but they were like pets. I noticed the angel still in the foyer, with a big smile on his face. There seemed to be no borders to the back of these aquariums.... they seemed to go on forever. I couldn't figure this out, and decided not to try.

Suddenly, I was back in the foyer with the angel, and was not wet. I looked up and wondered to myself, "how high is this foyer?" The angel answered me again in my mind "20 feet". Wow, was all I could say.

My gaze went straight ahead of me to the open windows to the garden in the back, and the double doors to it..... I felt a compulsion to go out to it. I stepped thru the doors and just stopped for what seemed like a long time and just tried to take it all in. The beauty was beyond comprehension. The garden was bordered by stone walls that went up about four feet., and trailing vines, with flowers draped over them, these walls surrounded the garden, making it an outdoor sanctuary, but it was huge. Within it the stone pathways went in several directions, and met each other at times. There were flower beds, fruit trees, and roses of many kinds. In one section a grape arbor was laden with vines and fruit, and under the arbor, an inviting bench.

I decided to take one of the stone paths to the left. While I had been in the house and upstairs, I had looked down and out and noticed that a single wide dirt road led out of the left side of this garden, and wandered over a brook, and to a huge barn in the distance, I had only been able to see the roof which was also dark green. Now, as I walked I looked for this path to lead me to the road, the angel walked along silently, but seemed to know where I was going; I could sense it. Around the bend, there it was, the road I'd seen upstairs. I decided to take it, I wanted to see this barn I had gotten a glimpse of earlier.

As I got closer I could hear the whinny of horses, they seemed to be calling to me. One especially seemed familiar to me..... and I knew it was a male horse. The road graced over the brook with a small bridge, as I crossed it, the barn came into view. It was long and narrow, white with green shutters; double doors on both ends, and stalls on both sides the full length of it. It looked to be about one hundred to a hundred and fifty feet long. The road sloped gently up to it, and as I walked along I could still hear the horses, they were greeting me, even though they hadn't seen me yet.

Then I heard a voice very familiar to me.... it was the voice of my husband coming to me from the barn. "Come on up, let me show you around." I continued walking and got to the front doors of the barn. Looking in I saw the most magnificent horses I've ever seen. They looked at me with intelligence, and as if they knew me, and shook their heads up and down in greeting. Halfway down the aisle, I saw a man bending over a piece of equipment. He stood up and turned around... It was Lynn. He smiled warmly to me, started walking to me, my heart was melting in me. He looked as he did when we first married, but even more handsome.

Suddenly, with a jolt, I heard a door slam..... and I was awake, back in the recliner in the living room. The first thing my eyes saw, was the clock. It was 3:36 in the afternoon.

My husband's steps came in from the kitchen, as he walked he said "Lorna, are you here?" I could not answer, I was frozen. He came around the corner and looked at me in the chair, then said "Are you ok? You look like you're in shock." All I could do was nod a "no". At this, he started relaying his day, while I sat there trying to come to my senses.

After a few minutes of acting like I was listening to him, I asked a crazy question, "Lynn, how high is our cathedral ceiling (which was what our living room was)". He looked at me with a question in his eyes, but answered "It is fourteen feet to the center". My mind was still in the foyer of that beautiful home.....

remembering."

Personal Notes:

There are some very interesting things I've taken note of about this visit that only God would know.

1. from a very little girl, I've had a fascination and love for tropical, and ocean fish of every kind. One of my first memories is of sitting on my Father's lap while he showed me a book of color pictures of ocean life, it was always the one I picked, to look at with me. I've been able to purchase aquariums, and have raised many kinds of tropical fish.

2. From the age of 3, horses have been another love of mine. I would sit and dream of owning Arabian horses. But I never thought I would own one. However, in 1984 I was able to purchase my first Arabian mare, and have owned several since. I also showed, trained and owned my own business for over twenty years. The Lord has blessed me beyond my dreams.

3. Green has always been my favorite color, especially for home decor.

4. My husband and I are country people, and like elbow room. We lived in a very rural setting at the end of a dead end road. Living in Northern Vermont, we both love mountains.

5. Lynn loved raising fruits, berries, and vegetables, and has done this for many years. The grounds around this house was graced with every kind of garden and fruit tree, and berry bushes in long rows, like he has had here.

6. The fact that he was already there was a prophetic message to me..... he is there now. My husband died in 2004 in my arms, of a heart attack. His military funeral was held at the Veterans cemetery in Randolph Vermont on July sixteenth, 2004-ten years to the day,

from the day I had this dream/vision.

There's many things that happened on this trip to heaven, that won't be shared. They were too personal, and would take another book, to relate.

Now, coming back to the story:

By the summer of 1994, we had several Arabians. My time became taken up with their care, and training. I began to work more extensively with two who had the most promise; Willow-now ten, and a young mare I'd bought as a foul, Naomi Roe-now four. As their abilities continued to increase, people began telling me I should show them in the show circuit. I listened, but had avoided doing that. I knew very well the tactics of those who followed the circuit; who schemed to win with envy, and jealousy. They had what I called "blue ribbon fever". There are some people who will stoop to anything to win, and I'd seen quite a bit of it just sitting and watching some of them, as a spectator at horse shows; I didn't want anything to do with it.

But, several people kept bringing it up. Then Lynn got in on it, and started trying to persuade me. I looked at him one day and said "Lynn, do you know what this would mean in terms of commitment, work, and who'd trailer these animals to all these shows?"

"Well, I've transported everything else, I guess I could transport these animals anywhere they'd need to go." He looked at me with that smile in his eyes, that I'd come to know well; he knew he had won.

So, I talked to the Lord about it, and knew it was His will. Then spent some time planning how to start a training program for the two we'd show, and went about putting this goal into my daily focus. I decided to aim for a regimen of at least schooling them five days a week, (rain or shine, or snow) sometimes more-until they were skilled enough to attempt putting them into a show ring. There are no shortcuts to a well-trained animal. It takes the commitment, focus, and hard work to spend quality training time, and know how to form a bond with the horse, so you both go into the ring with your minds working together-and that animal has a desire to give you the performance it's capable of, in willing obedience.

There were many precious memories of working with these animals, but one I'll share now, had nothing to do with showing; but everything to do with the simple joy of having them, and doing the unusual.

During the summers, and several times during a harvest moon in early fall, Lynn would harness Willow on a clear night, and a full moon, and we'd drive her up the dirt roads to places we knew, that overlooked mountain ranges-and stop and just gaze out over the landscape, and the beauty of the full moon shining down on the panorama before us. This was Lynn's idea of having a great time, and I agreed. These are the kind of memories couples need to make for themselves in their marriages-that makes a bond between them, that nothing can break. And, it's these kinds of memories, and enjoyment together, that costs nothing but the ambition to do it.

The first year of showing began in 1995, and the season ended in October with Willow earning several driving championships, and Naomi a reserve championship in Arabian Western Pleasure. I was happy with this outcome, being the first year. My goal for the next two years was to win the state championship with both of them, in their respective classes, and they did. In 1997, Naomi Roe won the state championship in Arabian Western Pleasure, and English pleasure. Willow won the state championship in driving-with Lynn doing the driving. Several more championships were won over the next few years, until I retired them in the year 2000. However, while these blessings took place, there was also ongoing problem situations and attacks in our family life, that many face.

The influence of people who bring disruption, their own evil agenda's, and turmoil. People who do not know the Lord, and haven't surrendered their lives to Him, are often what the devil uses, to destroy families. In my life, he's used unsaved, and uncommitted people to bring a lot of trouble, but we're told to expect it in this life:

> 2Ti 3:12 Yea, and all that will live godly in Christ Jesus shall suffer persecution.
>
> Act 14:22 Confirming the souls of the disciples, and exhorting them to continue in the faith, and that we must through much tribulation enter into the kingdom of God._

Carrie had come home from college, moved into a place of her own, and found work locally. One day she came to visit with a young man, introduced him to me, and let me know she loved him. He relayed his life, as much as he felt I needed to know; and also pulled out his wallet, showing me a picture of his young toddler son-from a woman he was not married to. I looked at Carrie, but said nothing. I looked back at him and said "I don't know what your situation is with the boy's Mother, but, don't you do this to my daughter." He knew exactly what I meant, and looked away, out the window.

I looked at Carrie, and in front of him said to her "Carrie, we raised you different than this. I hold nothing personally against this man, but he has a son already, by another woman between them. She is not married to anyone else right now, he's admitted this. If he really wants to do the right thing, he should seriously work on building a relationship with his son's Mother, and they should marry, and give that boy a family, and raise him and give him a home. What you're expecting me to approve of, I cannot. I don't believe the Lord will bless any relationship you have with him, because of the child he already has by the other woman. Carrie, you've professed being a Christian since the age of seven. You know better than to do this, I can't let you do it, without telling you how God see's this."

Her anger was evident, and the reply was one I expected "Mom, I'm not doing anything wrong with him, but we care for each other, and I'm going to keep going with him. My pastor says we need to forgive them, and says it's ok to go with each other, as long as there's no sex, until we marry."

"Your pastor is using his own human reasoning, and not seeing the whole picture of this. He's not thinking about that son, who needs two parents to raise him; if they would put aside their selfishness, and do the right thing, and marry each other, and give him a home-this is what God would approve of, and bless."

They both looked at each other, headed for the door, and left.

Over the next several month's the leadership of the church she attended continued to counsel them both that it was ok to stay in their relationship, and marry. I would not agree. Of course, Carrie took the counsel and advice from them, and they began making plans to marry. When the church women put on a wedding shower for her, I was not invited.

On a Saturday morning in July of that year, God gave me a dream/warning about Carrie's relationship with this man. In the dream, he was having his way with her-and looked up, and looking straight at me said "This is what I'm going to do to her, and there's nothing you can do about it. Then, as the dream went on, I heard a deep voice-which was the Lord's say to me "They will marry anyway, but it will only last three years." I awoke, my heart heavy as a rock. Then I heard the small voice of the Lord. "Get up, go to her once, and warn her what I've said and shown you."
I got up and drove to her apartment. She let me in, but I could see

she didn't want to hear what I had to say, before I even started. I relayed the dream, and what the Lord had said to me, then spoke my thoughts.

"I've come here Carrie, to try to warn you, that you're in for a lot of grief, and heartache, if you insist on doing this. I can't force you to listen, but I'll just tell you now, God wants you to stay with His word, and think about that little boy. They should do the right thing, and raise him together."

"Mom, I love him, and I'm going to marry him."

I left, and stayed away from then on. They planned a wedding for New Years eve, and let me know their pastor was going to do the service. His wife was greatly involved, along with several other women, in planning this without asking for my help. After Christmas of that year, I asked my brother, and he helped me do the work involved getting a church ready for the service, and the reception directly afterwards, downstairs in the basement of the sanctuary. Many of the people there knew the discord among us. Many I had known for years, took sides with the pastor and his wife-I was the outsider.

The final church service I attended after the wedding, the pastor's wife stood on the platform, and prayed a mother's blessing over Carrie and her new husband-taking my place; instead of calling me up to the front to pray for her. I stood up while she was still "praying", and with many eyes on me from the pew sitter's, walked out, and never returned.

During this ongoing situation, Lynn watched and said nothing, until the wedding was over. Then one night when we were home alone, seeing the sadness on my face, he looked at me and said "Watching this stuff go on among so-called Christians is why it's hard for me to believe it's real. Those people had no business telling Carrie what she was doing was right. They don't even believe the

Bible themselves, if they did, they never would have agreed to do what they did. It was wrong. I don't even claim to be a "Christian", and can see the wrong of this."

It took me a few minutes to say anything, but the Lord helped me find the words to answer him. "Lynn, we can't blame God for what people do, He's not to blame. I have to keep reminding myself of this too. One day they'll answer for what they did. I have to leave it alone now, and let Him take care of it, no matter how I feel."

He looked at me with the same matter-of-fact manner he always did, nodded, then went out to the barn. I watched him out the window, knowing he'd work on his wood projects, and get it out of his system that way. I decided to get on a horse, and take a long ride, and do the same thing; get it out of my system.

In relaying this part of our life, I'm giving the parents point of view; the reader can do with it what they want. I was brought up in a large family. Our parents loved us, but they didn't excuse us when we did wrong. We were punished, and if we intentionally disrespected our elders, or lied or stole anything, we were made to make restitution-and were taken to the person we stole from, and had to return it. There's a fine line between loving a kid-and idolizing them, and putting them on a pedestal. A lot that's wrong with society today, is there's many adults walking around who were raised to be spoiled brats, and they never grew up. These kind of people are the bullies, the arrogant loud mouthed people who have no sense of respect for others, and will do anything to get their way. We see the evidence of it everywhere. Many of them are the evil leaders of nations, and institutions. The meek, and the quiet among us live with the results of the evil policies these lawless people put in place-and rule over us.

I'm very aware this doesn't sit well with many. I'm used to being hated for making a stand for what is right, and what I believe in. When you have kids, and they get to a certain age, when you tell them "no" you'll start feeling their hatred, and it may last a life time. God doesn't give us kids to be their buddies, he tells us to train them in the way they should go;

> Pro 22:6 Train up a child in the way he should go: and when he is old, he will not depart from it.

Samuel describes the evidence of a righteous upbringing:

> 1Sa 12:2 And now, behold, the king walketh before you: and I am old and gray headed; and, behold, my sons are with you: and I have walked before you from my childhood unto this day.
>
> 1Sa 12:3 Behold, here I am: witness against me before the LORD, and before his anointed: whose ox have I taken? or whose ass have I taken? or whom have I defrauded? whom have I oppressed? or of whose hand have I received any bribe to blind mine eyes therewith? and I will restore it you._

We see a lot of evidence today, that most don't go by this counsel. There's kids killing their parents and other kids today, just because they don't get what they want, or are told "no" about something. In the last ten years, I've been harassed, cursed and spit at, and treated with total disrespect by kids, and young people, who I do not even know, and never had any association with; but have received the brunt of the effect of those who are raising them. When I was taking care of seniors, many told me stories of being treated the same way, and it's why many seniors become recluses.

Among this turmoil, other things began to evolve at the same time, bringing more pressure, and grief. Lynn's father passed away, leaving his elderly mother to keep watch of. We both took care of our parents on a regular basis. Now, it would take up more of our time, and cause significant changes in our lives. My mother was diagnosed with cervical cancer, that caused me to have to make regular trips back and forth to New York, helping care for her. I had applied to enter nursing school before this, and was scheduled to start that fall, but had to cancel it, and never able to follow through with it; because of the commitment to care for her. Lynn saw the toll this was taking on me, and said nothing. But he was a source of strength again, that helped me get through it. More was coming our way, it was a good thing we could only see one day at a time. Then Lynn's Mother came down with ovarian cancer. It began a long siege of him taking turns with his sister, to help care for her. This went on for almost a year, and he was with her when she passed away at her home. We were putting one foot in front of the other, and doing what had to be done. We both had learned to be people of responsibility, dealing with what was in front of us. But, sometimes we'd go someplace for a day, and just support each other, with silent love.

For the next two years, I rarely saw my daughter. It was just as well. Then, about the last quarter of their second year of being married, Carrie started coming to visit alone, letting me know some of the things going on with them. It wasn't good. I listened, but said nothing. I let her do the talking, while I silently I prayed.

Then in the first part of their third year, they separated. She began getting involved with other Christian people in another area, and eventually moved closer to the new people she hooked up with. She came once after she'd left her husband for good, and let me know her plans. Again, I put my foot in my mouth and said what I knew God would want, even though I knew it would be useless. "If you leave, and don't try to make this marriage work, now that you've made the commitment; you're doing it out of the will of

God. You know this is the case, but I have to tell you the truth, and make you face it, whether you want to hear it or not. I'm sure you're getting different counsel from your new friends you're involved with now."

Again, the expected anger. "I didn't think you'd understand, I won't come to bother you again about this. I have to make the decisions for my life, and these people are willing to help me get a new start." "I'm sure they are. I'll just remind you, I tried to warn you before you ever married him, to not do it. God told me it wouldn't last more than three years. I'm seeing it being played out in front of my eyes. These new people you're involved with, are just more influence, coming at a time the devil had planned for you. But, I'll believe God, that in this case; all things will work together for good, even if I can't see how right now. You are old enough and responsible now for your own future. I hope the best for you."

She looked at me, and left. There was nothing more to be said.

By this time, as Lynn watched this, the only thing he said to me was "If I were you, I'd stay as far away from whatever they do, as possible."

I agreed with him, and did.

In the last part of 1996, we decided to sell our house, and purchase some land and build a retirement home. He wanted to raise cattle. I hoped to continue to give riding lessons, and raise and train Arabians. Some family members felt this was only my idea, and that I was influencing Lynn to do it. The truth was, he'd wanted to do it long before me, and brought it up to me several times, years earlier. But, when people put their noses in your business, most of the time it's best to just let them believe what they want. The only remedy for gossip, is shut the door, lock it, and keep the troublemakers out. This is my approach to it most of the time.

When I found this piece of land, and walked over the field alone to a knoll that overlooked the landscape before me, the presence of the Lord enveloped me, and my mind went clearly back to when I was a small girl-and the dream I was given. It was vividly repeated as I stood there. I remembered the fields below, and the deep voice behind me as we traveled through the air above the fields; and being told one day I'd be living in Vermont. Then, I began to be told the rest of the dream, the part I couldn't understand as a little girl. The Holy Spirit relayed that a deeper service to Him would begin here, and continue the rest of my life. I indeed had lived in Vermont twenty years now with Lynn; but this was a significant turn in the road for us both. We purchased this twenty acre field, mostly open; and started the foundation.

One morning, while we were still in the house in East Corinth, as I sat at the kitchen table over breakfast; I decided to spend the day just doing something for the fun of it, got out my watercolor set and began to paint. As the day progressed, a picture developed on the page of a horse and rider traveling through the night- something very different from anything I'd ever done before.

THE NIGHTWATCHMAN

As it was finished, I sensed the presence of the Lord, and heard in my heart "You're the rider in this picture. I call you the Night Watchman. From a child, I've called you to be a watchman for me in these end of days. When you finish it, give it this name." It now hangs in my office, with the "NightWatchman" under it.

In the early spring of 1997, work on the house began, with a lot of planning and people involved. There was no spare time for anything, all our attention was spent on getting it done. At the end of the year, the house was finished enough to move into, just before Christmas. We had hopes of our lives slowing down, but it was not to be.

My Mother had recovered from cancer, and taken a trip to Alabama to visit one of my two older sister's. While she was there, a sore developed on her foot, and became infected. From what I was told, by the time the doctor's decided something needed to be done, it became so bad, part of her foot need to be amputated. The large toe, and ball of the foot. They sent her home to my sister with no antibiotics. The foot became badly infected. They became exhausted, trying to care for her, and at a loss to really know what to do. They called me saying they needed me to come as soon as possible, they needed help. Lynn and I had been in our new house less than two years.

I got a bus ticket and went down there. Lynn took me to the station, we embraced and he said not to worry, he'd take care of things while I was gone. He came on the bus with me, put my bags in the overhead hatch, and looked at me with that determined look "Be careful, and don't let strangers get near you." Our hands locked for a minute, then he left.

Seventeen hours later, I stood at a bus station in Alabama waiting for my niece to pick me up. I was weary. Already it was hot and muggy, and it was still morning. She found me, helped me put my bags in the back of her car, and we headed to her mother's. While on the way, she explained where my mother was, and what the doctors were planning to do. I just listened. I needed to see the foot myself, to be able to tell what it really looked like. I'd taken care of many serious situations like this in nursing homes. Just seeing it would give me a good idea what had to be done.

My two sister's greeted me when I made it to their house. We ate lunch they'd prepared for us, and they shared about Mom's condition. Then I spent the rest of the day getting some rest, before they took me to see her.

When we arrived at the hospital, Mother was very quiet, but glad to see me. Discouragement had set in. I could see it. I asked if the doctors were going to let her come back to my sister's house soon.

She said perhaps, if the infection could be taken care of. I asked to look at it.

A nurse's assistant came in, and I again asked to see the foot. She unwrapped the bandages. It was as I thought, a wound that had not been properly routinely cleansed, and infection due to a buildup of bacteria; a case of neglect.

Holding back my fury, in a low calm voice, I asked to see a nurse in charge of her care. Several minutes went by, finally a woman came in. I asked "How soon can my Mother be released to be brought to my sister's. I have the ability to care for her there, and would like an appointment made soon with her doctor to go over what should be done for a serious regimen of care, to get the foot healed."

"I'll look into it." She left and went back to the desk.

I spent the rest of the time visiting with Mother, asking questions, and telling her about things we were doing at home, to keep her mind in good spirits. I didn't let on to her, the utter disgust that was going through me; to see her in this condition, and know it was totally unnecessary. My mind began planning for making changes, as soon as possible.

The nurse came back, and said she'd called the doctor. He told her she could get papers ready, and let me take Mother back to my sister's house if I was going to be there for her continuing care. I said I was, so she left to get the papers ready to sign her out. I went to the closet, got the things Mother needed to get dressed, helped her to the toilet, and with her private needs, helped her get dressed, then my niece and I took her home. She was totally wheelchair bound. My heart was aching seeing how small, and frail she looked, and what this had done to her.

When we arrived, my sister had a room ready. We got Mother comfortable in the bed, gave her a cup of tea and a light lunch. I dressed the foot; and within minutes, she was asleep.

Back in the kitchen, my sister's asked me what I thought should be done. I said the doctor needed to refer her to a clinic or hospital that knew about wound care, and transfer her care to that kind of facility, or she would be in danger of dying. They said they'd get onto it in the morning, and tell the doctor what I said. "I hope you do tell him, he needs to know somebody sees and understands how bad this situation is. Maybe then, something will get done for her." Within a few days an appointment was set up for her at a hospital two hours away, that had a wound care section. One of my sister's did the driving. I rode along, with Mother in the back seat. When we found the office, a nurse called Mother for her appointment. I went in with her to hear what the doctor said, and get directions on what to do for her at home.

After the doctor examined her, and took tests, he came back and said he wasn't sure they could save the rest of the foot. They may have to amputate the rest of it, to the ankle. In my spirit the Lord said "No, don't let them do that. Follow the regimen he gives, and have them plan for a visiting nurse to help you for her care at home. She will heal."

"I'm willing to do whatever is necessary to treat the wound, and do her daily care. Can a visiting nurse be assigned to her, and come to our house, and train me to do what needs to be done?"

He looked at me and could see I was serious. "Yes, if you are willing to go that far. We can set up a nurse to come daily at first if needed, and also make sure you have all the medical supplies you'll need for the wound care, and medications."

"I'd like to go this route, and start as soon as possible."

Hearing this, he went on, and gave a brief overview of her condition, and what needed to be done. When the great toe of her foot had been removed, along with the ball of her foot, they had left it a gaping wound. No stitches, no medication of any kind, and no antibiotics. They sent her home in this condition, and because of the depth of the wound, developed puss from not being able to clean it completely. My sisters did the best they could, but didn't realize the extent of the wound, nor how to completely clean it; which is how infection took hold. He prescribed a port to be put into her chest, and an intravenous antibiotic would be pumped into her body every day. The gaping wound would be completely cleansed there that day by nurses, then packed with moist medicated gauze strips, and enough of these strips would be given to me, to take home and start a regimen of cleaning the wound every night, and replacing the gauze every time; packing it into the wound, to promote healing, and eventually it would close. The next day, the nurse arrived at the house, and began training me how to set up the intravenous tube into the port and how to monitor it to make sure nothing went wrong. This was to begin a daily schedule, with twice a week visits to the wound center for the next three weeks, then once a week, if the wound showed signs of healing. In all, it took six weeks to bring the wound to the place of being almost completely closed, and no sign of infection left. When we got to this point, my sisters talked about the best thing to do for Mother. Whether she should stay with them, and care for her, or she come home with me. I could see the apprehension on their faces. They didn't feel capable of doing this, but didn't want to say it. I knew what had to be done.

"I'll call Lynn, and have him set us up with plane tickets to Boston. He can pick us up there, and we'll bring her home. She'll be close to New York then, and be able to visit with her sister, when she's finally completely healed."

The relief was evident on their faces. They said they were grateful, and would make sure we were at the airport, and take care of everything for us, when we got ready to leave.

The arrangements were made, and when the plane landed in

Boston, Mother walked off the plane, with the help of a cane. I spent the time on the plane thanking the Lord silently for His goodness, and answered prayer for her healing. She had gone from totally wheelchair bound, to being able to navigate again on her own two feet. To God be the glory.

Lynn was standing waiting for us in the exit section where our plane was to unload. He got our bags, and took us to the car. I stood for a moment, enjoying the fresh, New England air. The almost two months in Alabama in over ninety degree muggy weather convinced me, I'd never be a southerner.

We arrived home in the early evening. God had won this battle; we spent the next few days in needed rest.

From this point on, Mother stayed with us. As she continued to improve, and there came times I'd take her back to her mobile home in New York, and she'd enjoy staying there for a few weeks at a time, but not any longer. She had diabetes and needed ongoing medical care, and her doctors were here in Vermont. Eventually, the mobile home had to be sold, and she was here permanently.

Shortly after this, I began working at a local retirement home, doing the night shift again. I was able to be home during the day with Mother and Lynn, work with my horses and give lessons; and still work during the night hours. Over the years I had developed a pattern of work, work, and more work. Eventually it would catch up with me, but I was now on a treadmill, and blind to what was happening to me.

During these night hours, after the residents had gone to their rooms for the night, many times I'd take my Bible, and study at the dining table under the lamplight. This way I could hear anything if someone needed help. At these times, He would show me things regarding national events, leaders he wanted prayer for, and how to pray for them. This was a ministry between God and I, of prayer, intercession, and fasting as He led. Several times during these years, I was shown things that would happen, and told I'd see them on national TV. Within a short time, I would.

From this pattern developed in my life, I do not depend on human reasoning for the answers to problems, or seek a position. God uses people to achieve His plans, but no one is any more special to him than another. If one person refuses to obey, and God wants something accomplished; he'll use somebody else, who will. He never forces anyone to follow Him, or obey Him.

By then end of 1998, Carrie let us know the divorce they filed for was finalized. She was now living on her own again. I just listened, and gave it to the Lord, asking Him to have His way. I had surrendered her, and the situation to Him, and put her in His hands.

Life was busy with the routine of training the horses, giving lessons, working, and caring for Mom. She had ongoing medical needs, and appointments to continue taking care of her foot, and controlling the diabetes.

Lynn became involved with neighbor's and their activities. I didn't have the time. When I did have any free time, it was used doing something at home, or getting some rest. As he continued to interact with these people, I began to notice a lack of interest in driving Willow, or involvement with the other horses. I sensed this was the probably due to things said by them. He was being drawn away; spending more time gone, doing things with them. I kept this to myself, it was his decision. I'd wait, and see how things progressed. I couldn't handle any more stress now. I just prayed about it, and trusted the Lord.

One afternoon Carrie called, and spoke of wanting to come for a visit. It had been a about a year since I'd heard from her. She asked when would be a good day. I said we were usually always here, to come anytime, just call ahead first. She said ok, saying it would probably be the following weekend.

When she came, she had a man with her. I could see this was again, a meeting for my "approval." She introduced him to us, and said his name was Richard Welch.

We went to the house, and sat in the living room. As she talked, and introduced him to me, a memory of a dream I'd had when I was the prayer chairman for the women's fellowship in the eighties came back to my mind. As I continued to look at him, I remembered the Lord had given me a picture of this man in my mind back then; when God had asked me to begin praying for men to be raised up in Vermont, and a ministry for men to be started. As I listened to him, I knew the Lord was showing me the beginning of the answer to those prayers.

He spoke of his addiction to drugs, and how his son brought him to Teen Challenge for help. He shared his salvation, and recovery; and now he had been working, traveling with a choir in the New England area for about ten years. He spoke of moving to this area, and being involved in the church Carrie was going to, and his desire to work with men. I listened, and felt the presence of the Lord. As he continued, the pieces of the puzzle came together, I did not share this with them, but kept listening.

After they left, Lynn said "You're not going to get involved in this, are you?"

"No, but I'm not going to shut the door to her either."

He understood, and we said no more about it.

They started coming occasionally, and their relationship, as I expected, became serious. I attended a service at their church in the early spring of 2001. They had a guest speaker that morning.

After the service was over he said if anyone wanted prayer, to come forward. Carrie and Rick went forward together. As he prayed for them, they held hands; and both of them went back to the floor, still holding hands. I saw this as a sign from God, of His bonding them together-in life, and ministry. It has proved to be the case to this day.

When this man was done praying for them, he turned around, looked at me, and pointed and said "God has called you to teach His word, with power."

He never touched me, but I went to the floor on my back. I opened my eyes to see my daughter and future son in law looking down at me.

Shortly after this, they let us know they planned to marry and live in the same area. I asked Carrie if she would like a wedding at our home. If so, I'd plan a lawn service, with a reception in the house afterwards. They agreed, and we began making arrangements. We located an open tent, and I ordered the cake, and made some of the meals to be served at the reception. Carrie's pastor's agreed to do the wedding ceremony. They set the date for September 1, 2001. Their ceremony was an all-day event. The house and yards were full of people, many from her church, and Rick's friends, family and ministry people he knew, who came and joined us.

They left that evening for their honeymoon, planning to go to Virginia. We wished them well. We had no way of knowing, that just eleven days later, we'd be watching the disaster in New York, of the Twin Towers destroyed, and the Pentagon hit.

I've come to see the significance of these events, as years have gone by. They were the beginnings I believe, of the destruction of this country from sources inside this government, called the "deep state". The entire thing was an inside job. They are committed to put into place what they call the "New World Order", and now 20 years later, we are seeing it being played out in front of us every day. It's plain, for those who have eyes to see. We are in the end of days, and this "New World Order", is going to end in the coming of Jesus Christ

After they returned from their honeymoon, they came for a visit and told us what it was like driving through the area, and the chaos they saw. They relayed the burning buildings, the massive destruction in New York City, and the atmosphere among the people as they drove to Virginia, and back.

Life at home for us the next couple of years was a steady routine. I worked nights at the retirement home, and days training horses and giving lessons. Mother was with us most of the time, unless I took her to New York for a couple of weeks. At this time, the Lord began speaking to me about several leaders, and directed me to pray for them specifically.

One was Benjamin Netanyahu. I was shown that one day he'd be the Prime Minister of Israel again. I put it in my journal, and added him to the list, but said nothing about it. The Lord gave several assignments also, regarding ministries here locally, to pray and fast for.

In 2003, Lynn began to lose energy, and have symptoms of trouble with his heart again. By the fall of the year, he decided to get checked at the Veterans hospital, and they said he should have another heart cauterization, but they'd have to schedule it to be done at the regional hospital; and they took care of that. They arranged for it to be done on October second 2003.

I made sure I'd have that night off, and planned to drive him there, and back home, when it was done. We were supposed to be there to sign in by 7:00 a.m., so we had to get up very early, to be there in time.
This was to be a day of destiny for us both. Below is the testimony

of his salvation, and the procedure.

From my journal:

October 2, 2003

"He agreed to have it scheduled, and for the last several weeks I could see he was heavy in thought, considering the possibility he may not make it. The doctor's had said there was a fifty percent chance he would not.

He needed to be there to fill out paperwork, then go to the same-day surgery unit. As I drove him there this morning, in the dark, I wondered if he had finally given in and talked to the Lord. There had been a number of times through the years that I had brought the subject up, hoping he would soften and accept Christ, but the response had always been the same-no. Now he was facing the possibility of this being his last day on this earth. My heart was heavy-almost twenty seven years of praying, and still no sign of change in his heart.

In a short time they had the paperwork prepared, and he was directed to a very small cubicle with curtains around it with a narrow cot and one chair.

He undressed-I took the chair. As he laid down on the cot, we chatted, then sat in silence, both of us thinking our own thoughts and watching the staff and other people in for various minor surgeries. I sensed a somber seriousness in Lynn that was not usually there. A nurse came in and inserted an intravenous needle in each arm. Shortly after this Lynn began to talk again, he took my hand, hesitated a few minutes, then said "You know, I do love you. I know it hasn't seemed like I do many times, but I do."

I leaned over and said "Lynn, I love you also. I have to ask you this, have you talked to the Lord about this day, and have you made things right between you?"

"Yes, I have. You may not think I have any communication with

Him, but I do."

"Are you saying, You know Jesus?" I asked.

"I believe in an Almighty Being."

I replied "Jesus said I am the way, the truth, and the life, no man comes to the Father but by Me." Do you believe in Him, or are you ashamed of His name?"

"I am not ashamed of Him" he said. Right at that point a nurse came in, breaking the conversation, and let us know it would be probably several hours more of a wait because of an emergency case being flown in by helicopter. I said nothing, but inside I felt frustrated, feeling her coming at that time was a demonic interruption, and the long delay was as well. It wasn't until the next morning, I realized that this was God's intervention to give Lynn more time to dwell on the prospects of what may happen to him-and give God more time to soften his heart. After she left, I felt it was better not to try to continue the conversation. In my heart I felt it best to wait for a while and see if another opportunity would come.

About an hour and a half later, my spirit felt an urgency again, so I brought the talk up again.

"Lynn, we were interrupted a while ago, and I need to ask you again, are you saying you believe in Jesus?"

He shook his head yes.

I stopped speaking-my spirit was seeking the presence of God. I was amazed at the response I got. Then I said "Lynn, it's a great comfort to know that no matter what happens in there, I will see you again-either here, or in heaven."

"Yes, you will see me again."

About five minutes later a nurse came in and said "I've been told to start medicating you for the procedure. They are ready to take you in." Just then a male nurse came in to move him to the surgery room. It was approximately 11:45 a.m.

God's timing is perfect.

As I waited, I was aware of the peace in my soul. I thought I'd be worried and anxious-but no, the Lord's presence was with me. Throughout the wait, at times it would hit me-Lynn is saved! Twenty seven years of praying-standing for him in faith-now swallowed up in a moment, and covered in Christ's blood.

The procedure was completed by 2:15 p.m., and they allowed me in his recovery room by 3:00 p.m. I went to a cafe downstairs and brought him something, and we ate together. Then we had to wait until 7:00 p.m., when they allowed him to leave.

I drove home with the verse going through my head "Old things are passed away, behold, all things are become new."

During the rest of that year, we talked quite a bit. He asked me a couple of times what I would do, if he died. I said I'd sell the farm, and purchase a smaller house, and sell our cattle and horses. Willow was already gone, we had to put her down that spring, because of serious inflammation in her joints. She had grown old, and was developing many health problems, and was suffering. Naomi was also retired, almost twenty now.

I knew as I listened to him, he wanted the assurance that I'd make the right decisions, and be alright. Over the years, we had melded together in such a way, that often when one of us would come into a room and look at each other, we'd know what the other was thinking, without saying anything.

We reminisced and went places together, making the best use of our time. But, sometimes when he was not feeling well, he would become irritable and I'd take a walk, or go someplace for a while.

There were times, I'd come home in the morning from working all night, and he'd be very angry at me, and I'd have no idea why. The doctor's told me to expect these mood changes, because he was dealing with end of life issues, and no matter how much we may care, there's some things people go through, that are between them, and God. Often, I'd go out to the bench looking out over the fields, and just pray for him.

The doctor's had him come in when they got the results from the cauterization, and they said what we expected. He'd lost more function of his heart. He only had about thirty five percent left, and there was more damage to the lower area, from the first heart attack. At home, he was sleeping more, and not able to lift heavy objects any more. We went home in silence. We had talked enough to know each other's thoughts. We just held hands.

One morning in late June, I came home from work, and Lynn was angry again, and again I asked him what the problem was; what had I done to him to make him this way. I wasn't prepared for what I heard.

"Have you been seeing other men, when you've gone on those weekend trips alone several times a year; that you've gotten in the habit of doing?"

I was speechless for a minute, looking at him, but finally replied. "You've known that my doctor's advised me to take those breaks because of the work schedule I keep, and caring for Mother, and trying to be here for you. I've never looked at another man, nor ever been with one. Where is this coming from, and who put this in your mind?"

"There's talk going around that you've been with somebody else." Again, the same demonic attacks against this marriage-it never ended. My stomach was churning, I was so angry, I didn't trust myself, knowing I may say something I'd regret. But, I looked him in the eye, and replied again;

"Lynn, if you can't trust me after all these years, and after you've watched me every day, and how I've lived my life-what could I possibly say, that would make any difference? But, I'll tell you this once, with God right here between us; I have never looked at, nor been anywhere with another man, and never will. You can either believe this, or not. It's your choice. I'm not going to answer this accusation again. Whoever the people are, who have put this in your ears, will answer to God for it someday. I'll be asking the Lord, to help me forgive them. Because I can't on my own."

He looked at me in silence, then went to the barn. I got in my car, and went for a ride, and prayed. Satan doesn't care where you are in life, or what you're dealing with. He'll hit you when you're already down, and kick you harder, and totally destroy you if he can. Now, I understood the mood swings, and periodic anger-he was festering with these accusations going on in his head, for a long time. Now I could put the pieces together. Certain members of the community were putting this in his mind, and Satan used them, to try to completely destroy our last span of time together, before he left this world. He was doing all he could, to break this marriage apart, even to the death.

My soul was weary, and physically exhausted from working all night. But as I sat parked looking out over a pond, I prayed and asked the Lord what to do. I heard no voice, but a surge of strength from my stomach arose, and the presence of God rose in me, and a prayer came up from deep within:

"In the name of Jesus Christ, Satan I come against you and every accusing spirit. I bind your power over my life, and my marriage. I block every accusation from the people you're using to bring this attack, and bind their mouths shut. I break every bondage from you and command you to cease your evil work in this marriage, and command every demon you're using to desist, and go to outer darkness."

I'd done this before, and knew he must heed it. I surrendered the rest of this to the Lord and asked for the strength to see this through to the end; to not let this attack destroy our final days together. When I drove up the driveway, Lynn was on the front porch, waiting for me. When I was parked he opened the door "Come on in, I've got coffee ready, and breakfast for us. Let's enjoy the morning, then you get to bed for a while, and rest." God had won this battle, again.

July eleventh 2004 was a Sunday, and most of the day was sunny and warm. I had to work that evening, and spent the day home, doing small household chores and resting, to be ready for the nights work ahead of me. Lynn had spent most of the day in his gardens, and berry patches.

At approximately quarter to three in the afternoon, a woman came to purchase some berries, and Lynn took her to the field to pick them for her. I was watering my flower gardens, and planned to be ready to go to work soon after. As I stood at the front corner of the house, I heard the woman calling for me, saying my husband had collapsed in the field, and was now at the corner of the garage. I dropped the hose, and ran around the corner. He was on the ground, his back leaning on the garage doorway. I reached for his shoulders "Lynn, don't try to get up, let me call 911".

He was determined to try to get in the house. He got up and attempted to get to the front door, but stumbled again. I held his shoulders, trying to get him to stop and sit down. He reached for the back tailgate of his truck, and collapsed again, as I continued to hold him. As soon as he fell to the ground I knew he was gone. As my hands held him, for about 10 seconds, I physically felt his spirit come up out of his body, and into mine-there's no other way to describe this. When this happened, I could not move. We were one, for those few seconds. Then I felt him go, straight upward.

I had to close his eyes, but refused to accept what had happened. I did CPR on him for seventeen minutes, until the fast squad got there, and took over. The poor customer had stayed and watched the whole thing. My heart now goes out to her; to have had to witness this. But, God has His reasons for everything, even when we don't understand. Mother was also there, feeling very helpless. I know she was reminded of her day of sorrow when she lost Dad. People in the fast squad tried to revive him, but we knew he was gone. They hooked him to oxygen and transported him to the local hospital.

A neighbor drove me, following behind the ambulance. When I went through the emergency room door, he laid on a gurney with the oxygen tube still in his mouth, and still in the soiled clothes he had been in at home from working in the fields. No one had cleaned his body, or removed the tube. Now, I was in shock, and sat beside him, not knowing how long-until a male nurse came to the other side and asked if I'd like to go to the chapel, and talk to somebody. I followed him out to the chapel. A woman minister came in and began to ask questions. I had no answers. She asked if I'd like to see him once more, before they called the funeral home, to come for him. I said yes.

After some time, they said I could go to the third floor, and gave the number of the room. I took the elevator, stepped out and went down the hall until I found the right number on the door, and went in. He laid on a single hospital bed, a sheet over his body. But the oxygen tube was still in his mouth, his body had not been cleansed, and still in the same soiled clothes he'd had on at home. I walked to his side, and said "What kind of a place is this, to let him stay like this." Now, after the years have gone by, I realize I should have went to one of the utility closets, gotten what I needed and cleaned him and removed the tube myself. But I was numb with shock. I had given this kind of care for other's in nursing homes. But now, my brain would not function.

While he was in this room, his sister and brother in law came in to see him, one last time. She also was disgusted at seeing him in that condition. But was in tears, it was not important; she had lost her brother. After a few minutes they left. I remained, for a while longer. Scenes of our married years went through my mind, as if watching a video. I was now sitting with him, finishing our last page of life together.

Looking out the window, seeing the sun was setting, I knew I had to leave. Mother was home alone. I looked at him one more time. Then turned and went out the door.

After getting back to the house, I called my sisters in Alabama, and other family members. Carrie and Rick were also contacted, they were in another state.

A ceremony was held in his home town, on July fifteenth, and the next day July sixteenth, a military funeral at the Veterans cemetery. At the family service at the funeral home, tables were set up with memorabilia and accomplishments of his life; along with photos from his childhood and our life together. At the end of the table I placed a plaque, which held a short summary of my assessment of this man:

Lyndon Gene Couillard
The Word he lived by

Proverbs 3:27 "Withhold not good from them whom it is due, when it is in the power of thine hand to do it."

Galatians 5:14 "For all the law is fulfilled in one word, even in this; Thou shalt love thy neighbor as thyself."
I, as his wife of 28 years have known him to live by these words....

always. And, as his partner thru life, have this to say of him;

Proverbs 31:23 "Her husband is known in the gates, when he sits among the elders of the land."

LYNN DRIVING WILLOW

TWELVE
PILGRIMAGE

During the last year of Lynn's life, the Holy Spirit had led me to study the book of Job and Ecclesiastes and Lamentations. These books teach us about the reality of the ebb and flow of life, of seasons of prosperity, plenty, blessing and the other side of that tide-the season of loss, suffering, mortality and death. I knew I was facing this coming my way. God had been merciful to us, and gave us time to talk about it, and make our peace with each other and the Lord. Now, I was on this pilgrim road, with God as my guide.

I've been asked if I was angry with God. If I blamed Him for the troubles and hardships in my life, or after Lynn's death. No, I don't blame God. Yes, I went through anger, frustration, as everyone does; even if they won't admit it. But when I look behind me, I see a pattern of God's steadfast love, mercy, and direction in our lives. I had no doubt, that whether I had a clear picture of the days ahead, or had to walk the rest of my days in a fog-God was there, and it would be alright. Job made a statement I used in the next several years, for my own circumstances;

> **Job 13:15 Though he slay me, yet will I trust in him: but I will maintain mine own ways before him.**

God had allowed us to achieve our goals, and know the joys of accomplishing our dreams, and we lived lives of purpose. No one could take that away from us. I had taken care of many seniors over the years who had gone through the losses of jobs, homes, and family, till they faced their end days. We were following in our parents and grandparents footsteps, learning as they did. We don't keep anything down here. We are only passing through this life and must leave it all behind. In this process, God is dealing with our hearts and spirits to see if we can do it with dignity, thankfulness, and peace. A verse in the psalms is one I have made a goal in my life;

> Psa 37:37 Mark the perfect man, and be-
> hold the upright: for the end of that man
> is peace.

I've had it said to me by several seniors that our greatest tests many times come in our later years, as the book of Job teaches us. To surrender, to let go, to learn again; we are but dust and these bodies will return to dust. The only thing we take into eternity, is what we've done with the souls and spirits God has given us. It's here, in this realm of life, we make the choices that will determine where we will spend eternity.

The rest of the summer was spent beginning the process of disassembling Lynn's cattle business, selling my horses, learning to take on the responsibilities he took care of, and eliminate what I would never use again. Equipment and his personal possessions. After two weeks of taking time off from my job, I went back to work, and continued to care for Mother. I didn't think about tomorrow, it was too much to deal with.

When the cattle and most of the horses were sold, I put the house on the market. After a couple of months of people looking at it, but no offers, the real estate person suggested lowering the price. I took this to the Lord, and got an answer "No, keep it at the price you're asking, and don't waiver."

That settled it for me.

After the six month term was up, and still no buyer, I just took it off the market, and decided to wait till spring to try again.

My younger brother came to stay with me, and help take care of the farm, and be with Mother while I worked. But, after only a short time, he developed blood clots in both of his legs, and needed hospital care. He went back to New York to stay with a sister, and get treatment. His doctor's said the clots were from many years of working and standing on concrete floors. His condition became very serious, and he almost died. All I could do was pray for him, and trust God to be with him.

Then Mother developed an open sore on the heel of her right foot. Even with diligent care, it would not heal. The doctor's said what I already knew, it was caused by multiple things, she was elderly, still smoked, and had diabetes. All of these issues played a part in it not healing. The diabetes, and continuing to smoke was stopping circulation to the foot. He tried to speak to her about it, but knew there was no chance of changing her, the addiction to tobacco was too strong. The future for her now, was becoming ominous.

On October 29, 2004, Mother fell in her room, and broke her leg. It was operated on the same day at 2:00 p.m., and from this point is was clear, arrangements would have to be made to place her in a nursing home. The ulcer on her foot, and the break in her leg would need intensive daily care. It was more than I could do now. Frustration of not being able to care for her anymore rose in me, but there was no other choice. It was now a situation that was out of my hands.

In the spring, I put the farm back on the market, and started looking for a place further north. Something in a quiet area.

Again, after a couple of months the real estate agent started trying to get me to lower the price. I refused. When the six month agreement ended, I took it off again. This time, I went to the Lord and said if He wanted it sold, to bring somebody to me, who was willing to pay the amount I heard Him give me. Then I waited to see what God would do.

Early one day in August of 2005, a woman called, and asked if I was still interested in selling the farm. I said yes, but I wasn't willing to lower the price I had listed it for. She said that was Ok, she would like to see it if I didn't mind. I said sure, and that I'd be home, if she wanted to come take a look at it.

She arrived about an hour later, and I showed her the barn first, then went back to the house. "I would like to take it, if you're sure you still want to sell it, and for the price you've asked."
"Do you have the finances to pay the amount I'm asking, without a mortgage?"

"Yes, if you want to go through a title deed company, we can set up a time, and sign the papers, and you'll have full payment that day."
"Yes, that's the way I'd like to do it."

By the end of August, the farm was sold, for the amount the Lord had given me to ask. I had found another place, and purchased it in September, after my house sold.

My Mother had been placed in a nursing home, close enough to visit her daily if need be. But caring for the farm through the last year, looking for another place to live, and going through the process of losing the farm, began to take a serious toll on me. One morning, coming home from work after doing another double shift (12 hrs., back to back), something in me began to crumble. The losses overwhelmed me.

I went in the house and looked out over the fields through the sliding doors, and thought of Lynn. The memories flooded over me. Life and purpose began to shut down. I had the next several days off, and spent them alone, talking to the Lord, asking what should I do. This answer came "Before you move, give your notice at work, and end the job there. Your life will change from this point on."

The next night I was scheduled to work, I went in early and spoke to my supervisor, telling her I'd sold the farm, and would be moving. I gave a two week notice, that I'd be leaving. She understood, and wished me well.

The house I'd purchased was in need of many repairs and renovations. It took six weeks to get it in livable condition. I moved in at the end of October of 2005. When I moved in at this time, the area was quiet, and thought it would be always be this way. I would learn I was mistaken, as time went by. But, I knew it was the place the Lord had chosen, for reasons I still do not fully understand.

Over the next several years, most time was spent learning to make independent decisions to maintain the upkeep of the house, continue to care for Mother, and my younger brother had recovered, and was with me again. His legs still had open ulcers that took a long time to heal. We helped each other with the everyday responsibilities of life, and keep the house in good repair.

I had kept Naomi, my champion mare, and moved her with me, and was able to enjoy having her for a while longer, but she also began having physical problems, as age crept up on her.

In 2006 I began to go to a local church regularly. During that time, significant events happened regarding my service to the Lord. He began to use me again, as He had years ago in the group I was in when I was first saved, with the gift of prophecy. The pastor said he knew they were given under the unction of the Holy Spirit, but there was ongoing controversy, because most in the group had not grown in their walk with the Lord. Most of them didn't take a Bible to the services with them. They didn't know how the gifts of the Holy Spirit were supposed to be used, or function in the church; this is the condition of most churches today.

However, the pastor allowed me to give some of the messages, because he understood the importance of the authority of the Holy Spirit in the meetings. During a Sunday evening service the Lord used me to speak a message concerning Benjamin Netanyahu; that he would become the Prime Minister of Israel again. It was written down, along with the date; this was 2007. For the next two years we waited to see what would happen. He was appointed Prime Minister again in 2009. It was noted and recorded. In the back of this book, several messages that were given by The Holy Spirit through me to the body of Christ are there; the reader can assess them for themselves, and take them to the Lord, and ask Him to show them if they were inspired by the Lord.

Someone reading this who may be called by God to a prophetic ministry, will understand the upheaval, adversity, and rejection that can come from those who do not believe, or understand the moving of God in using the gifts of the Holy Spirit. You will live a pattern of being rejected, and learn to stand and take it, or cave in and give up. It will be an ongoing lifelong battle. But if you are surrendered in your service to God; you'll do what He's given you, and let the chips fall where they may.

Also in 2007 the Lord opened doors for me to be able to teach for a couple of years, at Teen Challenge, in Johnson Vermont. Rick and Carrie had begun a ministry in 2005, and purchased property there; and began a Teen Challenge complex. This was a fulfillment of the word of the Lord given to me years earlier, of teaching His word. I would learn there is a cost to teaching God's word, that I had not experienced yet. Below is an excerpt from my journal:

"When I became a member of a church

in a local town, in 2006, the pastor approached me and said he felt I was called to be a leader, and wanted me to allow him to disciple me to become an assistant Pastor. At this same time, I was teaching at a Teen Challenge complex in my area as well. I am a spirit filled believer, and in the Pentecostal gifts of the Holy Spirit. The church I attended was also Pentecostal. God had given me prophetic messages that he wanted to be spoken to the congregation. I would go to the pastor and ask for permission to give them. Some of them he allowed me to speak, but some of the members objected, so he told me I would have to stop. (Over the years, I've sat and watched several of the prophetic messages given to me by the Holy Spirit as they transpired, on the news.)

I accepted what he said, but then he would come to me privately and tell me to give the messages to him, so he could speak them to the people. When I prayed about this, the Lord said, "No, don't allow him to speak them, I gave them to you to speak." When I told this to the pastor, he became very angry, and started to belittle me in public during the services. I knew things were not going to go well for me, but didn't know how bad they were really going to get.

In May of 2011, this pastor was found to be involved with a foreign exchange student that was staying with him and his wife. He had taken her to Boston and stayed there alone with her for three days. On his way back home, he had hit a moose, and had to be helped to get back home. His wife had to do the service that Sunday morning, because he was still in this situation. She had not been with them on the trip.

When I made a statement to some of the board members that he never should have been there with her alone, the members of the church turned on me and stood with the pastor. I was given the left foot of fellowship and a certified letter dismissing me from membership of their church.

The many years of trials, my husband's death, and the death of my loved ones, and this last event, caused me to become so weary and emotionally exhausted, I fell into discouragement. I have no excuses, this is simply the truth. From this point on, I went through a tunnel of defeat and failure. I didn't care about anything anymore. I loved the Lord, but wanted to die. This episode with this pastor destroyed my confidence in every church or organization. After years of watching the unethical actions of pastors and leaders in ministry, I had enough. I gave up on all of it.

At this time I was a member of a Christian forum on the internet that was monitored by two webmasters. But still, when I'd go to the site to interact with the members; out would pop nude pictures of men, and pornographic images that the webmasters would miss, or not delete. This is what the devil used to get me enticed to go to pornographic sites, it wore my resistance down.

If I had prayed, and cried out to God to help me, if I had turned off the computer and walked away, if I had told someone else, and asked for help in prayer; it would not have happened, but I didn't. The motives and reasons people do things is as important as the wrong done. Today's TV sitcoms are a revealing picture of what the world is like. When you fall, it becomes another source of mocking satire, with no regard to the broken lives they leave in their path.

Does God take into account the things we have to go through in life, and the level of attacks that come against us? Does He take into account the loneliness, losses, tragedies, and human frailties we deal with on a daily basis? I believe He does.

I have repented of the involvement with pornography, and asked the Lord's forgiveness, and the power of the Holy Spirit not repeat these sins. I know I am forgiven, once again. With Gods' help I intend to stay free, and his word is going to be my first line of defense in every situation from this point on. This has taught me much, and the strength I've regained is now enhanced with greater wisdom. When someone trusts me enough to tell me the truth about their failures, I take into account my own failures, and look at them and listen to them through the lens of compassion. God has stripped me of self-righteousness, and false pride. My feet are made of clay also. I can listen, and pray with them, and not condemn. But, point them to the One who can forgive, and restore them, give them renewed strength and get them started on the right road again.

As a minister, it may mean I never have much of what the world would term success. I've surrendered all of this to God. In God's eyes, the thing that matters is "come as you are". He does not refuse used goods."

If you're reading this, and have fallen on your face in failure, I hope God will use it to show you, you haven't gone too far. No matter what you may have done, how much you may have failed-there's hope for you, in Jesus.

There's no bottom to His love, mercy and forgiveness. Just admit what you may have done, repent, and get back up-and start again. He is for us, not against us.

Joh 10:10 The thief cometh not, but for to steal, and to kill, and to destroy: I am come that they might have life, and that they might have it more abundantly.

Joh 10:11 I am the good shepherd: the good shepherd giveth his life for the sheep._

In the early part of 2008, Mother began to show signs of failing, and talking of wanting to go and be with Dad. The year before, she had lost her sister from cancer. Now she talked about missing her also. I understood how she felt. She was wheelchair bound again, and the ulcer on her foot was growing worse every day. The doctor's said they didn't expect it would improve, but they kept a daily schedule of cleansing and changing the dressings. Her appetite was waning, and she was losing weight. I could see the signs of end-of-life conditions. I prayed for us both, to help us get through this. I asked the Lord what could be done about her appetite. I got a very good answer "Remember, she likes milk shakes." Of course, from then on, whenever I came to see her, or brought her to the house for the day-we made sure she had a milk shake.

While this was all going on, I started allowing deception to come into my life, and referred to myself as a nurse. I'd learned to do almost every procedure over the years, and though not willing to admit it, harbored a resentment toward some who I'd worked under, who would train me to do the treatments, while they sat at their desks many times, gossiping the night away.

I did the same work, without the credentials, or certificate on the wall, or the money they were making. I allowed myself to let the deception cause me to give myself a titled position, I didn't have. It took being confronted about it to get me to see I'd allowed lying and deception to creep into my life. I'm glad God didn't allow me to continue in this. I repented and confessed my wrong to those who needed to be spoken to.
Yes, believer's, and servants of God are just people; we stumble, we fall, but we get back up; and keep going again.

Psa 37:24 Though he fall, he shall not be utterly cast down: for the LORD upholdeth *him with* **his hand.**

Pro 24:16 For a just *man* falleth seven times, and riseth up again: but the wicked shall fall into mischief.

Rom 4:7 *Saying,* Blessed *are* they whose iniquities are forgiven, and whose sins are covered.

When God has disciplined me, and corrected me, I'm reminded again, that if it weren't for the mercy, and forgiveness of Jesus, none of us would have any hope.

> **Psa 51:5 Behold, I was shapen in iniquity; and in sin did my mother conceive me.**
>
> Rom 7:18 For I know that in me (that is, in my flesh,) dwelleth no good thing: for to will is present with me; but *how* to perform that which is good I find not._

It is His shed blood, His forgiveness, and mercy that is the only thing that we can cling to, and count on, to have the assurance of heaven, and any right standing with Him.

> Rom 13:14 But put ye on the Lord Jesus Christ, and make not provision for the flesh, to *fulfil* the lusts *thereof.*
>
> Eph 4:23 And be renewed in the spirit of your mind;
>
> Eph 4:24 And that ye put on the new man, which after God is created in righteousness and true holiness.
>
> 2Co 5:17 Therefore if any man *be* in Christ, *he is* a new creature: old things are passed away; behold, all things are become new.

In the Bible, when we read the stories of Abraham, Isaac, and

Jacob; all of these men were prophets, and God called Abraham His friend-but they were all liars, Jacob was a liar and a schemer. I'm not making any excuses, only making a point; these men confessed their sin, repented, and the Lord forgave them. They went on, and continued serving God. This is what we are supposed to do. Not wallow in self-pity, or self-condemnation. This is what the devil, and some people would love for us to do, and then give up. If you've slipped, committed some wrong; repent, do what needs to be done to make it right. Then get up, and go on with God. He's forgiven you, forgive yourself.

Below are verses relaying these men's errors:

Gen 12:17 And the LORD plagued Pharaoh and his house with great plagues because of Sarai Abram's wife.

Gen 12:18 And Pharaoh called Abram, and said, What is this that thou hast done unto me? why didst thou not tell me that she was thy wife?

Gen 12:19 Why saidst thou, She is my sister? so I might have taken her to me to wife: now therefore behold thy wife, take her, and go thy way.

Gen 20:3 But God came to Abimelech in a dream by night, and said to him, Behold, thou art but a dead man, for the woman which thou hast taken; for she is a man's wife.

Gen 20:7 Now therefore restore the man his wife; for he is a prophet, and he shall pray for thee, and thou shalt live: and if thou restore her not, know thou that thou shalt surely die, thou, and all that are thine.

Gen 20:8 Therefore Abimelech rose early in the morning, and called all his servants, and told all these things in their ears: and the men were sore afraid.

Gen 20:9 Then Abimelech called Abraham, and said unto him, What hast thou done unto us? and what have I offended thee, that thou hast brought on me and on my kingdom a great sin? thou hast done deeds unto me that ought not to be done.

Gen 20:10 And Abimelech said unto Abraham, What sawest thou, that thou hast done this thing?

Gen 20:11 And Abraham said, Because I thought, Surely the fear of God is not in this place; and they will slay me for my wife's sake.

Isaac and Abimelech

Gen 26:6 And Isaac dwelt in Gerar:

Gen 26:7 And the men of the place asked him of his wife; and he said, She is my sister: for he feared to say, She is my wife; lest, said he, the men of the place should kill me for Rebekah; because she was fair to look upon.

Gen 26:8 And it came to pass, when he had been there a long time, that Abimelech king of the Philistines looked out at a window, and saw, and, behold, Isaac was sporting with Rebekah his wife.

Gen 26:9 And Abimelech called Isaac, and said, Behold, of a surety she is thy wife: and how saidst thou, She is my sister? And Isaac said unto him, Because I said, Lest I die for her.

Gen 26:10 And Abimelech said, What is this thou hast done unto us? one of the people might lightly have lien with thy wife, and thou shouldest have brought guiltiness upon us.

Gen 26:11 And Abimelech charged all his people, saying, He that toucheth this man or his wife shall surely be put to death._

Now, Jacob deceives his father for his brother's blessing:

Gen 27:18 And he came unto his father, and said, My father: and he said, Here am I; who art thou, my son?

Gen 27:19 And Jacob said unto his father, I am Esau thy firstborn; I have done according as thou badest me: arise, I pray thee, sit and eat of my venison, that thy soul may bless me.

Gen 27:20 And Isaac said unto his son, How is it that thou hast found it so quickly, my son? And he said, Because the LORD thy God brought it to me.

Gen 27:21 And Isaac said unto Jacob, Come near, I pray thee, that I may feel thee, my son, whether thou be my very son Esau or not.

Gen 27:22 And Jacob went near unto Isaac his father; and he felt him, and said, The voice is Jacob's voice, but the hands are the hands of Esau.

Gen 27:23 And he discerned him not, because his hands were hairy, as his brother Esau's hands: so he blessed him.

Gen 27:24 And he said, Art thou my very son Esau? And he said, I am.

Gen 27:25 And he said, Bring it near to me, and I will eat of my son's venison, that my soul may bless thee. And he brought it near to him, and he did eat: and he brought him wine, and he drank.

Gen 27:26 And his father Isaac said unto him, Come near now, and kiss me, my son.

Gen 27:27 And he came near, and kissed him: and he smelled the smell of his raiment, and blessed him, and said, See, the smell of my son is as the smell of a field which the LORD hath blessed:

Gen 27:28 Therefore God give thee of the dew of heaven, and the fatness of the earth, and plenty of corn and wine:

Gen 27:29 Let people serve thee, and nations bow down to thee: be lord over thy brethren, and let thy mother's sons bow down to thee: cursed be every one that curseth thee, and blessed be he that blesseth thee.

Gen 27:30 And it came to pass, as soon as Isaac had made an end of blessing Jacob,

and Jacob was yet scarce gone out from
the presence of Isaac his father, that Esau
his brother came in from his hunting._

In relaying this incident, I'm bringing home the point, that no matter how old we become, in reality; we are still God's children. Throughout our life, no matter our age; God continues to deal with us, mold us, discipline and correct us. We are the clay, in the Potter's hands.

My oldest brother in New York was also suffering at this time from serious heart problems. My sister in law had brought him to the house in the fall of 2007, so he could visit Mother one more time. His doctor's didn't know how much longer he had to live. He spent the day with her, and we shared a meal together. God was with us that day, we all knew it would be the last time they'd see each other on this earth.

Now, as I watched my Mother declining, I decided to call my sister in law and check on him again. They had to put him in a nursing home also. His heart had become very bad. I asked her how she was doing, but already knew the answer. She said she didn't really know how to answer that. I said I understood, and if there was anything I could do, call me, and I'd be praying for them all. They were facing what I'd gone through with Lynn. More losses were coming my way.

By March Mom had lost a lot of weight, because she had no appetite. No amount of coaching would persuade her to eat any of her lunch. She survived on the milk shakes we brought her. Her foot was terribly infected, and the doctor's tried to persuade her to let them amputate it. She refused, she wanted to die.

By the middle of the month, she told me she had requested to sign papers releasing the nursing home from all responsibility, and refused any further medications to keep her alive. I knew what this meant. Several times in the past month, she had looked at me and said "Why doesn't God just take me?" I had no answers. All I could do was be there, love her, and listen. Now, she was taking steps to bring on her own death, and who was I to tell her she was wrong. But, everything in me fought this. I tried one more time "Mother, we love you, please, if you'd let the doctor's amputate the foot, you'd begin to heal, and feel better."

"No, my mind is made up. I'm tired of living like this, and I'm not willing to be in a wheelchair the rest of my life."

The nurse standing by and listening to this, saw my feeling of helplessness, and said "We can love them, try to care for them, but we can't control them. This is a situation where we have to allow them to make their own choices, whether we approve, or understand it, or not."

I knew she was right. I'd cared for other's in similar situations, and watched family members as they found they had to let their parents make their own decisions. Now, I was in the same place. I looked at Mother and said "Whatever you decide Mother, I love you, and I'm here for you."

We were able to have her come one last time for Easter, the last Sunday of March that year. She spent most of the day at the house with us, but had no appetite. Again, we gave her a milk shake. My brother took her for a ride in the country on the way back to the nursing home, but she was in pain, and could not enjoy it very much. The next day, he went back to the nursing home, and spent the day with her. She was beginning to fail, and the nurses let him know the end was close. He called me to let me know. I said I'd be there by 3:00 p.m., and replace him, and stay with her through the night.

When I arrived I could see she was losing the sense of her

surroundings. My brother's eyes were full of tears. He knew this was the last time he'd see her. As he got up, and started to leave, I told him I'd not be home that night. He nodded, going down the hall in silence. I closed the door, and helped Mother out of the wheelchair, realizing this would be the last time she would ever leave it, and into bed. Nurses assistants came in and helped her into a nightgown. She was unresponsive, she had gone into a coma, and never recovered.

She lingered for two days. I stayed in the room with her, keeping the door shut. I had determined she would die with peace and dignity. Nurses came in several times through the day, asking if I needed anything, and helping with her general care. But for the most part, we were left alone. At approximately 2:00 a.m., on March 28, 2008, Mother passed away. I made sure she was tended to, her body washed and clean sheets put over her. It was dawn when I got in my truck, and drove home.

A few months later, in June, my oldest brother passed away. The next month, I had to put down my last horse, my champion mare, Naomi Roe. Then in 2009, my oldest sister, living in Alabama passed away. I began to dread hearing the phone ring; never knowing if it would be a message of another loss.

I was still teaching at Teen Challenge at this time. One night I was scheduled to be there, I walked into the chapel, and found something I wasn't expecting. There was a pool table, slot machines, and other games set up, mingled in with the chairs for the class. When I saw this, my heart sank, my stomach felt like lead. I started praying, and asking the Lord what to do. I got this verse in my head, very clearly:

> **Mat 21:13 And said unto them, It is written, My house shall be called the house of prayer; but ye have made it a**

den of thieves.

When the men came in, I relayed this to them, and said this made my heart sick. I reprimanded the leadership, and said I was very disappointed that they could not see how wrong this was. God was not going to honor this. They may get people's approval, but not the Lord's. I did a short teaching on Jesus as he entered the temple and overthrew the tables of the moneychanger's, and related it to this kind of party spirit now in the chapel. When I ended for the night, I posted the teaching on my daughter and son in laws door, and left. They did not agree with my view of it, and let me know it. This was the last of my teaching there. I love them, but would not compromise. I do not claim to know all the reasons why this was allowed, but a few things have been made clear to me about it. 1. We will be tested to see if our commitment to the Lord is real, and if we will stand for the word of God, or give in to what the people want.

Psa 119:158 I beheld the transgressors, and was grieved; because they kept not thy word.

Psa 119:159 Consider how I love thy precepts: quicken me, O LORD, according to thy lovingkindness.

Psa 119:160 Thy word is true from the beginning: and every one of thy righteous judgments endureth forever.

Psa 138:2 I will worship toward thy holy temple, and praise thy name for thy lovingkindness and for thy truth: for thou hast magnified thy word above all thy name.

Rom 3:4 God forbid: yea, let God be true, but every man a liar; as it is written, That thou mightest be justified in thy sayings, and mightest overcome when thou art judged._

2. We love our family members, but we will be tested to see if we love God more than even our family.

Mat 10:34 Think not that I am come to send peace on earth: I came not to send peace, but a sword.

Mat 10:35 For I am come to set a man at variance against his father, and the daughter against her mother, and the daughter in law against her mother in law.

Mat 10:36 And a man's foes shall be they of his own household.

Mat 10:37 He that loveth father or mother more than me is not worthy of me: and he that loveth son or daughter more than me is not worthy of me.

Mat 10:38 And he that taketh not his cross, and followeth after me, is not worthy of me.

Mat 10:39 He that findeth his life shall lose it: and he that loseth his life for my sake shall find it._

3. Do the people have a desire to honor God, or their own lusts.

Psa 111:10 The fear of the LORD is the beginning of wisdom: a good understanding have all they that do his commandments: his praise endureth forever.

Ecc 12:13 Let us hear the conclusion of the whole matter: Fear God, and keep his commandments: for this is the whole duty of man.

Ecc 12:14 For God shall bring every work into judgment, with every secret thing, whether it be good, or whether it be evil.

Rev 19:5 And a voice came out of the throne, saying, Praise our God, all ye his servants, and ye that fear him, both small and great.

We can however, quote scriptures all day long, but the bottom line is, how much do we really love Jesus. Is He really first in our lives, or are we in the driver's seat. Is Jesus just a passenger in your life.

It has always been important to my daughter, to be well liked and have many friends. It's a slippery slope, because it's people's influence, and opinions that often override what God's will is. I love her. Someday we will understand each other better. But, perhaps not til we are in heaven.

In 2010 the Lord began to speak to me about starting an outreach ministry from my home, consisting of a website, and doing outreach work here in my area. It has proved to be an ongoing spiritual battle to this day. I have no doubt it's God's will, but the attacks against what I've been given to do-have come just as hard, and just as destructive from Christians, as from unbeliever's. I've learned like Jesus did-there's no one you can really trust, but God himself. Jesus loves man, but love and trust are two different things. I take

the same approach in life, and use these scriptures as my guide:

Psa 118:8 It is better to trust in the LORD than to put confidence in man.

Psa 118:9 It is better to trust in the LORD than to put confidence in princes.

Pro 29:25 The fear of man bringeth a snare: but whoso putteth his trust in the LORD shall be safe.

Joh 2:24 But Jesus did not commit himself unto them, because he knew all men,

Joh 2:25 And needed not that any should testify of man: for he knew what was in man._

When I began this ministry, the Lord asked it to be named "Two Sparrows Ministry", with these verses as its foundation;

Mat 25:34 Then shall the King say unto them on his right hand, Come, ye blessed of my Father, inherit the kingdom prepared for you from the foundation of the world:

Mat 25:35 For I was an hungred, and ye gave me meat: I was thirsty, and ye gave me drink: I was a stranger, and ye took me in:

Mat 25:36 Naked, and ye clothed me: I was sick, and ye visited me: I was in prison, and ye came unto me.

Mat 25:37 Then shall the righteous an-

swer him, saying, Lord, when saw we
thee an hungred, and fed thee? or thirsty,
and gave thee drink?

Mat 25:38 When saw we thee a stranger,
and took thee in? or naked, and clothed
thee?

Mat 25:39 Or when saw we thee sick, or
in prison, and came unto thee?

Mat 25:40 And the King shall answer
and say unto them, Verily I say unto you,
Inasmuch as ye have done it unto one of
the least of these my brethren, ye have
done it unto me._

As I began to create the website for it, and making visits to nursing homes in the area, doors began to open, and the Holy Spirit was directing it. There was good promise that I'd have Bible studies and home visits. I began in a local nursing home for a once a week service, and the people seemed open to my coming. But, within a few weeks, things took a turn, and people's countenances told me there had been talk going on. At one of the last meetings I held there, a man who was a resident, came to me and said "We've heard you want to take over everything, and be in control."

I responded "I've asked the head nurse here if it would be alright to have a simple Bible study, and share the scriptures and the love of Jesus with these people once a week, that is hardly taking over everything."

He turned and walked away, but I could see from what he said, there had been poison spread, and it had worked.
After that, the next time I came, nurses at the desk began mocking, and letting me know I was not welcome. I got the message, and could see from the looks on the faces in the meeting that gossip had

been spread further, and the doors were shutting.

There were hardly any who came to the last study, and when I went to my car to leave, a group of strangers, who apparently had family members in the home, were at my vehicle to confront me, and let me know I wasn't welcome to come back again. This kind of reaction has been consistent through the years.

When taking care of seniors, I watched, and found very few were ever interested in visiting the elderly; including churches. Yes, there are some who have good nursing home ministries, but not very many. Most nursing homes rarely get any ministry, and most of the time the staff doesn't care. A lot of religious politics and jealousy gets in the way of those who have a true calling, and desire to minister to these people, and many times gets hindered, and destroyed.

The Bible is full of stories we can relate to. Jesus had some harrowing experiences when He was here on earth. He knows what we may go through, He's had the same rejection.

Jesus Heals Two Men with Demons

Mat 8:28 And when he was come to the other side into the country of the Gergesenes, there met him two possessed with devils, coming out of the tombs, exceeding fierce, so that no man might pass by that way.

Mat 8:29 And, behold, they cried out, saying, What have we to do with thee, Jesus, thou Son of God? art thou come hither to torment us before the time?

Mat 8:30 And there was a good way off from them an herd of many swine feeding.

Mat 8:31 So the devils besought him, saying, If thou cast us out, suffer us to go away into the herd of swine.

Mat 8:32 And he said unto them, Go. And when they were come out, they went into the herd of swine: and, behold, the whole herd of swine ran violently down a steep place into the sea, and perished in the waters.

Mat 8:33 And they that kept them fled, and went their ways into the city, and told everything, and what was befallen to the possessed of the devils.

Mat 8:34 And, behold, the whole city came out to meet Jesus: and when they saw him, they besought him that he would depart out of their coasts._

Jesus heals two men with demons, and what do the people in the city do? They all come out, and when they saw him, the besought him to leave. They made it very clear, they didn't want him in their city-so he left.

Here's one more:

Joh 8:56 Your father Abraham rejoiced to see my day: and he saw it, and was glad.

Joh 8:57 Then said the Jews unto him, Thou art not yet fifty years old, and hast thou seen Abraham?

Joh 8:58 Jesus said unto them, Verily, verily, I say unto you, Before Abraham was, I am.

Joh 8:59 Then took they up stones to cast at him: but Jesus hid himself, and went out of the temple, going through the midst of them, and so passed by._

In these verses Jesus describes Himself as the same I AM, as addressed to Moses on Mt. Sinai. At this, the Pharisee's went mad; picking up stones to kill him. So, we see that in this world if they persecuted and eventually killed Jesus; we who follow Him can expect the same treatment, and often from the modern day Pharisee's.

But, even with these obstacles, I believe the most important things God wanted accomplished has been to spread the gospel of Jesus Christ, and give some warnings of world events, and the connection between them regarding the Lord's return.

In every circumstance through the years, the Lord has let me know it's not numbers that's important to Him; it's being faithful. Keep doing what I've been called to do. Don't worry who may, or may not be following. He's reminded me more than once; He never looked behind Him to see who was following when He was on the earth. He called the disciples, and let them decide if they wanted to come. He just kept walking.

Remember Noah; he preached 120 years, but converted no one. Only eight souls got on the boat. We aren't told in the Bible whether his family all believed in God, but they made it on the boat, because of Noah's righteousness. We are in the days of Noah again now, as Jesus tells us;

Mat 24:37 But as the days of Noe were, so shall also the coming of the Son of man be.

Mat 24:38 For as in the days that were before the flood they were eating and drinking, marrying and giving in marriage, until the day that Noe entered into the ark,

Mat 24:39 And knew not until the flood came, and took them all away; so shall also the coming of the Son of man be.

1Pe 3:20 Which sometime were disobedient, when once the longsuffering of God waited in the days of Noah, while the ark was a preparing, wherein few, that is, eight souls were saved by water.

2Pe 2:5 And spared not the old world, but saved Noah the eighth person, a preacher of righteousness, bringing in the flood upon the world of the ungodly;

As this story comes to a close, I'll ask the reader a question I'd often ask the men in the classes at Teen Challenge;

"When you come to the end of your life, and you look behind you, what do you want to see? What kind of pattern to your life, what level of commitment, what memories that you will have left family and loved ones? At the end of the day, this is all that's going to matter."

I wanted to give them something that would stay in their minds, and cause them to think of their lives, and the effect they were having right now, in everyday life, on the people they loved and associated with. Were they abusing, mistreating their wife and kids, parents, co-workers. Were they people of responsibility; or turmoil, corruption, and chaos, and causing those they loved misery and suffering.

If so, the day would come when they very well may look behind them and face the reality that their lives amounted to nothing but serving the devil; and now they were about to spend eternity with this destroyer forever in hell. We always have the choice to turn around and change direction. It's my hope and prayer that anyone reading this will heed this truth. If the Lord could save me, he can save anyone.

Consider these verses;

Choose Whom You Will Serve

Jos 24:14 Now therefore fear the LORD, and serve him in sincerity and in truth: and put away the gods which your fathers served on the other side of the flood, and in Egypt; and serve ye the LORD.

Jos 24:15 And if it seem evil unto you to serve the LORD, choose you this day whom ye will serve; whether the gods which your fathers served that were on the other side of the flood, or the gods of the Amorites, in whose land ye dwell: but as for me and my house, we will serve the LORD._

I'll never give any predictions or dates of the day of the Lord's return. But, the signs all around us, and we are seeing events unfold before our eyes in the news every day; that are telling us we should be watching, and be ready. He can come at any time. Jesus warns us:

Mar 13:35 Watch ye therefore: for ye know not when the master of the house cometh, at even, or at midnight, or at the cockcrowing, or in the morning:

Mar 13:36 Lest coming suddenly he find you sleeping.

I'll end with the very first prophetic message the Holy Spirit gave me at a Friday night prayer group, at a local pond, many years ago.

"Behold, I come quickly. Are you ready?"
Even so, come quickly Lord Jesus

END PAGE

Prophetic Messages

Below is a compilation of prophetic messages given by me in local churches with pastor's and people in attendance. These have been chosen to be put here, because they pertained to a national/ international context. I'm posting them out of obedience to the Holy Spirit.

July 30, 2006-I gave a prophetic message on this date, at a local congregation.

"How this generation loves its entertainment. It matters not whether it is real or an illusion, with no limits, and the bloodier the better. But the cup of indignation must be filled up. (Isaiah 26:20-21, Rev. 14:10)

And, I have an appointment with those who lust after blood, and will gather them together, and their lust will be filled to the full. (Zeph. 3:8, Joel 3:2)

But now let me change the scene, click the remote, and go to New England. From the ocean shores, thru the valleys, to the highest mountains, hear the word of the Lord.... The earth is the Lord's, and the fullness thereof, and all who live in it, and, Every knee SHALL bow and every tongue confess that Jesus Christ is Lord, to the glory of God the Father.

Now to every servant and to my angels I say, reap the harvest, and glean the fields, before the Great day of the Lord comes." (Lev. 19:10, Ru. 2:7)

Personal Note: This message disturbs me, and if I am in error in any way, may God forgive me. But as I researched this I found these scripture references- (Psalm 24:1, 1Cor. 10:26, Psalm 89:11, Rom. 14:11, Phil. 2:9-11) Note: When I asked the Lord why this was in the message this is the reply I received. "The Holy Spirit was using your mouth to speak the WORD to the spirits over New England, reminding them that they are subject to the authority of Christ, and must yield their dominion to Him, including the people in it. The Gospel preached in faith will yield a harvest, even in this dark hour."

December 2, 2006-At Sunday service today this message was given to me, my heart is so heavy, and the Lord gave me a tiny portion of His heartache over this, it is crushing me.

"Who can measure the value of one human life: I measured it by the blood of my only Son.

But this nation values life in terms of convenience, or inconvenience. I will not hold this nation guiltless. I am waiting to see the ultimate outcome of this nations decisions.

The blood of countless innocents cries out to Me from the ground, from one end of this nation to the other, and I surely hear them. Only those who walk in righteousness, and repent from their hearts will remain under My covering and protection."

December 10, 2006-This message was given to me to speak at the Sunday service at a local congregation.

"As My Spirit goes throughout this nation, and even the nations of the world; it is with great sadness that I see that so many have made their faces harder than a rock (Jeremiah ch. 5) against Me.

But, surely My mercy and My grace hovers over those who are My own, and I am a shield to all who trust in Me.

Do not be shaken, or in fear of whatever may take place in time to come, be comforted by My presence, and My peace. I will never forsake you.

For as I roam looking for those who love Me, know this; you are very precious in My sight."

December 11, 2006-Last night, the Lord woke me and spoke this to me.

"I'm asking you to join me in the sorrow I am in because of the conditions of this nation and Israel. As you mourn for your husband, I am mourning for these two nations, and indeed the nations of this world, because they have forsaken Me. My choices are few, and My heart is very heavy. I'm asking you to wear clothes of "sackcloth and ashes" as you continue to intercede until the day you join Me in heaven. There is a beautiful robe waiting for you here. But, the days ahead are going to be full of turmoil and trouble, especially for those who do not know Me.

I laid awake a long time after this, my heart is like lead. May God help me to be obedient.

January 7, 2007-This prophetic message was given by me at a local congregation.

"Again, battlelines are being drawn, and borders defined by many, to destroy the land I love. But it will be as in the days of Jehoshaphat. When he was surrounded on every side, he gathered all of Judah around him, with their wives and little ones, and he cried; We have no might against them, and we don't know what to do, but our eyes are on You.

My answer to him was, stand and see the salvation of the Lord, for the battle is not yours, but Mine. I will show myself strong again, and my arm strong to go into this battle. There will be great struggle, and horror.

And, I will raise up a man again, who knows my covenant, who has the strength of heart and spirit to fight to keep it. That man is Benjamin Netanyahu."

This prophecy was given two years before Mr. Netanyahu was in office.

Benjamin Netanyahu was re-elected Prime Minister of Israel in February 2009.

April 29, 2007- This prophecy was given at a local congregation, on this day at the morning service.

"Judgment rides on the wind, burns across the parched land, thru the raging seas, and it will come from the heavens. But, to those who call on My name, and who know me, I am a strong tower, a refuge and strength in time of trouble.

No matter what you see with your eyes, do not be afraid or dismayed. Know I am with you, and you are not alone.
And, be assured of this, it will all come to an end very soon."

May 13, 2007-This prophetic message was given at a local congregation.

"Rise with Me under My wings to the Throne of Grace, there you are seated with Me in heavenly places. Here there is no darkness, or shadow of turning. Here there is complete healing, wholeness, and light. As you worship Me here, receive this healing for your souls, then you can walk in this victory, even here on this earth."

August 19, 2007-This message was spoken at the morning service at a local congregation.

"This nation has rejected Me; and now their courts are allowing prayer to be offered to other gods, who are demons, but Me they do not want. Some of my people are calling to me, but not all; and this nation will not repent. What am I to do with it?

In My heart, I feel I would like to discard it like a worn out garment, just as it has forsaken Me. What do you say?

But, there are some in this last day that I've called to the front lines who I've made pillars of iron, and solid walls against the darkness, and wickedness of this hour. They are canopies of protection over my people, indeed, they are living sacrifices to Me. I've made their faces fiercer than the faces of their enemies.

I am calling all my people now to stand shoulder to shoulder, outward against the enemy the devil, not against each other. In their midst I AM a pillar of fire to protect them.

Now, stand ready, look up, for your redemption draws nigh, yeah it is even at the doors."

Sept. 2, 2007-This prophetic message was given by me at a local congregation.

"I am a God of covenant, and have pledged myself to Israel, and Jerusalem. She is my beloved, even thou she has rejected me, and hardened her heart against me.

I have not changed my mind, and I will not allow this Land that is Mine to be divided, nor Jerusalem. In time to come, those who oppose her will know this.

And when He sets His foot on that mountain, all of Israel will look on Him whom they have pierced, and know He is the only God, and there is no other. His name is not Allah, nor Mohamed, and all will know this.

He only is the One, and His Name is One."

October 7, 2007-This message was given by me at the morning service at a local congregation.

"When you arise to meet Me, your horses are ready for you. Their bells will chime to "The Song Of Moses", and their breastplates have written "HOLINESS UNTO THE LORD".
Time is very short, be encouraged; your horses are ready."

October 26, 2007-This message was given to me by the Lord in the middle of the night, which He wants to have spoken. I'm going to give it to my pastor.

"One by one the mega churches have risen, filling their storehouses with merchandise which they've acquired by using My Name. They have made them dens of thieves, full of perversion, twisting my Words to fit their plans, and fill their lusts.

But, as I took Ezekiel by his hair to see the abominations in Jerusalem, I've taken some of my servants by the Spirit and shown them the abominations of these corrupted pastor's, and ministers in these mega churches. My true servants wail to me and cry for justice with great weeping. Because of my longsuffering mercy I've held back, seeking them and convicting them by My Spirit to come to repentance, but they will not. They are drunk and blind with pride.

They preach my Word with compromise, and trickery, while they live in debauchery, and pomp and pride. They think I do not see, or hear. The gods they serve are demons of lust, excess, and fraud, and they teach their sons and daughters the same.

My sheep are being destroyed by them, and led into hell, because of the error being preached. Hell will be hotter for those who are teaching them.

But now the stench of rotten fruit has come up to My throne, and I can no longer bear it. As a house of cards, and dominoes in a row; with one touch of My finger they are going to fall. I will lay low all who have corrupted themselves, and no one will be exempt. As they have brought reproach and shame to My Name, I will expose them, what is done in secret will be brought to the light.

My Father's house is to be a house of prayer; and it is time to clean His house once again."

On October 28, 2007 the message was given. I could see and sense the opposition. Praise the Lord anyway. I pray the He will come soon or take me home soon, I'm getting very weary in this work.

January 7, 2008-In the middle of the night; The Lord has spoken this to me concerning Bush, and this nation:

"Bush has sealed his fate, and his destruction is sure. He has had many warnings from servants I've sent to him to not continue in these dealings with Olmert to divide My land. But, he has closed his heart, and will not listen. They are both headed for hell.

This nation will follow close behind, the disasters will continue. There will be weeping and wailing; the likes this nation has never seen.

Anyone who is not with Me; is against Me, it is as simple as this. Each person will be tested to see where their heart truly is. I'm coming; and nothing the devil can do will stop Me. The church I come for will be pure, full of light, and there will be no darkness in her at all.

Gird yourselves now with the Word of God, it is the only thing that will last in the times to come."

February 10, 2008-This message was given this morning at a local congregation.

"My Spirit hovers over this body; you are a precious and peculiar people to me"
However; am I to conform to man, and the deeds of the flesh? No, man is to conform to me in My holiness.

As Moses went up to the mountain to separate himself to Me, and consecrate himself to Me; so the same.

Come away, and be separate, be holy as I am holy.

I am no respecter of persons; how I blessed him, is the same way I will bless anyone who truly comes out of the world and follows Me. When I see this kind of consecration; it is then that the manifestations of My glory will come down."

Vortex of Evil

5/12/2008

Last Thursday night, the Lord gave me a vision and a prophetic message; and has asked me to share it with you. I've been very reluctant, because of the gravity of it. It made me sick to my stomach for several days, and my heart is like lead. I've prayed about this and checked it with all the knowledge, scriptures, and discernment I can think of; I'm sure I've heard correctly, but it is very hard to do this. I pray the Lord will show you His heart in this.

In the vision, I was taken up into space; and looking down on the globe of the earth, I saw a funnel cloud form from about the center of Florida. It grew, and grew until it went up to the heavens, and was enormous. Then, it slowly started to move; still growing as it went. It continued to move slowly, weaving back and forth, consuming everything in its path; until it had circled the globe.

Then I saw smaller funnel clouds being birthed from this first one; and doing the same thing; growing and growing and beginning to move these funnels moved in a rhythm together and I knew as I watched that they were the "children" of the first vortex. Then, my eyes became like telescopes; and I could see great details within these funnels even from where I was. I saw multitudes of people being sucked into them; and falling headlong into the center; as they fell they became aware of the trap they were in and started screaming for help; but it was too late, and they were sucked into the bottom.... and disappeared. I perceived it was like being drawn into a black hole, once you're in; there is no way out. There were millions upon millions being sucked in, never to be seen again.

As I watched in horror; I cried to the Lord, "What is this; what are you showing me; and why?"

This is the answer I received.

"This main huge funnel, is the "Lakeland Outpouring", of Todd Bentley's crusades, and his doctrine. This is only the beginning; and it will grow to cover the world. He will not receive any correction, and he will infect the entire Body of Christ, worldwide. Every denomination, and every church on the globe will be affected by this ministry."

Then, I was given this prophetic message:

"Now the doors of darkness are open even wider; and My Body is given over to the ways of Eli, and his sons. Todd Bentley is igniting his own strange fire; is being endorsed by the leadership behind him, and anyone who has tried to correct him has been dismissed, and rejected. He, and those who follow him are saying: "Tickle me, tell me I'm ok, do not show me my sin, don't tell me I must change my behavior and my ways. Let me worship you; as I remain the same, don't show me where I need to align myself with the Word of God. It is a day now when only those who will go deep into my

Word, and prayer that will be protected as this vortex of evil swarms over the land; and consumes many in its path. For those who want to worship the God of their own imaginations; they will be sucked in; and there will be no way out. They are making their choices; and I am making Mine. I am calling out to those who will hear "who will say as Joshua; as for me and my house, we will serve the Lord."

This is the beginning of the "great falling away", and as I have said "even the elect will be deceived."

Whoever chooses this strange fire, will be allowed to; and ultimately destroyed. I will cleanse My House. I'm coming for a bride without spot or wrinkle."

I've wept bitter tears over this vision and message. My heart is like lead. But, I know the Lord wants you to know what is coming; and be prepared for it.

Recommended Reading

Prayer/Fasting/Intercession-Spiritual Warfare

Alice Smith-Beyond The Veil
Betty Malz-My Glimpse Of Eternity, and Prayers That Are Answered
C.S. Lewis-Mere Christianity, The Great Divorce, The Screwtape Letters, and A Severe Mercy
Brother Lawrence-Practicing His Presence
Corrie Ten Boom-The Hiding Place, Tramp For The Lord
Don Piper-90 Minutes In Heaven
Florence Bulle-Lord of the Valleys
Fred Stone-Fire On The Alter
Joy Dawson-Ruined For The Ordinary
John Bunyan-My Sojourn in Heaven and Stopover in Hell
Lilian B. Yeomans M.D.-The Great Physician
Norman Grubb-Rees Howells Intercessor
Madame Guyon-Autobiography, and Experiencing The Depths Of Jesus Christ
Watchman Nee-The Spiritual Man, A Table In The Wilderness, Spiritual Authority
Scenes Beyond The Grave-Visions of Marietta Davis Edited by Gordon Lindsey

Spiritual Warfare

Derek Prince-Spiritual Warfare, They Shall Expel Demons, Blessing Or Curse, Secrets Of A Prayer Warrior-Derek Prince can also be Googled, and many Youtube videos of his teachings can be found
Dr. Walter Martin-The Kingdom of the Cults- Dr. Walter Martin can also be Googled, and many teaching videos can be found on

Youtube

Win Worley-Battling the Hosts of Hell, Diary of an Exorcist, Conquering the Hosts of Hell, An Open Triumph, Warfare Prayers - Win Worley can also be Googled, and many videos of his teachings are on Youtube

Rebecca Brown M.D.-He Came To Set The Captives Free, and Prepare For War

Frank and Ida Mae Hammond-Pigs In The Parlor

The NightWatchman

If ye then be risen with Christ, seek those things

which are above,

where Christ sitteth on the right hand of God.

Set your affection on things above,

not on things on the earth.

For ye are dead, and your life is hid with

Christ in God.

When Christ, who is our life, shall appear, then

shall ye also

appear with him in glory.

Col 3:1-4

Lorna Couillard